FRONTIERS OF
COMMODITY CHAIN
RESEARCH

FRONTIERS OF COMMODITY CHAIN RESEARCH

Edited by Jennifer Bair

Stanford University Press
Stanford, California

Stanford University Press
Stanford, California
©2009 by the Board of Trustees of the
Leland Stanford Junior University

Printed in the United States of America on acid-free, archival-quality paper

Library of Congress Cataloging-in-Publication Data

Frontiers of commodity chain research / edited by Jennifer Bair.
        p. cm.
  Includes bibliographical references and index.
  ISBN 978-0-8047-5923-6 (cloth : alk. paper) — ISBN 978-0-8047-5924-3 (pbk. : alk. paper)
  1. Commercial products. 2. International trade. 3. International division of labor. 4. International economic relations. I. Bair, Jennifer, 1973–
  HF1040.7.F76 2009
  382—dc22   2008011829

Designed by Bruce Lundquist
Typeset by Classic Typography in 10/14 Minion

Contents

Acknowledgments

T HE IMPETUS FOR THIS VOLUME CAME FROM A PROJECT THAT
I organized together with Richard Appelbaum titled "Global
Networks: Interdisciplinary Perspectives on Commodity Chains." An initial
meeting of the group involved in this project was made possible by the gen-
erous support of several organizations at Yale: the Council on Latin American and Iberian Studies through the Edward J. and Dorothy Clarke Kempf
Memorial Fund; the Center for Comparative Research, Department of Sociology; and the Institution for Social and Policy Studies. Among the individuals who provided support and encouragement, I am grateful to Phil Gorski,
Donald Green, Gil Joseph, Gus Ranis, and Ivan Szelenyi. I would also like to
thank the staff at the Council on Latin American and Iberian Studies and the
Yale University Center for International and Area Studies for their assistance,
especially Jean Silk.

In addition to the authors whose work is included in this collection, the
following presenters enriched the Yale meeting: Richard Appelbaum, Emily
Erikson (and coauthor Peter Bearman), Peter Gibbon, Sanjaya Lall, David
Levy, Nelson Lichtenstein, Tina Mangieri, Will Milberg (and coauthors
Melissa Mahoney, Markus Schneider, and Rudi von Armin), Enrique Dussel
Peters, and Katie Quan. Collectively, this project benefited as well from a set of
wonderful discussants, whose criticisms and insights are reflected in this vol-
ume: Julia Adams, Michael Denning, Teresa Lynch, Chick Perrow, Andrew
Shrank, and Meenu Tewari. Of course, I greatly appreciate the efforts (and

patience) of the thirteen authors whose work appears in this volume. Emily Hollerman provided excellent assistance in preparing the manuscript. Thanks are due also to our editor, Kate Wahl, as well as to Judith Hibbard and Joa Suorez at Stanford University Press, and to David Horne at Classic Typography for a careful and thoughtful copyediting of the volume.

As editor, I would like to acknowledge the support provided by a Junior Faculty Fellowship from Yale University. I would especially like to thank Professor Uli Jürgens and the other members of the Knowledge, Production systems, and Work research unit at the Wissenschaftszentrum Berlin für Sozialforschung (Social Science Research Center Berlin) for giving me an institutional home during my fellowship, where most of the work of editing this manuscript was completed.

In closing, I would like to note with sadness the passing of two scholars who were involved, directly or indirectly, in this project. Professor Sanjaya Lall was a renowned and prolific development economist whose work included seminal contributions to our understanding of multinational corporations and foreign direct investment, technology transfer, and trade and competitiveness. The paper that he presented at the Yale meeting shortly before his untimely passing, *Global Value Chains and Networks: Opportunities or Challenges,* demonstrated Professor Lall's continued interest in finding new ways to analyze the relationship between globalization, industrialization, and development. Finally, when we conceived the idea of an interdisciplinary project on commodity chains, Stephen Bunker was among the first scholars invited to participate. I was delighted both by his willingness to share his work at the Yale meeting and by his enthusiasm for this project more generally. Though Stephen's illness ultimately prevented him from contributing to this volume, his influence on the ideas presented here is significant. In particular, I hope that the third chapter, in which David Smith and Matthew Mahutga call for "bringing in Bunker" by acknowledging the importance of extractive industries for commodity chain analysis, might be seen as something of a tribute to his important work.

Jennifer Bair
Boulder, Colorado
September 2008

The Authors

Jennifer Bair is assistant professor of sociology at the University of Colorado at Boulder. Previously, she taught at Yale University, where she was the director of undergraduate studies for the Program in Ethics, Politics and Economics. Her research interests lie at the intersection of economic sociology and political economy, with a particular focus on the organizational dynamics and developmental implications of cross-border trade and production networks in the global economy. She is the coeditor (with Gary Gereffi and David Spener) of *Free Trade and Uneven Development: The North American Apparel Industry After NAFTA.*

• • •

Gary Gereffi is professor of sociology and director of the Center on Globalization, Governance, & Competitiveness at Duke University. His books include *Manufacturing Miracles: Paths of Industrialization in Latin America and East Asia; Commodity Chains and Global Capitalism; Free Trade and Uneven Development: The North American Apparel Industry After NAFTA;* and *The New Offshoring of Jobs and Global Development.* Gereffi's research interests deal with the competitive strategies of global firms, the governance of global value chains, industrial upgrading in East Asia and Latin America, and the emerging global knowledge economy.

• • •

Julie Guthman is an associate professor in the Department of Community Studies at the University of California, Santa Cruz. At its core, her research is about various efforts and social movements to transform the way food is produced, distributed, and consumed, focusing primarily on California. Her book *Agrarian Dreams: the Paradox of Organic Farming in California* won the 2007 Frederick H. Buttel Award for Outstanding Scholarly Achievement from the Rural Sociological Society.

• • •

Gary G. Hamilton is a professor of sociology at the Jackson School of International Studies at the University of Washington. He specializes in historical/comparative sociology, economic sociology, organizational sociology, and Asian societies, with particular emphasis on Chinese societies. He is the author, with Robert Feenstra, of *Emergent Economies, Divergent Paths: Economic Organization and International Trade in South Korea and Taiwan.*

• • •

Thalia Kidder is the Global Adviser on Labour and Gendered Economics at Oxfam Great Britain. Beginning as a union organizer in the United States, she later worked closely with women workers in the garment industry in Central America and has supported grassroots workers' campaigns in Asia, Latin America, Africa, and the United Kingdom.

• • •

Matthew C. Mahutga is assistant professor of sociology at the University of California, Riverside. His research investigates macro-structural change and its effect on various forms of inequality at the global level, as well as social network methodology in general.

• • •

William A. Munro is associate professor of political science and director of the International Studies Program at Illinois Wesleyan University. He has conducted extensive research on state formation and agrarian change in sub-Saharan Africa, and is the author of *The Moral Economy of the State: Conservation, Community Development and State-Making in Zimbabwe.*

• • •

Kate Raworth is senior researcher at Oxfam Great Britain and is author of Oxfam's report *Trading Away Our Rights: Women Working in Global Supply Chains*. Prior to joining Oxfam she was a coauthor of the United Nations Development Programme's *Human Development Report* for four years.

• • •

Rachel A. Schurman is associate professor of sociology and global studies at the University of Minnesota. Her areas of interest include biotechnology and agriculture, development sociology, the sociology of the environment, and political sociology. She is coeditor of *Engineering Trouble: Biotechnology and Its Discontents*.

• • •

David A. Smith is professor of sociology at the University of California, Irvine. His research interests include globalization and inequality, world city networks, and global commodity chains and development. His recent coedited books include *Labor Versus Empire: Race, Gender and Migration* and *Raw Materials and Political Economy*.

• • •

Timothy J. Sturgeon is senior research affiliate at the Industrial Performance Center at the Massachusetts Institute of Technology; co-organizer of the Global Value Chains Initiative (www.globalvaluechains.org); and research fellow at the Institute for Technology, Enterprise, and Competitiveness at the Doshisha Management School in Kyoto, Japan. Tim has conducted field research in dozens of countries, and published heavily cited articles in international peer-reviewed journals including *Industrial and Corporate Change, Review of International Political Economy, Journal of East Asian Studies,* and *Journal of Economic Geography*.

• • •

John M. Talbot is a senior lecturer in sociology at the University of the West Indies, Mona Campus, Jamaica. He is the author of *Grounds for Agreement: The Political Economy of the Coffee Commodity Chain*, which was awarded the 2005 Distinguished Book Award by the Political Economy of World-Systems section of the American Sociological Association. He is currently working on a history of Jamaican Blue Mountain coffee.

• • •

Steven Topik is professor of history at the University of California, Irvine. His previous work ranged from political economy (*The Political Economy of the Brazilian State, 1889–1930*) to international relations (*Trade and Gunboats: The United States and Brazil in the Age of Empire*) to commodity studies (*The Second Conquest of Latin America: Coffee, Henequen and Oil; The Global Coffee Economy in Africa, Asia and Latin America 1500–1989*, coedited with William Clarence-Smith; *From Silver to Cocaine: Latin American Commodity Chains and the Building of the World Economy, 1500–2000*, coedited with Carlos Marichal and Zephyr Frank) to world history (*The World That Trade Created: Culture, Society and the World Economy, 1400 to the Present*, coauthored with Kenneth Pomeranz).

• • •

Immanuel Wallerstein is senior research scholar in sociology at Yale University. He is author of *The Modern World-System* and most recently *European Universalism: The Rhetoric of Power.*

FRONTIERS OF COMMODITY CHAIN RESEARCH

1 Global Commodity Chains

Genealogy and Review

Jennifer Bair

O VER THE PAST TWO DECADES, A VOLUMINOUS LITERATURE on international trade and production networks has accumulated. Such networks were described first as commodity chains, later as *global* commodity chains, and most recently as global *value* chains. Although the sheer size of this flourishing literature underscores the appeal of global chain constructs as a way to conceptualize and analyze globalization, the dynamic and rapid proliferation of this research program also poses challenges. The significance of new theoretical formulations and empirical findings must be assessed, as scholars examine the extent to which they contradict, complement, or correct our extant knowledge about the ways in which people, places, and processes are linked to each other in the global economy. This volume, containing new work from an interdisciplinary group of scholars, aims to offer such an assessment of what we know about commodity chains, twenty years after the term was coined by Terence Hopkins and Immanuel Wallerstein.

In this introductory chapter, I describe the three approaches that collectively constitute what we might consider the field of global chain studies: (1) the world-systems tradition of macro- and long-range historical analysis of commodity chains; (2) the global commodity chains (GCCs) framework developed by Gary Gereffi and colleagues as a blend of organizational sociology and comparative development studies; and (3) global value chains (GVCs) analysis, the newest variant, which draws inspiration from its GCC predecessor but also, in some of its formulations, from the quite distinct tradition of transaction cost economics. Although often used interchangeably to describe the sequence of processes by which goods and services are conceived, produced, and brought to market, each of these chain constructs has its own history, its own theoretical and disciplinary affinities, its own substantive emphases and empirical concerns, and, arguably, its own political valences. In providing the reader with a modest exegesis of the commodity chain, my aim in the first section of this introduction is not to evaluate the relative merits and weaknesses of these constructs but rather to underscore the similarities and differences between them. The second part of the chapter then reviews three areas of debate within the study of global chains. Via brief summaries of the nine chapters that follow this introduction, I explain how the collection engages these debates and extends the frontiers of commodity chain research.

A Genealogy of the Commodity Chain

One way to understand the relationship between the actors and activities involved in creating goods and services in the global economy is to describe them as links in a commodity chain. Hopkins and Wallerstein define such a chain as "a network of labor and production processes whose end result is a finished commodity" (1986: 159). Later, I elaborate on the distinctive meaning of this analytical construct within world-systems theory, and contrast this understanding of the commodity chain with that found in the GCC and GVC frameworks. Through this genealogy of the chain concept, I aim to show the variation that exists among these approaches; however, because I also want to compare and contrast what I am referring to as the composite "global chains" literature with alternative perspectives on international production networks, I begin by reviewing some other chain-like concepts or constructs that aim to describe the organization and geography of production in the global economy.

Other Variations on the Chain Theme

In their discussion of commodity chain research as it pertains to agriculture and food, Jackson, Ward, and Russell (2006) locate two nearly contemporaneous but distinct sources of inspiration for this work. The first is world-systems theory, discussed in greater detail in the next section of this chapter. The second is the "new political economy of food and agriculture," and particularly the work of William Friedland and colleagues (1981) on technological change and its impact on the organization of work in U.S. farming.[1] Friedland's approach, which he described as "commodity systems analysis" (Friedland 1984) influenced others studying the organization of agricultural production, and increasingly, the relationship between production and consumption in food chains. Jackson and colleagues point out that though the agro-food literature has been influenced both by the world-systems and commodity systems approaches, "Friedland et al.'s key work made no reference to Wallerstein and vice versa. These are distinctly different traditions in their conceptual drivers, objects of study and modes of analysis" (2006: 131).

A later framework that would also prove influential within agro-food studies—systems of provision—was developed by Ben Fine and Ellen Leopold (1993; Fine 2002). Rather than beginning with production, as is typical of work in the new political economy of agriculture, Fine and Leopold sought to devise a more integrated approach to the relationship between consumption and production that would avoid the "productivist pitfall" typical of commodity analysis (Leslie and Reimer 1999: 406). Specifically, Fine and Leopold argued that one needed to consider the specificity of the consumption-production relationship as it pertained to particular commodities, and showed how commodities are "distinctly structured by the chain or system of provision that unites a particular pattern of production with a particular pattern of consumption" (Fine and Leopold 1993: 4).

A third and final chain-like tradition in agro-food studies is the filière approach, which pre-dates the commodity systems and systems of provisions frameworks, having been developed in the 1960s by researchers in France at the Institut National de la Recherche Agronomique and the Centre de Cooperatión Internationale en Recherche Agronomique pour le Développement. The application of the filière approach in developing countries "was heavily influenced by the needs of the colonial and post-colonial French state, since state (agricultural) development policy in former French colonies was commodity-centered and required a matching analytical framework" (Raikes, Jensen, and Ponte 2000: 391).

Each of these concepts—commodity systems, systems of provision, and filière—describe production (or production and consumption) in terms of a chain linking together different activities and agents. Perhaps for this reason, they are sometimes conflated with each other, or with what I later suggest is a more delimited commodity chain construct. For example, Leslie and Reimer use commodity chains and systems of provision interchangeably (1999; see also Hughes and Reimer 2004). In her discussion of commodity chain analysis, Jane Collins subsumes the filière tradition and the commodity systems approaches under the overarching rubric of commodity chain analysis, but her review contains no reference to the founding contributions of Hopkins and Wallerstein and mentions the world-systems tradition of chain research only in passing, when describing Gary Gereffi's global commodity chain paradigm as "operating within what is nominally a world systems perspective" (2005: 6).

Like their counterparts who study primary commodities, researchers investigating manufacturing industries have also been drawn to the chain metaphor as a way to capture the links connecting firms and other actors to each other across space. However, few references to the world-systems tradition of commodity chain research are found in such studies, and constructs that were developed specifically to analyze production processes in agriculture, such as commodity systems and filiére, are also largely absent. Instead, a variety of other concepts have been used to describe the highly internationalized production processes for manufactures such as cars, clothing, and computers (Borrus, Ernst, and Haggard 2000; Ernst 1999; Henderson, Dicken, Hess, Coe, and Wai-chung Yeung 2002).

Among these various approaches, the "Manchester school" of global production networks (GPNs) is closest to the commodity chain tradition.[2] Developed as "a relational and specifically geographic approach to the study of the global space-economy" (Hess and Yeung 2006: 1196–1997), the GPN framework evolved in dialogue with, and as critique of, the GCC framework, and Gary Gereffi's work in particular (Czaban and Henderson 1998; Dicken, Kelly, Olds, and Yeung 2001; Henderson and others 2002). Specifically, the proponents of the GPN approach argue that research carried out under the GCC banner has tended to ignore the spatial dimension of such chains. In contrast, the GPN approach seeks to reconcile an appreciation of the multiscalar dynamics of globalization with close analysis of specific networks in situ, and specifically the extent to which global networks are also local in the sense that they are embedded in different kinds of social or institutional contexts (Hess and Coe 2006; Hess and Yeung 2006). Despite the different emphases of the GPN framework and the efforts of its proponents to distinguish their approach from the GCC framework, most research carried out under the banner of the former consists of detailed and empirically rich case studies, and thus does not differ greatly from analyses of global commodity chains in terms of methodological approach (Bair 2008).

Though antecedents of contemporary work on international production networks in manufacturing are various, I will mention only two here. A 1973 article by Gerry Helleiner, which discusses the role of multinational corporations (MNCs) in the shift to export-oriented industrialization in developing countries, anticipates the transformations that Feenstra (1998) would describe a quarter century later as "the integration of trade and the disintegration of production."[3] Although foreign investment in the developing world focused first on resource exploitation and later on serving domestic markets protected by import-substituting industrialization, Helleiner predicted that MNCs would "move increasingly into the internationalization of production and marketing, knitting the less-developed countries into their international activities as suppliers not only of raw materials but also of manufactured products and processes" (31). Helleiner pointed to the implications of this "processing, assembly, and component manufacture" model for extant explanations of the internationalization of corporate activity, as well as for the industrialization and development prospects of host countries. By the end of that decade, the future Helleiner envisioned had, to large degree, materialized. The emergence of export-oriented manufacturing in many developing countries was famously interpreted as a new international division of labor, manifest in the proliferation of export-processing zones throughout the Third World (Fröbel, Heinrichs, and Kreye 1980).

Stephen Hymer's work on MNCs was a second important predecessor to the contemporary literature on cross-border production networks in global industries. If Helleiner assumed that the expansion of manufacturing for export in the developing world would take the form of foreign direct investment by multinationals in overseas subsidiaries, Hymer anticipated not just the geographical relocation of manufacturing but also its externalization to networks of independent enterprises (Strange and Newton 2006). In a 1972 paper, Hymer describes a cycle that "traces the operational flow of activities organized by the corporation through the phases of science, invention, innovation, production, marketing, distribution, and consumption" (Hymer, quoted in Cohen, Felton, Nkosi, and van Liere 1979: 151). In a passage that is resonant with Gereffi's description of buyer-driven commodity chains, Hymer hypothesizes that "where product design becomes the dominant element, investment in development and marketing is more important [than production.] The large corporation might then prefer to allow small businesses to own the plant and equipment (along with the associated risks) while it concentrates on intangibles" (Hymer, quoted in Cohen, Felton, Nkosi, and van Liere 1979: 248; compare Gereffi, Humphrey, Kaplinsky, and Sturgeon 2001: 6).

Decades after these pioneering discussions, two more variations on the chain theme emerged from milieu quite different than the literature on MNCs to which Helleiner and Hymer were contributing. The first is *supply chain management* (SCM), a term coined in 1982 by Keith Oliver, a vice president in the London office of the international consultancy firm Booz Allen Hamilton. Oliver developed an integrated approach to inventory management that sought to balance the trade-off between his client's goals and the needs of the client's customers; his idea was to analyze the "management of a chain of supply as though it were a single entity, not a group of disparate functions" (Laseter and Oliver 2003). Oliver referred to his approach as supply chain management; not only did the name stick, but this project of integrating logistics with materials and information flows mushroomed in the 1990s with new point-of-sale technologies and electronic data interchange (EDI).

The second is the notion of the *value chain,* which entered the lexicon of strategic management via Michael Porter's well-known 1985 book, *Competitive Advantage.* For Porter, value chains are tools for analyzing the relationship between various actors and activities *within* an organization. Businesses can secure a competitive advantage by successfully managing the linkages between these internal functions in a way that creates value for the firm's customers. Porter uses the term *value system* to describe the set of *inter-firm* linkages through which different enterprises (and their value chains) are connected to each other. These larger interconnected systems of value chains, which extend backward from an individual firm to its suppliers, and forward into its distribution channels, are often international in scope. For this reason, within the strategic management literature they are sometimes referred to as global supply chains, or occasionally global value chains.

The first set of chain concepts discussed earlier—commodity systems, systems of provision, and filière—shares some similarities with commodity chains as understood by world-systems theorists, whereas the various network approaches used to describe global manufacturing arrangements, as well as supply chain management and Porter's value chains, are closer to the GCC and GVC frameworks. Yet these variants differ from the three camps of commodity or value chain research summarized further on insofar as the latter share common roots—specifically, in a political economy perspective in which the chain construct is used to investigate interconnected, cross-border processes of trade and production. Although the discussion of these three chain approaches later in this chapter points to some of the ways in which the GCC and later the GVC approaches diverged from the original commodity chain formulation offered by Hopkins and Wallerstein, they can nevertheless be regarded as stemming from a single intellectual lineage, in the sense that the GCC framework grew out of (though modified) world-systems theory, and

GVC analysis grew out of (though, again, also modified in important ways) the GCC framework. The extent to which this lineage outweighs salient differences between these camps, and the relationship between this composite global chains literature, so conceived, and other network approaches such as the GPN framework mentioned earlier, is an ongoing question, and one that is addressed, implicitly or explicitly, in several of the chapters that follow.

From Commodity Chains in the World-System to Value Chains in the Global Economy

The term *commodity chain* dates from a 1977 article by Hopkins and Wallerstein in which the authors sought to differentiate their understanding of capitalism's territorial scope from the orthodox way of thinking about globalization. Instead of seeing the global economy's development as a sequential process whereby national markets evolve in the direction of expanded foreign trade geared to an international market, the authors suggest starting with

> a radically different presumption. Let us conceive of something we shall call, for want of a better conventional term, "commodity chains." What we mean by such chains is the following: take an ultimate consumable item and trace back the set of inputs that culminated in this item—the prior transformations, the raw materials, the transportation mechanisms, the labor input into each of the material processes, the food inputs into the labor. This linked set of processes we call a commodity chain. If the ultimate consumable were, say, clothing, the chain would include the manufacture of the cloth, the yarn, etc., the cultivation of the cotton, as well as the reproduction of the labor forces involved in these productive activities (128).

Three features characterize the world-systems tradition of chain research. First, commodity chain analysis focuses on how the global division and integration of labor into the world economy has evolved over time: "In terms of the structure of the capitalist world-economy, commodity chains may be thought of as the warp and woof of its system of social production" (Hopkins and Wallerstein 1994: 17). Historical reconstruction of commodity chains suggests that they have been global in scope since the emergence of modern capitalism. Thus, contra a presentist view of globalization, world-systems theory maintains that "transstate, geographically extensive commodity chains are *not* a recent phenomenon, dating from say the 1970s or even 1945, . . . they have been an integral part of . . . the functioning of the capitalist world-economy since it came into existence in the long sixteenth century" (Wallerstein 2000a: 2).

Second, commodity chain analysis seeks to understand "the unequal distribution of rewards among the various activities that constitute the single overarching division of labor defining and bounding the world economy" (Arrighi and Drangel 1986: 16). The question for researchers is what we can learn from commodity chain analysis about the process of capital accumulation at a particular point in the evolution of the world-system, and what it tells us about the distribution of the total surplus-value created in a particular chain between its various links (or boxes, in the terminology of Hopkins and Wallerstein). Some links in a chain will tend to be located in core (that is, developed) countries of the world-system, and others in the less-developed zones of the semi-periphery and periphery, but the spatial distribution of these links can change over time, as can the configuration of the chain itself, as when the boundaries around boxes are redrawn (for example, activities previously performed in one box are divided into two separate boxes). Boxes that are characterized by a high rate of profit are typically monopolized by a small number of producers and are usually located in core countries, although any highly profitable link is subject to competitive pressures that tend toward its demonopolization over time.

Third, the spatial and social configurations of chains are linked to cyclical shifts in the world economy. During phases of economic contraction (Kondratieff B-phases), the geographical scope of a chain is often reduced, due to increased concentration and a decline in the overall number of producers participating in it, while the degree of vertical integration characterizing a chain tends to increase (that is, more links of the chain are incorporated within the organizational boundaries of the firm) (Hopkins and Wallerstein 1994). The reverse is true of expansionary periods, or Kondratieff A-phases.

The first book-length manuscript devoted to commodity chains appeared in 1994. *Commodity Chains and Global Capitalism* was edited by Gary Gereffi and Miguel Korzeniewicz and contained a number of papers presented at the sixteenth annual conference of the Political Economy of the World-Systems (PEWS) research group. Most reviews of the commodity chain approach cite this volume as "the beginning of GCC analysis as a relatively coherent paradigm" (Daviron and Ponte 2005), and emphasize the framework's roots in the world-systems orientation (Dicken and others 2001; Fine 2002; Thompson 2003), the dependency tradition (Henderson and others 2002), radical development theory (Whitley 1996), or structuralist development economics (Cramer 1999).[4] However, as I have argued elsewhere (Bair 2005), there is a disjuncture between the world-systems tradition of commodity chain research and the GCC framework, and these differences were already evident in the Gereffi and Korzeniewicz volume. Most of the chapters in the book, with the exception of those on the shipbuilding and wheat flour commodity chains during the sixteenth and seventeenth centuries (Özveren 1994; Pelizzon 1994), focus on contemporary manufacturing industries, and in particular on inter-firm networks linking developing country exporters to world markets. In addition, most contributors neglected to investigate the cyclical dynamics of commodity chains that are of great interest to world-systems theorists.

The most widely cited contribution to *Commodity Chains and Global Capitalism* was a chapter by Gary Gereffi that described a framework for the study of what he called global commodity chains, or GCCs. Gereffi (1994) identified three dimensions of such chains along which they could be analyzed: (1) an input-output structure, which describes the process of transforming raw materials and other inputs into final products); (2) a territoriality, or geographical configuration; and (3) a governance structure, which describes both the process by which particular players in the chain exert control over other participants and how these lead firms (or "chain drivers") appropriate or distribute the value that is created along the chain. In a later contribution (1995), Gereffi added a fourth dimension: institutional context, which describes the "rules of the game" bearing on the organization and operation of chains.

As Gereffi and his coauthors make clear in their introduction to the volume, part of the appeal of the commodity chain construct is its ability to move across different levels of analysis: "Our GCC framework allows us to pose questions about contemporary development issues that are not easily handled by previous paradigms, and permits us to more adequately forge the macro-micro links between processes that are generally assumed to be discreetly contained within global, national, and local units of analysis" (Gereffi, Korzeniewicz, and Korzeniewicz 1994: 2).

Global commodity chains are structures that connect actors across space—not only to each other, but also to world markets. They can thus be thought of as the infrastructure of international trade, and their analysis reveals cross-border flows and intermediate processes of production and exchange that are concealed by statistics referring only to trade in final products. For this reason, Gereffi's GCC framework proved particularly appealing to scholars in development studies, who having witnessed the widespread adoption of export-oriented industrialization (EOI) strategies across much of the global South throughout the 1980s and 1990s were eager to find a paradigm that would help shed light on these policies and their consequences. The shift to EOI among developing countries was auspicious for the reception of Gereffi's GCC framework among academics and policymakers alike, and although the timing was fortunate, the substantive relevance of the GCC approach for development issues was rooted in the evolution and trajectory of more than two decades of Gereffi's own work—first, on the pharmaceutical industry in Mexico and the dynamics of dependent development (Gereffi 1983), and later on the comparative trajectories of East Asian and Latin American economies (Gereffi and Wyman 1990). Although his early writing was strongly influenced by dependency theory, Gereffi's comparative research later highlighted differences in the industrialization strategies being pursued across regions, especially with regard to how these domestic policies and regimes intersected with the organization of global industries.

As an approach linking development trajectories to the dynamics of industrial sectors, the GCC framework provided a way to codify and extend the insights generated by Gereffi's studies of comparative development. Chief among these was Gereffi's assertion, contra the world-systems view of commodity chains, that *global* commodity chains are an emergent organizational form associated with a relatively recent and qualitatively novel process of economic integration: "One of the central contentions of the GCC approach is that the internationalization of production is becoming increasingly integrated in globalized coordination systems that can be characterized as producer-driven and buyer-driven commodity chains" (1996: 429). This distinction between producer-driven and buyer-driven commodity chains (PDCCs and BDCCs) highlighted distinct patterns of coordination and control in global industries. The emergence and proliferation of buyer-driven chains in light manufacturing industries seemed to capture well the experience of many developing countries, which were becoming integrated into global markets as exporters of toys, footwear, apparel, and consumer electronics. In addition to Gereffi's own early work on apparel (Appelbaum and Gereffi 1994; Gereffi 1994), dissertations written by Gereffi's students at Duke University contributed to the emergent literature on BDCCs in several industries throughout the 1990s (Cheng 1996; Haji-Salleh 1997; Leung 1997; Pan 1998).

The GCC approach departs from the original world-systems research agenda on commodity chains in two ways. First, its analytical emphasis on the activities of firms, and especially the chain drivers that play the lead role in constructing and managing international production networks, gives greater weight than a more orthodox world-systems approach would to the role of firms as capitalism's organizing agents. Second, its interest in analyzing—and later, in more policy-oriented work, harnessing—the dynamics of commodity chains to advance the industrialization and developmental objectives of states marks a further break with the world-systems tradition, which inveighs against the myopia of this "developmentalist illusion" (Arrighi 1990; Wallerstein 1994). Although studies of GCCs frequently focus on the prospects for firms, nations, or regions to upgrade via incorporation into particular commodity chains, world-systems theorists emphasize that for understanding the world-capitalist economy, "[w]hat is central is the fact of unequal exchange operating through a set of mechanisms . . . that continually reproduces the core-periphery division of labor itself—despite massive changes in the areas and processes constituting the core, periphery and semi-periphery" (Arrighi and Drangel 1986).

The GCC framework outlined by Gereffi in his contribution to *Commodity Chains and Global Capitalism* proved widely influential, and within a decade a wide range of global commodity chains in the manufacturing, agricultural, and (to a lesser extent) service sectors had been studied.[5] Several international institutions embraced the GCC (and more recently, GVC) framework as well. The International Labour Organization sponsored a multiyear project looking at the implications of this kind of analysis for employment; the United Nations Commission for Latin America and the Caribbean has drawn on the GCC approach in research on regional production clusters; and the United Nations Industrial Development Organization funded a series of sectoral analyses assessing the prospects for developing-country firms in various global chains, including those for autos (Humphrey and Memdovic 2003), apparel (Gereffi and Memdovic 2003), and furniture (Kaplinsky, Morris, and Readman 2001).

By the close of the 1990s, and in the context of this burgeoning literature on global chains, some scholars began to reappraise the original GCC approach. First, the very description of these chains as *commodity* chains was questioned, because the term *commodity* is generally taken to denote either primary products (for example, agricultural staples) or low-value-added, basic goods (such as plain t-shirts as "commodity" garments).[6] Second, Gereffi's original distinction between producer-driven and buyer-driven chains was thought to miss important features of chain governance that were revealed by new studies, suggesting the need for an expanded typology. Finally, some scholars noted that there was relatively little exchange between researchers working within the GCC framework and those who, although working on similar topics, were using different concepts to describe international production networks. This became especially evident when, as Timothy Sturgeon's chapter in this volume explains in greater detail, a group of researchers, with support from the Rockefeller Foundation, began an interdisciplinary initiative in 2000 to examine different approaches to the study of global production networks. Out of their conversations and collaborative work came the conviction that a common terminology would foster dialogue and promote a sense of intellectual community among scholars studying global industries. With the aim of selecting a term that would be inclusive of various constructs, this group decided to describe their project as *global value chain analysis*. The GVC rubric was favored over alternative concepts such as *commodity chains* or *supply chains* "because it was perceived as being the most inclusive of the full range of possible chain activities and end products" (Gereffi, Humphrey, Kaplinsky, and Sturgeon 2001).

There is no clear consensus regarding the relationship between the GCC framework and GVC analysis, however. For example, scholars at the Danish Institute for International Studies adopted the new vocabulary in a multiyear research project analyzing the experiences of African exporters in global markets. Although the two books that resulted from this research are the first manuscript-length works to refer to GVCs, the authors appear to regard the shift from "commodity chains" to "value chains" as a purely terminological one devoid of substantive theoretical implications (Gibbon and Ponte 2005; Daviron and Ponte 2005). Indeed, Daviron and Ponte refer to the GVC approach as one "that first appeared in the literature under the term 'global commodity chain' (GCC) analysis" (2005: 27), suggesting that GVCs and GCCs are more or less interchangeable constructs.

However, a somewhat different perspective is offered by Timothy Sturgeon, whose chapter here both elaborates his view of GVC analysis as a broader intellectual project and situates within this overarching GVC research agenda a specific theory of GVC governance, which he has helped formulate. In Sturgeon's view, GVC analysis draws on the GCC tradition of chain research, but it is also influenced by transaction cost economics and a broader literature in the economics of organization. A paper coauthored by Sturgeon, Gary Gereffi, and John Humphrey, which appeared in the *Review of International Political*

Economy in 2005, was a key moment in the development of a GVC approach distinct from Gereffi's GCC framework. In this paper, the authors identified a typology of five possible governance structures that can be found at the inter-firm boundary linking suppliers to lead firms in global value chains. According to this theory, the type of governance prevailing at the link between two firms is determined by the values (measured as "low" or "high") in three independent variables: the complexity of transactions, the codifiability of information, and the capabilities of the supply base. These variables are intended to capture characteristics of the industry structure or production process, including the nature of "the knowledge transfer required to sustain a particular transaction, particularly with respect to product and process certifications, the extent to which this information and knowledge can be codified, and therefore, transmitted efficiently and without transaction-specific investment between the parties to the transaction, and the capabilities of actual and potential suppliers in relation to the requirements of the transaction" (Gereffi, Humphrey, and Sturgeon 2005: 85).

Thus far I have offered a genealogy of the commodity chain concept that distinguishes between the world-systems tradition, the GCC framework, and GVC analysis. One might interpret these as three *generations* of chain constructs, insofar as they roughly succeed each other in a temporal ordering, with the original commodity chain concept dating from the 1980s, the GCC framework being elaborated in the 1990s, and the global value chain variant emerging only in the 2000s. However, a generational schema of this sort is somewhat misleading because these literatures overlap, and work in all three traditions of chain research continues, including some by scholars who have been influenced by, and whose present research references, more than one of these frameworks. For example, though Gary Gereffi has been actively involved in the development of global value chain analysis, and was one of the architects of the GVC governance theory, it is the GCC framework and its conceptualization of governance as "drivenness" that informs his analysis in Chapter 7 of this volume, authored jointly with Gary Hamilton.

In fact, the construct of the buyer-driven commodity chain figures prominently in Hamilton and Gereffi's discussion of the relationship between global buyers and local producers in Korea and Taiwan. This suggests that the new typology of governance proposed by Gereffi and colleagues (2005) is not intended to replace the GCC framework's original buyer-driven versus producer-driven distinction. Rather, because these different classificatory schemes correspond to different conceptualizations of governance (as I discuss in the next section of this chapter), the question of which typology to apply in a particular piece of research may well depend on the specific analytical or theoretical issue that is being addressed. Hamilton and Gereffi use the BDCC construct to explain how networks between global buyers and local suppliers can shape the organization of a national economy. Given their interest in demonstrating the macro-level consequences of these networks, the GCC framework provides a better analytical lens than that of the GVC governance theory, whereas the latter might be preferable if the researcher wanted to focus instead on the dynamics of a particular industry, or to explain the variation that exists within a set of buyer-driven chains.

As the preceding discussion as well as the chapters that follow suggest, the extent to which a clear differentiation between the world-systems, GCC, and GVC versions of commodity chain research can and should be made is open to dispute, and so too is the question of how one might distinguish between these various approaches as they are applied in empirical work. Readers of this volume can make their own judgments about the analytical utility of such a distinction, and likely will arrive at their own assessments.

Three Debates in the Study of Chains

I turn now to a review of key debates within the commodity chain literature that contributions to this volume engage. These deal with central methodological and theoretical questions about what and how we learn from the study of global chains, and include (1) issues of analytical scope and operationalization of the chain construct, (2) chain governance, and (3) the sociological and political implications of chain analysis. The remainder of this chapter is divided into three sections, each of which provides an overview of one of these debates, followed by brief summaries of how the chapters in this collection address and extend them.

Issues of Operationalization, or "Which Is It Anyway—Commodity or Value Chain?"

Of necessity, every contributor to this volume takes a position with regard to the first of these debates by deciding to use either the term *commodity chain* or *value chain*. Although some might dismiss as inconsequential the decision to use *value* or *commodity,* the genealogy of the commodity chain concept traced in the previous section suggests that the choice for one term versus another is meaningful insofar as it has implications for how chains are studied, starting with the fundamental question of how the very object in question is analytically defined.

The commodity chain of world-systems theory is the most inclusive of extant chain constructs. Like its GCC and GVC counterparts, it includes the sequence of activities through which raw materials or components are transformed into final products, but this tradition of chain research also emphasizes that labor power is a critical input into every commodity chain and thus seeks to identify the various modes of labor control and reproduction that one can find along a chain, or even within a single box (Hopkins and Wallerstein 1994). Depictions of historical commodity chains as they have been reconstructed by world-systems researchers also include the transportation and storage of intermediate and final products as boxes in the chain. In this sense, the commodity chain is more like a web than a chain. World-systems analysts are not only, or perhaps not even primarily, interested in the sequential flow of materials and transformations that produce a final commodity. Instead of this "forward" view, they may want to look outward from any particular box in a chain and analyze the various processes which created the product in *that* box. In other words, what may be the last link in one chain is itself an input or intermediate link in another. It is the overlapping and intersecting nature of different commodity chains that Hopkins and Wallerstein meant to evoke when referring to them as the warp and woof of the capitalist world-economy.

Moving from this conceptual understanding of commodity chains to their empirical study poses a number of daunting challenges for the researcher. Hopkins and Wallerstein suggest that one possibility for commodity chains research is "to develop a mode of evaluating the entire network of commodity chains at successive points in time, so as to locate shifts in which chains are the major loci of capital accumulation" (1994: 49). However, in reality most studies focus on a single chain, or more accurately, a segment of a single chain or even a single box. This raises a methodological question for chain researchers: how *should* a chain be defined and made manageable as an object of study? For example, if the buyer-driven and producer-driven constructs are Weberian ideal types, how is a particular buyer-driven or producer-driven chain—say, those for apparel and automobiles, respectively—operationalized in empirical analysis? Or put differently, how does one differentiate between a global commodity chain as a stylized representation of inter-firm networks in a global industry and the many sets of specific linkages that constitute "real world" chains?

One of the benefits that primary commodities offer to chain analysts is manageability. Studying the entire length of a commodity chain is a task more easily accomplished for coffee and cocoa than for cars and computers. Another "comparative advantage of tropical commodity chain analysis" (as described by John Talbot in Chapter 5) is the tendency of these chains to highlight issues of global inequality that may be less obvious in other industry contexts. This is because the ecology of tropical commodities requires them to be grown in the global South, whereas markets for these products are located primarily in the North. Thus tropical commodity chains are almost always truly "global"—not only do these chains cross national borders, they also connect producers to consumers across the boundaries of the world-system zones (Talbot 2004).

But are all commodity chains so extensive in their territorial dimension? Put differently, are all global commodity chains, in fact, global? It was a premise of Gereffi's original GCC framework that transnational production systems are becoming increasingly integrated and coordinated across space, but the extent to which the territoriality of any specific commodity chain is global is an empirical question. Geographically concentrated chains can be found in global industries for a variety of reasons, including product characteristics and market factors. For example, clothing retailers in the United States might prefer domestic or regional (say, Latin American) suppliers when speed-to-market or quick replenishment pressures are critical. For some products, "shorter" and less dispersed chains are part of the product's very definition and appeal; this may be the case for fruits and vegetables sold at a local farmer's market when, for example, the consumer values the increased transparency and freshness that spatial proximity between "farm and fork" is thought to provide. Yet although particular chains—that is, discrete sets of linkages between specific actors—may not be global, the GCC framework leads us to ask how these are nevertheless shaped by the broader organizational field of the global commodity chain to which they belong.

Several critics have faulted the chain construct for its linearity, suggesting that it is incapable of conveying the complex and interactional nature of networks (Henderson and others 2002; Cook and Crang 1996). Some argue that an analytical vocabulary of networks better captures the role of actors than do more structural chain approaches, which Arce and Marsden accuse of verging on a functionalist determinism that "suppresses the significance of contextualized human agency" (1993: 296; compare Collins 2005). Leslie and Reimer (1999) worry that "horizontal" dimensions receive inadequate attention when analytical priority is given to the flow of materials or processes along the chain. For example, aspects such as place and gender are relevant for each link in the commodity chain, yet may be neglected by chain approaches focusing on the connections between links, as opposed to the common elements bearing on the organization of actors and activities across the chain.

These and other critical discussions of the global chain literature highlight some of the methodological weaknesses or confusions that chain researchers should address, and underscore the need for greater attention to the question of how we operationalize the commodity chain as an analytical construct. Raikes, Jensen, and Ponte point to the need for this kind of clarification in their review of Gereffi's global commodity chain framework: "Is a GCC just any channel, or set of channels, by which products cross the world, or should the notion itself include the specific power and governance structure seen by Gereffi to define GCCs?" (2000: 400). Similarly, Thompson asks "[w]hat are the 'limits' of GCC/value-chain analysis, and what is the 'beyond' of its particular analytical formulations? Is there anything that cannot be included as a commodity/value chain that can claim to be called economic production?" (2003: 211).

The chapters in Part I speak to several of the methodological issues at stake in analyzing commodity chains in comparative and historical perspective. These authors reflect on how we define the commodity chain as an object of study, implicitly pointing to the challenge that researchers face in deciding on an operationalization of the commodity chain that is feasible in terms of empirical study and yet still sensitive to the complexity, multidimensionality, and variability of these networks across time and space.

In the only chapter authored by a historian (Chapter 2), Steven Topik's discussion of the global trade in coffee underscores the importance of approaching commodity chains as concrete social relations between historical actors. In contrast to the GCC approach's emphasis on the role of lead firms as the organizational drivers of chains, Topik shows how changing patterns of popular consumption in foreign markets, as well as particular characteristics of the locations in which production takes place, shape the geography of international production and trade networks. Within the vast literature on the coffee trade, analyses of the contemporary coffee chain highlight the power of large, multinational roasters and specialty coffee retailers and the collapse of the International Coffee Agreements in explaining the precipitous decline in the price of green coffee beans (Talbot 2004). Others emphasize that the ability of brands and coffee retailers such as Starbuck's to capture the majority of value-added in the coffee chain reflects their control of symbolic or immaterial aspects of production, such as the in-person services or atmosphere provided on-site at the local café (Daviron and Ponte 2005).

These analyses provide valuable insight into the organization of the coffee chain (including the enormous volumes of coffee traded on the futures market), but Topik's sweeping historical analysis, which begins *before* coffee became constituted as a commodity, enables a different perspective. Challenging the standard view of coffee-growing countries as victims of powerful U.S. or European corporations, Topik describes Brazil's importance as a "market maker" for coffee in the late nineteenth century and its later role as a global "price maker," following the government's implementation of the valorization plan in 1906. In short, historical analysis is capable of underscoring agency and contingency in commodity chains, and can show how power among actors in chains shifts over time—all of which helps one to avoid the temptation of seeing the organization of contemporary commodity chains as necessary or inevitable, the functionalist determinism that Arce and Marsden, among others (Henderson and others 2002), caution against.

David Smith and Matthew Mahutga provide a similar warning about what Topik refers to as the problem of "tunnel vision" in analyzing commodity chains. In their contribution (Chapter 3), Smith and Mahutga argue that extractive activities, which produce the raw materials used in so many commodity chains, merit far more attention than they have received in the chain literature—an omission they aim to address. Drawing on the "modes of extraction" concept developed by Stephen Bunker (1985; Bunker and Ciccantell 2005), Smith and Mahutga suggest that analytical attention to these forgotten links in the commodity chain foregrounds critical factors, such as the importance of transportation in enabling geographically extensive chains, and the role of the state, given that governments are often intimately involved in administering and supporting the infrastructure required for large-scale extractive activities. An operationalization of the commodity chain that "starts at the beginning" (Smith 2005) is part of the authors' project to link the analysis of international trade and production networks to a country's structural position in the world-system, as well as to broader debates about the degree and nature of global inequality. In this sense, Smith and Mahutga's chapter is the most faithful extension of the world-systems research agenda on commodity chains among those collected here. However, their quantitative network analysis departs from the historical reconstruction of commodity chains that has characterized this tradition, and thus extends world-systems analysis of commodity chains in a new methodological direction.

Like Smith and Mahutga, Immanuel Wallerstein points in Chapter 4 to the importance of the state in shaping commodity chains, and like Topik, he is interested in the implications of this insight for appreciating the historically contingent and politically constructed nature of chains. Wallerstein elaborates the various ways in which governments shape what the GCC framework refers to as the institutional context within which chains operate, but he emphasizes that the influence of the state over global production networks is not restricted to setting "the rules of the game." The configuration of chains sometimes reflects struggles between the state and producers, as the latter try to avoid or circumvent government-imposed restrictions on their activity that they find onerous. In addition to these internal struggles between states and producers, Wallerstein observes that international trade and production networks are often objects of political and ideological contestation between countries, as was starkly apparent when a unified front of developing countries (the so-called G-20 plus) challenged the legitimacy of the global trade regime during the WTO meeting in Cancun, Mexico, in September 2003.

Wallerstein's chapter provides a fitting conclusion to the first section of this volume, because he speaks directly to the question of how we should study commodity chains. Rather than offering a specific set of recommendations, Wallerstein reminds us that even the most careful operationalization of the chain concept, and the most rigorous empirical analysis, will yield only a partial perspective on the dynamics of production and exchange in the world capitalist economy that he and Hopkins developed the commodity chain concept to explore: "Studying commodity chains is for the political economist something like . . . looking through the Hubble telescope for the cosmologist. We are measuring indirectly and imperfectly a total phenomenon that we cannot see directly no matter what we do. . . . It requires imagination and audacity along with patience. The only thing we have to fear is looking too narrowly."

Governance: Beyond the PDCC-BDCC Distinction

Gereffi's (1994) differentiation between producer-driven and buyer-driven commodity chains is the most widely cited proposition in the global commodity chains literature. Producer-driven chains are characteristic of more capital-intensive industries in which powerful manufacturers control and often own several tiers of vertically organized suppliers (for example, motor vehicles); buyer-driven chains refer to industries, apparel being the classic case, in which far-flung subcontracting networks are managed with varying degrees of closeness by retailers, marketers, and other "intermediaries" (Spulber 1996) that generally make few or none of the products that are sold under their label. Ownership is more closely correlated with control of the production process in PDCCs than in BDCCs. In the latter, non-equity ties between lead firms (or "big buyers") and first-tier suppliers, as well as between suppliers and several tiers of contractors, are more prevalent than either vertical integration or one-shot, arm's-length market transactions. What is most significant about this dichotomy is the recognition of the role played by commercial capital in BDCCs. These companies, mostly retailers and brand-name marketers, call the shots for the many firms involved in the buyer-driven chains they manage, although they generally have no equity relation to the producers making goods on their behalf.

One of Gereffi's main interests was to show that even chains with more "market-like" governance structures require coordination, and that these coordinating tasks are assumed by lead firms that determine much of the division of labor along the chain and define the terms on which actors gain access to it (Appelbaum and Gereffi 1994). Thus outcomes for suppliers are strongly affected by the behavior of lead firms, leading researchers to examine the implications of a chain's governance structure for the upgrading efforts of suppliers and the developmental prospects of the regions in which they are located (Gibbon 2001a; Schrank 2004; Daviron and Ponte 2005).

Although the analytical utility of these Weberian ideal types was confirmed by studies using the producer-driven and buyer-driven constructs as templates for analyzing various industries, the PDCC-BDCC distinction was criticized for being too narrow, overly abstract, or both (Clancy 1998; Fold 2002; Gellert 2003; Henderson and others 2002). Other studies suggested that the buyer-driven and producer-driven categories did not adequately capture the range of governance forms observed in actual chains, leading to a proliferation of variations on the original theme of "drivenness." Although the PDCC-BDCC distinction had been elaborated with reference to manufacturing industries, Peter Gibbon (2001a) proposed that true "commodity" chains—that is, those along which basic agricultural products such as coffee and sugar are harvested, processed, and marketed—are international trader-driven chains, with large trading houses often playing the lead firm role. Based on his study of the chocolate chain, Niels Fold (2002) proposed that a bipolar governance structure can emerge when two types of lead firms (in the case of chocolate, cocoa grinders and brand-name chocolate manufacturers) control different segments of the chain. Sean O'Riain (2004) argued that research-intensive industries such as software are best understood as technology-driven chains. Gereffi himself proposed that Internet-based developments such as B2B (business to business) networks were producing new forms of coordination and control described as Internet-driven chains (2001a). Yet another governance structure—the modular network—was proposed by Timothy Sturgeon (2002). The modular network, which is discussed in more detail later this in this section, describes relations between brand-name companies in the electronics industry (such as Apple, Compaq, Silicon Graphics) and the contract manufacturers that supply them (for example, Solectron, Flextronics).

Among the four dimensions of the GCC framework outlined by Gereffi, governance structure has received the most empirical and theoretical attention (Gereffi, Humphrey, and Sturgeon 2005; Ponte and Gibbon 2005; Petkova 2006). To understand current debates about governance in the chain literature, and how the chapters in this volume contribute to them, we must first consider how the concept of governance in the GCC and GVC frameworks differs from the view of networks as organizational "hybrids" in transaction cost economics, as well as from the view, prevalent within much of economic sociology, that relational networks are a distinct, trust-based governance structure.

Sociological research on economic networks in the 1980s was largely a response to, and more specifically a criticism of, transaction cost economics. The latter field developed as part of the new institutional economics in the 1970s, when economists, armed with the much earlier work of Ronald Coase (1937), began to look inside the "black box" of the firm. If Coase argued that the problem of the firm—that is, why the economy features large organizations that internalize transactions that could occur in the market—is to be explained by the fact that transacting on the market implies costs, Oliver Williamson set out to formalize this observation, asking under what circumstances do the costs of transacting on the market make the internalization of those exchanges within a firm the more efficient solution? Williamson's answer hinged largely on asset specificity: transactions were more likely to

be conducted within the organizational boundaries of the firm when they required particular, dedicated investments. In Williamson's view, investments of
this kind increase the mutual dependence between the actors in an exchange
(for example, between buyer and supplier). The mutual dependence implied by
high levels of asset specificity create the conditions for opportunistic behavior
on the part of one or both parties to the transaction, which, in turn, creates
costs, such as the building-in of safeguards to prevent possible malfeasance
(Williamson 1975).

Although Williamson's theory initially focused on elaborating the circumstances under which hierarchy (that is, firms) may represent an efficient
alternative to markets, he later acknowledged that intermediate forms of organization that mix elements of market and hierarchy are also possible. In an
analysis of the way in which different organizational forms depend on and
are supported by distinct traditions of contract law, Williamson identifies a
"hybrid" organizational form between market and hierarchy, which describes
various kinds of long-term contracting arrangements or other situations in
which there are repeated exchanges between autonomous parties that share
some degree of mutual dependence (Williamson 1991).

Sociologists challenged Williamson and the new institutional economists on three grounds. First, they argued that the hybrid form Williamson
described was not an *intermediate* organizational form between the poles of
market and hierarchy but rather a *distinct* network governance structure that
was, in Powell's classic formulation, "neither market nor hierarchy" (1990).
They further rejected Williamson's assumption that what he called intermediate forms of organization were relatively infrequent, arguing that because
"the network form of organization has a number of distinct efficiency advantages not possessed by pure markets or pure hierarchies," it is empirically
more common than transaction cost economics would predict (Podolny and
Page 1998: 59). Finally, the very tenability of Williamson's distinction between
different organizational forms was questioned, because there are "strong elements of markets within hierarchies" and vice versa (Perrow 1986).

In a highly influential and widely cited article published in 1985, Mark
Granovetter argued that transaction cost economics operates with an "under-
socialized" conception of human action. His claim is that standard economic
accounts obscure the fact that interpersonal relations between economic actors, and the obligations and expectations that derive from them, can constrain the malfeasance and opportunistic behavior at the core of Williamson's

explanation of the firm (Granovetter 1985). However, if trust-producing social relations can "solve" the malfeasance problem, they do not necessarily do so, leading Granovetter to eschew a predictive model specifying when interpersonal ties generate particular outcomes in favor of grounded analyses examining how concrete social relations affecting economic activity emerge and evolve in specific contexts.

The research agenda proceeding from Granovetter's intervention has since been pursued by many authors seeking to demonstrate how socio-structural contexts shape economic activity (see also Hamilton and Gereffi, Chapter 7 in this volume). Many of these contributions focus on a particular organizational form—inter-firm networks—and a particular manifestation of the social-interpersonal relations, between, for example, firms and venture capitalists (Powell, Koput, and Smith-Doerr 1996) or between manufacturers and their suppliers (Uzzi 1997). In fact, a focus on social networks as dyadic ties between individuals or firms is a hallmark of the new economic sociology (Granovetter 1992; Swedberg 1997; Grabher 2006). Thus, although one could read Granovetter as suggesting that *all* economic activity and *every* form of economic organization is embedded in a social context—in which case, embeddedness is a process that bears on hierarchies and markets as much as on hybrid forms—sociological work proceeding from Granovetter's challenge to economics has focused primarily on the inter-firm network as a uniquely "social" organizational form (Bair, 2008).

Understood in this sense, networks are unlike either markets or hierarchies because they generate mutual expectations and relations of trust, which arise from repeated exchanges that become "overlaid with social content" (Granovetter 1985: 490). It is because of their "distinct ethic or value-orientation" that networks are "not reducible to a hybridization of market and hierarchical forms, which, in contrast are premised on a more adversarial posture" (Podolny and Page 1998: 61). The benefits of networks relative to other organizational forms derive in large measure from the kind of interactive and collaborative learning that trust is presumed to enable. Brian Uzzi's discussion of networks in the New York City garment district is typical in this respect:

> Unlike governance structures in atomistic markets, which are manifested in intense calculativeness, monitoring devices, and impersonal contractual ties, trust is a governance structure that resides in the social relationships between and among individuals and cognitively is based on heuristic rather than calculative

processing. In this sense, trust is fundamentally a social process, since these psychological mechanisms and expectations are emergent features of a social structure that creates and reproduces them through time. This component of the exchange relationship is important because it enriches the firm's opportunities, access to resources, and flexibility in ways that are difficult to emulate using arm's-length ties (1997: 45).

Sociological analyses of the network form often highlight, as Uzzi does, the functional advantages that networks provide. But what if a different governance structure is capable of generating similar benefits? This is the question both posed and answered by Timothy Sturgeon's work on contract manufacturing in electronics. Sturgeon hypothesizes that value chain modularity represents a form of governance that is not only neither market nor hierarchy but, equally important for the purposes of this discussion, also not a network form exhibiting the "open-ended, relational" features that Powell argued "greatly enhance the ability to transmit and learn new knowledge and skills" (1990: 304).

As Sturgeon explains (2002: 480), "trust, reputation and long-term relationships are not the only way to buoy external economies." For example, the development of industrywide standards and the codification of knowledge in the electronics industry enable lead firms and highly competent suppliers to exchange rich information (such as detailed specifications) about transactions without need of deeply relational ties. "Turn-key" suppliers provide their clients with "a full-range of services without a great deal of assistance from, or dependence on lead firms" (2002: 455). In modular networks asset specificity remains relatively low because there is "a highly formalized link at the inter-firm boundary, even as the flow of information across the link has remained extremely high" (468). The linkage between lead firms and these key component suppliers, which often work for multiple clients, enables external economies of scale that cannot be realized in the trust-based, relational networks described by Granovetter, Uzzi, and Powell. Comparatively, modular networks are characterized by lower degrees of mutual dependence and a greater reliance on codified instead of tacit knowledge. In a sense, Sturgeon is arguing that standards and codification mimic "trust"—they produce an outcome that is similar to what may be observed in long-term, relational networks, but via a different mechanism.

Sturgeon's concept of value chain modularity implicitly underscores the extent to which sociologists posit the relational features of networks as constitutive of, or synonymous with, networks as an organizational form. This is not surprising, because it is precisely these attributes of network relations (the degree to which they consist of interpersonal communication, generate or express trust, and so on) that point most clearly to the independent effects of social structure on economic action, and are therefore most auspicious for developing a sociological alternative to transaction cost reasoning. But if the project of economic sociology is largely to *dispute* transaction cost economics, Sturgeon's work and the GVC governance theory elaborated by Gereffi, Humphrey, and Sturgeon (2005) are in *dialogue* with it, as is made clear by the weight that these authors give to transaction costs as a factor shaping the coordination and configuration of value chains in global industries.

Pursuing the path opened by Sturgeon's identification of the modular network, Gereffi, Humphrey, and Sturgeon (2005) develop a typology of the various forms that inter-firm relationships can take in GVCs, effectively elaborating a continuum of governance structures between the poles of hierarchy and market. In addition to modular networks, this continuum includes relational networks, in which interaction between firms is frequent and interpersonal communication important, and captive networks, which refer to relationships that are more asymmetrical, as lead firms that have invested in developing the skills of their suppliers seek to lock them in to the relationship, thus making them "captive." Thus, like institutional economics and economic sociology, the theory of GVC governance asks why we sometimes find networks between firms instead of markets or hierarchies, but it operates with a more diversified understanding of the network forms that may exist at the inter-firm boundary, and thus also seeks to explain why one *kind* of network is found instead of another.

As was also the case with the earlier dichotomy between producer-driven and buyer-driven chains, the utility of the fivefold typology outlined in the GVC governance theory is already being questioned by scholars asking how well these modes of inter-firm coordination capture the overall dynamics of various chains (Gibbon and Ponte 2005; Bair 2005; Palpacuer 2008). Within the GCC framework, the BDCC-PDCC distinction aims to describe the composite power structure of a chain but offers no predictions about the way in which particular activities or the relationship between specific links are coordinated; the opposite would seem to be true of the GVC governance theory. As Sturgeon acknowledges in his chapter here, the GVC governance framework is best suited for analyzing a *particular* link in the chain—that is, the transaction between lead firms and first-tier suppliers[7]—whereas more work is needed to understand to what extent and how the mode of coordination prevailing at this link affects inter-firm dynamics farther down the chain.

This brings us to the first of several questions regarding chain governance that are addressed in this book: *Are chains characterized by a single governance structure, or are multiple forms of governance possible? If the latter is the case, how do we understand and theorize the relationship between them?* This issue is raised by John Talbot's analysis of tropical commodity chains (Chapter 5). Talbot explains that the commodity chain for coffee forks into two branches after the growing, harvesting, and initial processing of the beans—one branch results in roasted and ground (R&G) coffee, whereas instant coffee is the final product of the other segment. Because these branches are different from each other, but both part of the larger commodity chain for coffee, Talbot follows Sturgeon (2001) in suggesting that they be referred to as threads. However, both industrial R&G and instant coffee differ from fair trade and specialty coffees, and Talbot proposes the term *strand* to denote the distinction between these "upscale" coffees and their industrial counterparts. Unlike the fork after the green coffee stage, which leads to two distinct forms of coffee, the production process for specialty or fair trade coffee may not differ greatly in terms of activities and inputs from that for industrial coffee. Yet even if the processing of these beans is similar, this occurs in the context of distinct governance structures and institutional contexts, meriting the recognition of specialty and industrial coffee as distinct strands that together constitute the coffee commodity chain.

As Talbot's findings seem consistent with earlier work on the bipolar governance structure of the cocoa chain (Fold 2002), one hypothesis is that multiple governance forms more commonly characterize agricultural or other primary commodity chains, which often feature one "local" segment or set of links for the harvesting and initial processing of the product and another segment devoted to transportation, further processing, and eventual marketing; these later links in the chain tend to be located closer to the consumer. Is it also possible to identify somewhat analogous forks or splits in manufacturing commodity chains, and if so, do these give rise to or reflect different governance structures?

A second question regarding governance is, *How is governance best understood—as "drivenness" or as "coordination"?* In the GCC framework, governance describes the power relations between actors that shape the flow of tasks and the distribution of costs and profits along the chain. Within any two chains of the same type the specific coordination of activities might be handled differently. For example, in the language of Gereffi, Humphrey, and Sturgeon's

GVC governance theory, the retailers and branded marketers that are the lead firms in the apparel chain opt to establish more relational networks with their suppliers, whereas other inter-firm relationships between buyers and suppliers are better described as captive networks. Yet rather than explain this diversity, GCC analyses of the apparel chain have emphasized the extent to which the overall dynamics of this industry conform to the buyer-driven governance structure—that is, the greater relative power that virtually *all* lead firms have vis-à-vis manufacturers to decide how, where, and by whom products are made, regardless of the particular mode of coordination governing specific relationships.

In his contribution (Chapter 6), Timothy Sturgeon clarifies the relationship between the earlier PDCC-BDCC distinction and the new typology of governance structures laid out in the GVC theory of governance. Although Gereffi's buyer-driven category gestured toward the importance of external networks in the coordination of global production processes, it did not differentiate between different network forms, and so failed to capture the diversity of inter-firm relationships that exist. The GCC framework was also unable to model how the possibilities for coordination between links in the chain are affected by dynamic processes of technological change and learning at the firm and industry level. The GVC governance theory was developed, in part, to compensate for these limitations of the GCC approach. In formulating their theory of GVC governance, Gereffi, Humphrey, and Sturgeon drew on many rich empirical analyses of specific global industries. Their intent was to build on the inductive, case study method typical of the GCC tradition, while developing a deductive approach that would allow for the formulation and testing of hypotheses.

Sturgeon's chapter aims to clarify the relationship between this discrete theory of GVC governance on the one hand and the broader research agenda of GVC analysis on the other. He offers a clear assessment of the GVC governance framework's strengths as well as its limitations, and acknowledges that governance is conceived in this theory as the coordination between two links in a chain—a definition that is analytically narrower and theoretically distinct from the conceptualization of governance as "drivenness" on offer in the GCC framework, which characterizes governance structure in terms of the composite power relations characterizing ideal-typical chains (also Gibbon, Bair, and Ponte 2008).

The third and final question about chain governance that is addressed in this volume is, *How do governance structures change over time?* Because global chains are dynamic, chain analysis is necessarily historical. Although the GVC and GCC approaches depart from the sweeping, long-range studies characteristic of the world-systems tradition, these frameworks also acknowledge the importance of understanding how changing forms of governance affect the organization of global industries over time. In fact, Gary Hamilton and Gary Gereffi argue (Chapter 7) that not only have buyer-driven commodity chains reconfigured the geography of global manufacturing, this governance structure has also played an unappreciated role in the much-debated East Asian miracle.

Hamilton and Gereffi explain that in the decades after World War II, U.S. retailers became "global market makers"; their overseas sourcing activities created a market of international suppliers for goods such as footwear, apparel, and electronics. These buyer-driven commodity chains critically enabled the rapid economic growth characterizing the Korean and Taiwanese economies from the 1960s through the 1980s, but this causal factor has been omitted from the prevailing statist or institutional accounts of East Asian development. Hamilton and Gereffi assert that the economic organization of Korea and Taiwan reflects a process of iterative matching between global buyers and local suppliers, which, over time, gave rise to distinct patterns of sectoral specialization and an eventual divergence between these economies. By linking the emergence of buyer-driven commodity chains and the rise of demand-responsive economies in East Asia, Hamilton and Gereffi not only provide a new interpretation of that region's successful industrialization but also more generally underscore the need for economic sociologists to take globalization—as a historical process and an ongoing set of organizational dynamics—more seriously than has been the case to date.

Workers and Activists in Global Chains

The final section of this volume engages two related debates about the social and political implications and possibilities of chain research. First, what can we learn from commodity chain analysis about how global industries shape outcomes for developing-country firms and workers? Second, in what ways can commodity chain analysis inform forms of activism designed to promote ethical production, mitigate globalization's social and environmental costs, or both?

Many contributions to the GCC and GVC literatures have been made by scholars working in development studies. This is not surprising, because the advent of the commodity chain approach coincided with a period of searching within the development field for new paradigms capable of illuminating the relationship between national development and a changing global economy. By the 1980s, the apparent failure of import-substitution industrialization regimes and the massive Third World debt crisis were widely interpreted as evidence that existing development strategies were misguided or unviable. Export-oriented industrialization (EOI) strategies were a key feature of the new conventional wisdom, famously summarized by John Williamson as the "Washington Consensus." More or less rapidly, countries across the developing world embraced the turn toward EOI, often as part of broader reform packages that included trade and financial market liberalization and privatization of state-owned enterprises. The international financial institutions emerged from the debt crisis with an expanded and changed focus vis-à-vis developing countries (Krueger 1997), leading to much debate, considerable criticism, and eventually talk of a post–Washington Consensus, with an expanded agenda that includes issues such as poverty reduction and institution building.

The orthodox version of EOI maintains that economies should export goods in which they have a comparative advantage, and open their domestic economies to imports in order to help secure access to markets abroad. But as a way of examining how export-led policies become applied in practice, GCC research shows that participation in global markets is not restricted to trade in final goods. Instead, countries become linked to the global economy in a variety of ways via participation in commodity chains. Unlike conventional trade theory, which assumes that trade patterns reflect comparative advantage, and further that comparative advantage in turn reflects differences in factor endowments across countries, the global commodity chain approach examines the relationship between trade and production as a set of activities that is organized by particular economic actors. Analyses of GCCs often focus on the role of lead firms as particularly important actors in a chain, and potential agents of upgrading and development (Gereffi 1999, 2001a).

This opens up a way of looking at trade and production networks as opportunity structures for organizational learning on the part of developing countries. Not only can local firms access international markets via such chains, but the implication is that firms can actively seek to *change* the way that they are linked to global chains in order to increase the benefits they derive from participating in them—a process of repositioning that is called upgrading. Early discussions of upgrading within the GCC framework focused largely on the export roles that countries or regions perform in the global economy.

Drawing on comparative research analyzing development trajectories in East Asia and Latin America (Gereffi and Wyman 1990), Gereffi argued that firms in the former had parlayed basic assembly subcontracting activities into a wider repertoire of export roles, giving East Asian exporters a more secure and more profitable niche in global markets than the one enjoyed by their counterparts in Latin America (Gereffi 1994, 1999). Although initially the upgrading concept was used to analyze the trajectories of national or regional *economies,* it was increasingly used to describe the position and capabilities of (developing-country) *firms* in particular global value chains.

Analyses of upgrading have figured prominently in both the GCC and GVC variants of the chain literature (Humphrey and Schmitz 2001; Kaplinsky 2000a), and this accumulated body of research has engendered several critical appraisals of upgrading, both as an empirical phenomenon and as an analytical concept (Bair 2005; Rammohan and Sundaresan 2003). There is vigorous debate and substantial disagreement among academic researchers and policymakers alike about the extent to which participation in GCCs can promote positive development outcomes. In part, this lack of consensus reflects a fundamental unit of analysis problem plaguing research on global chains: At what level do commodity chains have an impact on development processes? At the level of the firm or the cluster, for example, or at the level of the local, regional, or national economy? And if participation in such chains can facilitate development, who benefits from these outcomes? In what ways, if any, do workers gain from upgrading processes that benefit owners and managers?

In their contribution to this debate, Kate Raworth and Thalia Kidder (Chapter 8) underscore the connection between the how and who questions, arguing that particular strategies to increase the competitiveness of suppliers in global chains may look like upgrading from the vantage point of the firm but in fact constitute a form of downgrading for the workers involved. Raworth and Kidder draw on research conducted by Oxfam and partners to analyze the value chains for apparel and fresh produce and find strong evidence that the adoption of a "lean production" philosophy by lead firms in both chains has strong (and strongly negative) effects on workers in developing and developed countries alike. As implemented in these value chains, lean production is transformed from a "high road" to competitiveness to a set of practices that entail squeezing employees at the bottom of the chain in order to lower costs and increase flexibility.

Raworth and Kidder's analysis also speaks to the difference between defining governance as coordination (as in the GVC governance theory) and understanding governance as drivenness (as in the GCC framework). Whereas Gereffi, Humphrey, and Sturgeon (2005) describe the governance structures of the apparel and fresh produce chains as a mix of relational and modular networks (chains that they contend are characterized by relatively low power asymmetries between actors), Raworth and Kidder show that these networks are compatible with significantly asymmetrical relations between buyers and suppliers. They find that the apparel and fresh produce chains alike are highly driven by retailers or importers, who put intense and growing pressure on their suppliers to reduce costs, increase services, or both. When managers lack the will, resources, or knowledge necessary to find other routes to increased competitiveness, these demands are offloaded onto employees, and take the form of deteriorating working conditions and more precarious employment.

Shifting from a focus on workers to a focus on activists and consumers, the final chapters in this volume ask how commodity chain analysis can enrich our understanding of the social and political implications (and possibilities) of globalization. In volume 1 of *Capital,* Marx introduces the notion of commodity fetishism to describe the way in which the commodity circuit transmogrifies relations between social actors such that they assume the "fantastic form of a relation between things." Critical scholars have enlisted the commodity chain as a way to interrogate this "fetishism which attaches itself to the products of labour, so soon as they are produced as commodities" ([1867] 1992: 77). The most influential formulation along these lines was that of David Harvey, who reported asking students where their last meal came from as a way of conveying the meaning of commodity fetishism. His description of the exercise resonates with the concept of the commodity chain as elaborated by Hopkins and Wallerstein:

> Tracing back all the items used in the production of that meal reveals a relation of dependence upon a whole world of social labor conducted in many different places under very different social relations and conditions of production. That dependency expands even further when we consider the materials and goods used in the production of the goods we directly consume. Yet we can in practice consume our meal without the slightest knowledge of the intricate geography of production and the myriad social relationships embedded in the system that puts it upon our table (Harvey 1990: 422).

Harvey goes on to explain how the diner can consciously engage the concept of the commodity chain to learn about the conditions under which his or her food was produced. True, the "grapes that sit on the supermarket shelf are mute;

we cannot see the fingerprints of exploitation upon them or tell immediately what part of the world they are from," but further inquiry makes it possible to "lift the veil on this geographical and social ignorance and make ourselves aware of these issues. . . . [I]n so doing we have to . . . go behind and beyond what the market itself reveals in order to understand how society is working" (423). What Harvey points to here is the use of the commodity chain as a tool of critical inquiry—a way to "penetrate the veil of fetishisms with which we are necessarily surrounded by virtue of the system of commodity production and exchange," laying bare the social (and geographical) relations characterizing this system. Because the spaces of production and the spaces of consumption are distinct, analysis of the relationship between them is necessary if we are to avoid the danger of not looking beyond the latter, the fetishism constituted by taking "the realm of individual experience . . . as all there is" (423).

If we accept commodity chain analysis as a mode of critical inquiry, it is perhaps not a great leap to imagine how it might also constitute a form of politics—not only a method for unveiling the prevailing social relations of production but also a means for resisting the exploitation and alienation that these entail. Indeed, several commentators have noted the "political 'edge' [the commodity chain] appears to offer in the critical analysis of contemporary production systems" (Jackson, Ward, and Russell 2006: 132). Leslie and Reimer observe, for example, that "commodity chain analyses provide a space for political action by reconnecting producers and consumers" (1999: 402; also McRobbie 1997).

In fact, many activist organizations have made use of the commodity chain approach in precisely this way, using it to map connections between First World consumers and workers in Mexico or China or southern California who sew the t-shirts and grow the produce they will purchase. A desire to ensure that production processes are carried out in a particular way (for example, avoiding child labor, insuring worker safety), concerns about the health or environmental consequences of these activities (such as promoting organic farming methods, preserving local biodiversity), or an interest in establishing a particular distributional outcome (for example, that growers of "fair trade" coffee secure a minimum price for their beans) orient various commodity chain analyses conducted by NGOs and other consumer groups.

As a form of politics, these strategies are rife with contradictions. Chief among these is that ethical consumption is a form of politics that uses the dynamic of market competition in the realm of capitalist circulation to resist the social and ecological degradation that occurs in the realm of capitalist production. The logic for initiatives that are "in the market while not quite of it" (Taylor 2005) is that consumers will vote with their dollars to support producers who bring goods to market while ensuring that certain standards (such as sweat-free, bird-friendly) are met. In spite of the practical difficulties that these initiatives encounter (Who pays for developing-country firms to be certified and monitored? How can sufficient market demand for ethical products be created?), labeling and other forms of alternative trade help to produce better-informed consumers and, more controversially, positively affect the workers and communities that are the intended beneficiaries.

But to work, alternative trade initiatives depend on the continued existence of conventional markets. Fair trade coffee, to take one example, is only meaningful when it is contrasted with the industrial coffee that accounts for 99 percent of the global market. Because these initiatives are necessarily limited in scope and impact, there is a danger of fetishizing the de-fetishizing move they ostensibly represent. This is the risk that Julie Guthman invites us to consider when she attempts to "unveil the unveiling" of commodity chain analysis as it applies to voluntary, ethical food labels (Chapter 9). Guthman explains how certification and labeling schemes, though often in pursuit of politically progressive or socially desirable ends, constitute barriers to entry for producers. Labels that are intended to serve a redistributive function (for example, fair trade) are only effective when they generate rents for producers; Guthman's point is that as a form of "created scarcity," such rents cannot be universally, or perhaps even widely, available. Thus these schemes are necessarily exclusionary—an insight of critical importance for understanding and evaluating protective labels as a form of politics.

As a mode of critical or strategic analysis, the commodity chain construct is most frequently used in the way endorsed by Harvey and problematized by Guthman—that is, to reveal links between producers and consumers that would otherwise be concealed by the commodity form. The goal is often to create an implicit alliance between workers (typically though not exclusively in the global South) and consumers (usually in the global North) vis-à-vis employers, in pursuit of shared goals and objectives, such as better working conditions. But if commodity chain analysis can be applied strategically by activists in designing consumer campaigns, it can also help make sense of why some efforts along these lines prove more efficacious than others.

This is the task that William Munro and Rachel Schurman take up in the final chapter of this volume (Chapter 10), which examines why the movement against genetically modified organisms (GMOs) was more successful in

Europe than in North America. They show that differences in the structure of the food commodity chain are important in explaining these divergent outcomes. The pro-GMO faction in the United States, consisting of an alliance between the agro-technology companies and the farmers who use their products, presented a united front that was difficult for anti-GMO activists to penetrate, whereas the configuration of the chain in the United Kingdom, and the organization of the retail link specifically, created a more propitious environment for strengthening consumer opposition to the importation of what was largely regarded as a "foreign" technology. Munro and Schurman's discussion points to the utility of chain analysis for understanding processes of interest formation and identity construction among various constituencies and stakeholders in the chain. Consumer struggles for social or ecological objectives are not just shaped by the production networks they target; they are also simultaneously and necessarily struggles to shape the organization and the operation of global chains.

. . .

In this introduction, I charted the development of the commodity chain concept over the past several decades and reviewed several key debates within this literature. In the chapters that follow, the authors advance the frontiers of the field I have reviewed here in multiple ways. Some examine methodological and theoretical issues regarding the conceptualization and study of global commodity chains, while others explore the extension of this approach to novel forms of analysis and even activism, including chain-inspired politics. In doing so, these authors draw on the world-systems, GCC, and GVC traditions to a greater or lesser extent, and in ways that reflect the different disciplinary formations, theoretical commitments, and substantive interests they bring to the study of global chains. It is my hope that this collection provides ample material to help researchers understand what is at stake in these various approaches in terms of the kind of questions they open up, as well as the kind that they might foreclose.

PART I
OPERATIONALIZING GLOBAL CHAINS: THEORETICAL AND METHODOLOGICAL DEBATES

2 Historicizing Commodity Chains

Five Hundred Years of the Global Coffee Commodity Chain

Steven Topik

A BRIEF HISTORICAL ANALYSIS OF THE CREATION AND DEVELOPMENT of coffee commodity chains will allow us to appreciate the multiple forces and factors that have been involved over time in a crop going global. Embracing many of the characteristics of the tropical commodity chain that John Talbot so expertly outlines elsewhere in this volume (Chapter 5), the coffee commodity chain discussed here covers a five-hundred-year sweep of history.[1] Coffee differs from many other tropical commodities: it is a food whose variations in taste are valued; it is less perishable than many tropical fruits; it is a psychoactive drug because of caffeine; and it has enjoyed a long partnership with humans. These characteristics have often made it an integral component of ethnic, religious, or national identities.

But there is no unanimity about what coffee is. Estate owners, cooperative coffee growers, specialty coffee house owners, not to mention botanists would all give different answers. This chapter will chart the formation of the coffee commodity chain over time, recognizing that even today it is a complicated arena. Although the word *chain* implies something deterministic, rigid, unidirectional, and functionalist, in fact the flows from producers to consumers have been flexible, dynamic, and varied. Even a small country such as Costa Rica can have multiple coffee commodity "segments" (Samper K. 2003: 135) or, as John Talbot refers to them in this volume, "strands." I have adopted "commodity chain" because of current conventions, but could as easily use "circuits," "networks," or "flows." And commodities themselves are volatile.

They can have "social lives" with numerous phases and competing meanings and values over time, and even at the same time (Appadurai 1986; Polanyi 1957). Use and exchange value are plastic and interchangeable.

Commodity chain analysts should also guard against tunnel vision. Participants in the coffee commodity chain are also involved in broader production systems, social networks, commercial circuits, and markets. Coffee farmers have often harvested other crops and sometimes raise livestock; many of them allocate their time among several economic activities, including off-farm labor, so coffee plays different roles in their livelihood strategies. Growers, processors, and traders in coffee actively negotiate their respective interests amongst each other and with other socioeconomic and sociopolitical actors, whether locally or on a broader scale. Thus when we think about coffee, we have to think about what Mario Samper K. (2003: 122) calls "the coffee complex." The commodity chain should also take into account what Albert Hirschman (1981) calls "linkages," multiplier effects for the rest of the economy and for state building.

The shape of today's world coffee economy was neither predestined nor predictable over six hundred years ago when coffee arrived in Yemen from Ethiopia and began its commercial life. The early coffee farmers and drinkers could not foresee that the seed of the coffea Arabica trees would become one of the most valuable internationally traded commodities in history, drawing in growers and consumers on every continent in the world. The use of commodity chain analysis allows us to unveil the connections between people who are distant and unfamiliar to each other and permits us to palpably understand the links between people who not only occupy different continents with markedly diverse lifestyles and cultures but sometimes work under contrasting modes of production.

To study the coffee commodity chain is to understand and historicize the intimate, though sometimes contested and contradictory, connections between production, intermediation, processing, marketing, and consumption in what has been one of the world's two or three largest international markets for over two centuries. It allows us to integrate insights from economic and business history as well as from political economy, anthropology, sociology, geography, and literary studies and to understand how these facets of coffee interacted over time and space.

Why Study Coffee?

Why focus on coffee? As an internationally traded commodity, it is one of the few goods that dates back to the days of the fifteenth-century spice trade. It has connected Africa, the Middle East, Asia, Europe, and the Americas. Because hundreds of millions, if not billions, of people have been intimately involved in the growing, trading, transporting, processing, marketing, and consuming of coffee, we are dealing with more than just a case that is illustrative of broader trends. Rather, coffee itself has been central to the expansion of the world economy. In addition to being long-lived and well traveled, coffee is one of the most valuable goods in world commerce and the most popular legal drug. And it is a food with nutritional value (derived from additives such as sugar and milk). It occupies a central place in the worlds of work and of sociability. It has fed national treasuries and corporate coffers, helping to develop some economies and, arguably, to underdevelop others. Coffee sales and consumption have helped sustain states by providing revenue and energizing armies, whereas coffee cultivation has sparked revolts against other states. Coffee has fueled world trade and manufacturing and inspired protective reactions to the dominance of the international market, such as the International Coffee Organization and today's concerns with fair trade and ecologically friendly and ethical commodities.

The nature of the international coffee chain has changed dramatically over the centuries as it has grown in length and complexity. Geographical location, modes of production, the cultivar being grown, transport and processing technologies, markets, marketing, and end use have varied greatly. Governance of the chain moved away from the grower (or wild harvester) to the exporter in the sixteenth century; then in the nineteenth century to the grower and the importer; and in the twentieth century to the roaster, governments, and international institutions; and finally today to a few multinational firms that are being contested by NGOs. The evolution not only reflects changes in botanical knowledge, technology, notions of property rights, economic institutions, and transformations in the consuming societies but also mirrors changes in the nature of demand. What was considered "coffee"; how, why, and where it was consumed; and the extent to which it was commoditized are historical issues that reflect not only personal preferences but also social preferences that are embedded in shifting concepts of time, sociability, fashion, status, gender, work, and leisure. State power and the later developing civil society and public space loom large in shaping consumption because the value of coffee is as a social product as well as a plant (Roseberry, Gudmundson, and Samper K. 1995).

The Creation of a Commodity

To study a commodity chain, one presumably should have a commodity to study. This chapter, however, starts with coffee *before* it became a commodity. Central to understanding the historical coffee commodity chain is appreciating that coffee was a plant that appeared without human help and became a "thing" (Appadurai 1986), with many uses besides commerce.

The coffee that became internationally popular, Arabica, originated in what is today Ethiopia, where it grew wild natively. Over one hundred species of genus *Coffea* have been identified, yet only two of them became widely popular (the Arabica and the canephor or Robusta) (Davis, Goeverts, Bridson, and Stoffelen 2006). The popularity of Arabica and its global diffusion were human decisions, which, as the name implies, began not in Ethiopia but across the Red Sea in Yemen.

In Ethiopia humans consumed coffee more as a food or as a stimulant than as a drink. Oromo and Haya tribesmen did not agree that its fruit was more consumable than its leaves or stems, but they did relish chewing fried coffee in religious and hospitality rituals. Coffee was a holy sacrament used by indigenous peoples to honor God, *Waqa,* in communal ceremonies and sometimes used as a fetish to divine the future (Bartels 1983; Weiss 2003). Markets were little in evidence. The Oromo accepted *Waqa*'s gift from naturally appearing trees; they were forbidden to plant stands of Arabica trees. In this sense, in the beginning coffee was not only *not* a commodity, it was not even a "crop." Ethiopians remained very minor coffee producers and exporters until the twentieth century.

The coffee *drink* gained popularity before 1500 in Yemen, where coffee was planted in the mountains and became a trade good (Tuchscherer 2003). Although it was also chewed, fried, and infused as a tea using coffea cherry husks, the Sufi of Yemen made a drink out of the roasted cherry pit or "bean," which was much less perishable than other parts of the plant. This taste choice would prepare coffee for its precocious long-distance trade.

At first, however, it was a local affair. The Sufi faithful in Yemen met at night in prayer vigils using the drink as a communal religious ritual. Caffeine

was a vital aspect of the attraction. As in Ethiopia, it was a religious aid. Pil-
grims visiting Mecca for the Hajj and Ottoman officials and soldiers asserting
the power of Constantinople diffused the coffee practice to lands from Indonesia to West Africa, from Somalia to the Balkans.

Coffee became closely associated with Islam, in which it substituted for the
social role of alcohol, forbidden by Mohammed. Indeed, the Arabic word for
the drink, *qahwah*, was an epithet for wine, and coffee was often referred to
as a "liquor." The new drink became acceptable only after theological battles
with Muslim Ulamas, who sometimes ruled the new beverage forbidden by
the Quran, and after secular fights with Ottoman officials, who sometimes
enforced the edicts (Hattox 1985). Eventually the secular pleasure of coffee
sociability and the profits this demand promised overcame religious objections. Coffee houses replaced taverns. Schivelbusch (1992) has even argued
that the opening of cafés was a marketing device to create new customers,
though studies of Syria show that coffee roasting guilds and roasting shops
preceded cafés (Rafeq 2001). Coffee houses and peddlers hawking hot coffee
proliferated, creating demand by offering a new space for (male) hospitality
and lighting the night with what could be called the first night clubs. Coffee
was a socially revolutionary beverage that created ever-more links to its chain.
Still, coffee provided a limited market in the Ottoman Empire because it was
mainly a luxury beverage for the urban affluent.

Initially coffee was neither a producer-driven or buyer-driven chain. Both
the growing and the brewing ends were fragmented. It became an international trader-driven chain as mercantile-minded Arabs and Indians with
much experience in long-distance, market-oriented commerce of the spice
trade incorporated it into the circuits of the Red Sea, Mediterranean, Indian
Ocean, and Middle Eastern shipping and caravan commerce. Merchants prof-
ited from Ottoman imperial dominance that left trade routes safe and homogenized means of payment. For over two centuries, Eastern trade diasporas, not
Europeans, dominated caffeinated cross-cultural commerce (Curtin 1984).

Coffee became a commercial commodity, but trade was slow to convert
growers into full-time, market-oriented profit seekers. They had harnessed
nature by bringing the Arabica to the irrigated terraces they built high in the
mountains, where they grew it in small plots that included subsistence crops.
Surplus production was slowly brought down the mountains to market towns,
where Arab and Indian merchants purchased small batches and dispatched

them overseas, overland, or a combination of the two. Many small-scale merchants and transporters moved each batch to market in cargos lumped together with other goods. Cairo was a major center from which large-scale merchants distributed it to West Africa, the Hejaz, the Levant, and Constantinople's Egyptian Market (Faroqhi 1994).

Outside of the major markets, information about production levels, amounts on sale in markets, prices, and consumer demand was scarce and partial. The coffee was homogenized as "Mocha," the name of the major export port, not the name of the growing areas. Indeed it seems that few merchants ever climbed up into the growing areas. As a result, although coffee played an important social and fiscal role in the sixteenth and seventeenth centuries, production was so low that gardens in Yemen and apparently some in Ethiopia satisfied world demand. This was an economy centered in the Middle East and the Indian Ocean. The trade involved only green coffee beans, which had been processed to that point in Yemen's mountains. In the country of final destination it was treated as the same species and cultivar, a rather undifferentiated commodity, though in Yemen price varied according to where the coffee was grown. The coffee brewer in the household or in the coffee house undertook the artisanal tasks of roasting, pulverizing, brewing, and flavoring the coffee. Consumers differentiated coffees by the café in which they drank them, the itinerant peddler who served them a cup, or the retailer who sold them beans. The Yemeni grower and even the merchant who sent the Arabica on its many-step voyage were obscured from the coffee drinker. Because growers, traders, transporters of coffee, roasters, and brewers also engaged with numerous other goods and pursuits, they would have had difficulty identifying themselves as agents in a specific "commodity chain." It was certainly more a mental construct than a palpable institution.

Clearly, the coffee trade was not a European invention. Only after more than a century of the Arab-centered international market did British, Dutch, and French monopoly companies become involved as an extension of their spice trade (Cowan 2005). Although Europe was still a small luxury market, its demands outstripped Yemen's production possibilities.

A growing taste for coffee in Europe and the desire for a profitable commodity and self-financing colonies led Dutch, French, and British merchant companies to move from commerce and transport to production. They began overseeing coffee planting in their newly conquered colonies. Whereas 90 percent of Amsterdam's imports in 1721 were from Mocha, by 1726 90 percent were from Java (the Dutch colony today part of Indonesia), where peasants were coerced into cultivating and selling coffee to the Dutch East India Trade Company. The small French colony of Reunion in the Indian Ocean became a major producer by importing Arabica seedlings from Yemen and for the first time introducing large-scale African slavery into production (Campbell 2003). Consignment merchants helped create demand for this international trader-driven chain. The central role of the mercantilist state meant that there were several separate imperial chains that sought to keep production and consumption within each empire. Belatedly, the Dutch were able to overtake Mocha and Mediterranean ports such as Alexandria, Constantinople, and Marseilles to transform Amsterdam into the world's leading coffee entrepôt for over a century.

By 1750 Amsterdam's imports of American production almost matched its purchases of Javanese coffee. Initially the American good was mostly colonial production from Dutch Guyana. But soon the price of French production from St. Domingue (today Haiti) made that island more attractive and turned it into the world's wealthiest colony. At first a poor man's crop, coffee came to rival sugar as Haiti's and the Caribbean's leading export. Dutch willingness to trade in the coffees of other empires, and German and Scandinavian desire for coffee in the absence of coffee colonies, undercut the hold that monopoly companies had over the world coffee market. The strands of the coffee commodity chain became more homogeneous and fungible. This was clearly commodity production, though not capitalist production, because it used Indian Ocean coerced peasants and African slave labor.

By the 1770s over 80 percent of the world's production originated in the Americas, as Mocha, Java, and Reunion could not keep up with expanding Latin American production. In 1800 coffee was the most widely spread tropical commodity in the world. But it was, and still is, centered in the Americas. Asia and Africa raised their combined coffee exports to about one-third of international trade by 1830 and remained at that level in 1860. Nature in the form of a coffee disease drove them back to 5 percent of world trade by 1913, however (Clarence-Smith 2003). Although in the past twenty years Asian production returned to prominence, Latin America still produces most of the world's coffee.

The market for this urban luxury good remained small at the beginning of the nineteenth century. Only green Arabica coffee beans were sold. Now their provenance—Mocha, Java, Reunion, Guyana, Jamaica, or Haiti—was taken into account in the reckoning of price, with the spreads between cultivators as large as 100 percent (Posthumus 1946, vol. 1: 75–79). But origin identifications were often not officially enforced, so fraud and adulteration were common. Green coffee was sold at auction in Europe by consignment merchants who dealt in mixed cargos. Merchants and shippers—who were often the same people—governed the chain.

Merchants and planters were the main entrepreneurs in expanding the coffee trade because European states did not play a major role in the development of coffee production after the middle of the nineteenth century. Dutch Java's production fell sharply because of the attack of leaf rust after the 1880s, returning to a position of prominence only in the late twentieth century after independence (Fernando 2003: 162–163). In the Americas, the Dutch preferred to serve as traders and shippers; they never developed or expanded their small colonies. The British preferred the mercantilist possibilities in exploiting the Chinese and then the Indian tea trade. The Spanish and Portuguese preferred cacao, so Iberian Americans had to wait until well after independence to become significant coffee producers. When states asserted their control over the world coffee market in the twentieth century, it was independent states of growers or consumers, not colonial regimes.

Brazil Changes the World Coffee Economy

Coffee was treated differently from sugar and rubber in the nineteenth-century Age of Empire because its low technological demands meant that an independent former colony, Brazil, could begin producing on an unprecedented scale. Cheap, fertile virgin land and abundant and relatively inexpensive slave labor due to the proximity of Africa allowed Brazil to cause world coffee prices to plummet after 1820 and remain low until the last quarter of the century, creating supply-induced demand. Brazil's success was not just because of European colonial know-how or because of natural resource endowment (Nugent and Robinson 2000). Brazil emerged as the world's major coffee exporter partly because of its independence in 1822. More important to Brazil's rise to caffeinated dominance were exogenous changes in the world market: the collapse of Haitian production after the revolution, welling European and later U.S. urban markets, and capital and transportation revolutions brought by industrialization. Brazil's bountiful exports financed a "hollow state" that guaranteed property (especially in slaves until 1888), kept the roads relatively free of bandits, and maintained social peace while limiting civil and international wars (Topik 2002; Saddi 2002).

Not only did Brazilian production largely satisfy growing world demand, Brazilians stimulated and transformed the place of coffee on overseas tables. The dependency view of agricultural producers as servants or as providers of brute labor-power, willingly serving up their produce to thirsty European buyers who were the masters of the trade, misrepresents the nature of the relationship. Brazilians, either native born or African or Portuguese immigrants, developed new production techniques, discovered productive cultivars, constructed an elaborate domestic transportation network in a geographically unpromising setting, and developed market standards and financial instruments as well. They were able to outproduce all the European colonial growers in this age of empire.

To give the *dependentistas* their due, Brazilians were also successful in the nineteenth century because of British neocolonialism in the form of inexpensive and reliable shipping and insurance, loans, infrastructure investments, and protection of sea routes (Platt 1977; Graham 1968; Miller 1993; Cain and Hopkins 1993: 298–306). So although the tea-drinking British did not export or import much coffee from their own colonies, they exported and reexported a lot of coffee from Brazil. Most of it went to the two other fastest-industrializing countries in the world, the United States and Germany.

Even with Brazil, Ceylon, and Java greatly expanding world coffee production in the first half of the nineteenth century, the essential nature of the commodity chain remained the same. All the coffee exported was still green Arabica sent overseas by consignment merchants who represented factors who, in turn, provided planters (though not peasants) with the working capital to bring crops to port. Larger plantations set the standards for cultivation, though smaller-scale slave-worked holdings in Brazil and coerced-peasant production in Java competed. Sail ships carried coffee packed in leather pouches or cotton and jute bags to major markets, where it was often sold at auction to wholesalers. Roasting, grinding, and brewing were still done in the home or in the coffee house. The commodity chain was a hybrid: partially producer-driven because many of the improvements in expanding cultivation were financed by reinvested profits of planters, partially international-trader-driven in the context of what Gallagher and Robinson (1953) called free trade imperialism (Stein 1985).

The creation of the liberal export economy in the Americas, which contrasted with and complemented the expanding European colonialism in Africa, Asia, and Oceania, transformed the nature of the demand for coffee. Coffee went from being a noble and then bourgeois beverage before 1800 to become a mass drink in the last part of the nineteenth century. The slaves of Brazil slaked the thirst of the factory workers of the industrial countries, particularly the United States, the German realms, and the Netherlands.

Brazil, which produced over half the world's coffee by 1850, was responsible for about 80 percent of the unprecedented expansion of world coffee production in the nineteenth century.[2] By 1906 Brazilians *produced almost five times as much as the rest of the world combined.* And this was no marginal market. At the dawn of the twentieth century the value of internationally traded coffee trailed only grains and sugar.

How did this happen? As I suggested, Brazil's remarkable expansion of the world coffee economy and the increase in the chain's length and complexity resulted from a unique confluence of Brazil's internal natural endowment; such externalities as the availability of foreign laborers in Africa until the Atlantic slave trade was abolished in 1850 and in Southern Europe after Brazilian slavery was outlawed in 1888; economies brought by revolutionary advances in transportation and communication technology; and vast transformation in the coffee business in the United States and Western Europe.

The explosion of coffee in the nineteenth century was not brought about by new production methods (Wickizer 1961). Until the last quarter of the century, cultivating, harvesting, and processing continued to be done manually by the same sort of slave labor Brazilian planters had previously used for sugar and French coffee planters had used on the African island of Reunion, and on a greater scale, in Haiti. Indeed it was known at the time as the "West Indian" cultivation system. But the vastness of some Brazilian plantations and industrial-scale picking, which lowered both the cost and the quality of coffee, were new.

Still, slave labor has been given too much credit for the coffee export boom. The abolition of Brazilian slavery in 1888 did not diminish Brazil's place in the market. In fact, coffee exports expanded at a more rapid rate in the first decade of free immigrant labor than they had before. Spanish American *fincas* rapidly expanded exports after the 1870s using domestic labor, though often peasants were coerced into work through debt peonage.

Technological improvement was more evident in transportation than in cultivation. The train reduced cargo tariffs, but not dramatically. By the turn of the twentieth century, rail transport still contributed from 15 to 22 percent of production costs. But the quality of coffee was better and, more important, cheaper; more fertile lands were now accessible in the interior, and ever-larger amounts could be brought to market faster, reducing interest charges on working capital. In other words, the railroad allowed Brazilians to take advantage of their country's vastness and *continue* their boom. They thereby escaped the geographic trap that had prevented much smaller Yemen, Java, Martinique, Dutch Guyana, and Haiti from qualitatively transforming the world market and from taking advantage of economies of scale.

Railroads were useful but not *necessary* for a coffee export economy—no other coffee producer had much track until the twentieth century (though Costa Rica's relatively short line was important). But the great amount of low-priced Brazilian coffee making its way to international ports on iron tracks expanded and reconfigured the world market because Brazil produced more than the rest of the world combined in the second half of the nineteenth century. Rail-deprived producers such as Colombia, Chiapas, Mexico, and Guatemala then took advantage of niches in the larger market that Brazilian rail-transported mass production had started, as American roasters blended the more expensive Spanish American milds with lower-cost Brazilian beans.

Coffee commodity chains grew also as a side-effect of transformations of the broader world economy. A clear case of an externality that revolutionized the relationship of Brazil's coffee (and later that of competitors) to the Atlantic world was the shipping revolution, which shrank the world (Greenhill 1977; Bairoch 1974: 606; North 1958: 537–555). At first European sail ships, which had a three-centuries-long tradition of carrying Brazilian dyewood, sugar, and gold overseas, added the Arabica to other cargos on board. Then increasingly after the 1860s steamships increased their carrying capacity and speed. Regularly scheduled freighters docked at ever-larger and more efficient ports ever-better served by warehouse capacity. Eventually some ships were dedicated to carrying only coffee.

The mode of transportation had considerable weight in the construction of the coffee commodity chain. It is not simply an incidental event between production and consumption. In the era before today's enormous container ships, the mode of transport helped select which areas could join the world economy and in what capacity (Levinson 2006).

In the nineteenth century railroads and ships allowed the apparently paradoxical situation of growers receiving a greater share of the final foreign selling price while consumers abroad enjoyed lower retail prices. The new, cheaper methods of conveying freight and European industrialization permitted the supply of coffee to grow quickly enough to satisfy and even stimulate continually growing demand abroad without a jump in nominal price. Because manufactured imports from Europe and then from the United States became cheaper, Brazil and other coffee producers could enjoy steadily improving terms of trade; that is, the real price of coffee—what it could buy in imported goods and services—increased more rapidly than did its nominal price, which was fairly steady until the late 1880s (Bacha 1992: Leff 1982; Harley 1996).

The nature of the era permitted Brazil to gain from international technological, financial, and institutional externalities. This again underlines the importance of the historical epoch for appreciating the commodity chain and the relative winners and losers. The gains during the 1875–1929 period reverted to agricultural producers as well as to industrial ones; indeed, the terms of trade improved for tropical agricultural goods as luxuries became necessities (Lewis 1978). Because of their free-trade, liberal attitude, Brazilian statesmen did not use their market power to win monopoly rents as mercantilist trading companies had; therefore, nominal coffee prices remained relatively low. The fact that Spanish American producers such as Costa Rica, Venezuela, and Colombia began producing coffee instead of indigo, tobacco, sugar, and cacao demonstrates that world coffee prices were sufficiently high to make them attractive for growers, even while low enough to seduce ever-more overseas consumers. The secret was not only the low price of vast, fertile, and well-watered land but also the self-provisioning of slave and then free coffee workers. They were paid mostly in usufruct rights rather than money, so that workers could reproduce and even multiply despite very low monetary wages. Clearly, the coffee commodity chain linked different modes of production. Over time, trade, foreign investments, and the political organization of the agrarian working class increased homogeneity between the trading partners, though the gulf between the income of agrarian workers in the coffee lands and that of urban consumers remained and remains very large, and in some cases probably grew.

Strikingly, Brazil's coffee boom was slow to lower transaction costs. Brazilian coffee planters (*fazendeiros*), as well as slavocrat growers in Haiti, Jamaica, and Puerto Rico, were clearly market-oriented. But even *fazendeiros* were buffered from the market in the interior by poor roads and communications until the twentieth century. They had to negotiate a complicated chain in which small growers sold to larger growers or mill owners, who sold through factors (*commissarios*), who often sold to sackers, who blended the coffee and then sold to exporters, who initially were consignment merchants (Laerne 1885; Sweigart 1987; Greenhill 1993).

Despite the fact that inexpensive and plentiful Brazilian production quenched the thirst of ever-more North American and European consumers, its remarkable increase in cultivation did not create a monopoly. Yes, in 1906 Brazil produced some 80 percent of the world's coffee. But the institutionalization of the market with scheduled large steamers, railroads, warehouses, standards, futures market, and, as we shall see, new convenience coffee products opened North American and European ports to other Latin American producers. Rather than a zero-sum game, this was a mutual gain for all coffee producers. In most years until 1929, all Latin American growers increased output. Latin America turned much of the Western world into coffee drinkers. In other words, Brazil was not just a passive bystander in the world market; it was a market maker and would become a price maker beginning in 1906 with government price intervention (Abreu and Bevilaqua 2000).

The Transformation of Consumption

Coffee's heroic nineteenth century occurred not only because of Brazilian and gradually other Latin American production, but also because of burgeoning United States and Western European consumption. The transportation revolution and lowered international transaction costs reduced the cost of the lengthiest section of the commodity chain and accelerated the commercial relationship between Brazil and the United States, which was strengthened by ever-closer diplomatic ties (Topik 1996).

Another stroke of luck for coffee shippers was the construction of the world's most efficient internal transportation systems, in the United States and Western Europe (Cronon 1991). Rail, canals, and rivers integrated the swelling westward-bound American population into international trade, giving birth to an elaborate processing and marketing network. Coffee became truly a mass product for the first time in the United States, followed by wider consumption in Western Europe.

U.S. government policy also helped. The United States was the only major market to import coffee tax free, as duties declined from a high of 10 cents a pound in 1812 to free for all but a decade after 1832. This probably was a consequence of colonial resentment of import taxes such as the tea tax. Coffee taxes in Western Europe were all substantially higher because of the Europeans' mercantilist traditions. Consequently, per capita consumption of coffee in the United States grew from one-eighteenth of a pound in 1783 to nine pounds a hundred years later. The political economy of taxes has to occupy a central place in the commodity chain. It was based not only on revenue needs and state fiscal capacity but also on consumption preferences that were cultural as well as economic.

Low taxes and the U.S. population's fifteenfold explosion in that century meant that total coffee imports grew 2,400 percent. Half of the growth in world consumption in the nineteenth century was due to increased United States purchases![3] Almost all the rest was in Western Europe, especially in the north (Samper K. and Fernando 2003: 443, 446–447; Rischbieter 2005). Coffee producers were very fortunate to find such favor in the countries whose GNPs were growing the fastest in the world (Bairoch 1974). U.S. per capita consumption would continue to grow, with some fits and starts, until the 1940s.

The confluence of vast U.S. coffee consumption and its unparalleled economic boom was not just coincidental. Caffeine and coffee served both as rewards for workers and as stimuli for work. Coffee intensified labor and labor paid for coffee. Western Europe, with a time lag, enjoyed the same combination. The point here is that a historically sensitive commodity chain analysis takes into account specific flows that are affected by the histories of both trade partners. The coincidence and complementarity of Brazilian production; U.S. consumption; and British finance, carrying, and insurance in the mid-nineteenth century provided a synergy in ways that were not then found in other parts of the international coffee economy until decades later. Eventually coffee's economies of scale, new technologies, and economic institutions would spread across the globe.

Coffee's rapid expansion in the nineteenth century was due to peculiar demand conditions that were specific to coffee because of its cultural reception in the United States, as well as Brazil's ability to meet that demand cheaply. Demand in the nineteenth century, in both the United States and Europe, was initially both income-elastic and price-elastic. The more people earned the more likely they were to purchase coffee, and the lower coffee's price the more likely they were to buy it.

Surprisingly, in the twentieth century this was not the case in the established Western consumption countries, despite better quality, more accessible coffee, and rapidly expanding discretionary incomes. In the early nineteenth century coffee was viewed as a luxury item, a sign of aristocratic and bourgeois distinction. As it became available to lower-class urban inhabitants and eventually even to rural populations at a relatively low price, they chose it over ersatz coffees and teas they had previously drunk because coffee symbolized affluence. So powerful was this appeal that the income-elasticity for coffee in developed countries between 1830 and 1900 has been estimated at 1.3. As it became an accepted part of the working class's breakfast, coffee became rather price- and income-inelastic. Neither greater income nor lower price made much of a difference in coffee purchases. The United States Federal Trade Commission estimated income-elasticity in 1954 at only .2, almost stagnant. (1954 39–40). Total coffee consumption in the United States accompanied the growth of the population, though after 1946 per capita consumption steadily declined until the very end of the century (Buzby and Haley 2007).

Western European countries did not face the same market pressures because the wars, depressions, and rebuilding of the twentieth century had made coffee a prized rather than a routine purchase. But the global growth of demand in the twentieth and twenty-first centuries in countries new to the coffee habit repeated the U.S. nineteenth-century experience. By 1970 Western European countries were importing almost half of all world coffee exported; thirty years later their imports had grown a bit and were double those of the United States (Fridell 2007: 229). The desire to emulate U.S. and Western European consumption patterns has created new coffee addicts in Asia, especially the most prosperous countries such as Japan, South Korea, and Taiwan.

Coffee was one of the few major internationally traded commodities to enjoy a real price increase in the second half of the nineteenth century and still have a per-capita consumption increase (Ocampo 1984: 302–303; Bacha 1992). Again the coffee chain benefited from an externality: the plunging price of many staples in the 1870s due to overproduction and cheaper transport in what Alfred Crosby (1986) calls "neo-Europes" reduced the price of basic necessities for the working class of North America and Europe. They therefore found themselves with greater discretionary income to spend on newly available luxuries such as coffee and sugar (Mintz 1985). Thus commodity chain analysis should take into account goods that competed for consumers' dollars, pounds, and francs. The issue was not just how much coffee was available at what price and how much discretionary income consumers had, but also which other goods were filling similar perceived needs. Once coffee's status declined in the early twentieth century from luxury to necessity, its income-elasticity did also (Okunade 1991). This would only change in the last decades of the century, as specialty coffee purveyors and coffee houses again convinced more buyers that coffee was a luxury and a youth drink.

The rapid expansion and transformation of the U.S. and Western European markets led to institutional restructuring and new layers of intermediaries, which gradually brought governance of the longer chain to importers and then to roasters. Overseas merchants lost control in 1874 when a submarine cable tied South America to New York and London by telegraph. Information about prices, standards, and demand and supply gradually became easily available in consuming countries. Warehouses that held a substantial share of the world's visible stocks were built, strengthening the market position of importers.

Exporters ceased being consignment agents, becoming instead agents of importers, who controlled the trade and set the prices. Traders such as the German Theodor Wille and Edward Johnston of England started their careers in Brazil, expanded their commercial business to other ports and countries, and moved up-country. They invested in complementary activities such as insurance companies, banks, warehouses, and, reluctantly, plantations (Zimmerman 1969; Greenhill 1993, 1995). Rarely did they become roasters. Coffee had to be processed to the point of green or parchment coffee in the cultivating countries because the cherries spoiled too fast to be exported. Green coffee was durable. But early on, the roasting and grinding had to be done in the end-consuming countries because the final processed product quickly lost its flavor and aroma. Although later technology permitted the export of roasted and even ground coffee from growing countries as well as instant coffee manufactured in the global South, tariffs in consuming northern countries and the market power of roasters in the North prevented finished coffee exports.

As the trade grew so did the size of the largest exporters, most of whom were Western European or American. By the end of the nineteenth century the five largest exporters shipped over 40 percent of Brazil's exports and the ten largest over 60 percent (Marcellino Martins and Johnston 1992: 371). The growth of the trade brought merchants to found the Le Havre exchange and then the New York Coffee Exchange in 1882 to attract trade to their ports and capital in the form of a futures market. They were also concerned with preventing commercial corners from provoking rapid and unpredictable fluctuations in price. The exchanges institutionalized access to standardized information. Hamburg and London soon followed with major coffee exchanges. The telegraph created the possibility of an integrated international commodity market and increased the market power of importers and processors in consuming countries. Prices and grades thereby became more standardized.

Social practices in the largest markets, the United States and Germany, very much affected the nature of demand and the ability of roasters to respond to and modify it. The fact that in the United States, Germany, the Netherlands, and Scandinavia coffee was consumed in the home much more than in coffee houses had important implications for the organization of the trade. Because coffee in the United States was overwhelmingly sold in grocery stores, a few roasting companies such as Arbuckles and the Woolson Spice Company took advantage of the invention of industrial-scale roasters in the late nineteenth century to create brand names. The proliferation of brands meant that roasters were no longer selling a commodity—the green bean—but were selling a trademarked product such as Arbuckle's *Yuban*. Advertising and other marketing tactics such as colorful cans and trading cards attempted to whet the appetite for particular brands and to appeal to the expanding retail grocery sector.

But the ever-larger roasters could not overtake the thousands of grocers and small roasters who sold green beans or custom roasted until they found a way to prevent ground coffee from quickly losing its flavor, a way to win consumer confidence in the quality of packaged beans they now could not see, and a stable price. The first problem was easily solved when vacuum sealing was invented in 1900, though it would require two decades for vacuum packing to gain wide acceptance. By the 1920s "convenience" had started to become an important attribute of roasted coffee, as the Jazz Age heightened the desire for speed and leisure.

The second problem—the questionable quality of canned beans—required government interventions to take command of the market away from importers, who often adulterated coffee stocks. In the United States, the Pure Food and Drug Act of 1907, based on a British pure food law some thirty years earlier, set standards (Anderson 1958; Friedman 1973). It decreed that imported coffee be marked according to its port of exit. Thus "Santos" became a specific type of coffee, as did "Java" or "Mocha."

By gaining the confidence of consumers and providing mass-produced roasted coffee, large industrial roasting firms began to control the market and the chain (Spice Mill 1912). They lengthened the chain by industrializing and commoditizing roasting and grinding, formerly the domain of the housewife. Brands segmented the market by selling various roasts and blends depending on region. By 1935, 90 percent of all coffee sold in the United States was sold roasted in branded packages. The branded coffee that housewives purchased at their neighborhood grocery store was not a commodity; it was a proprietary product.

The largest brands also lengthened the chain by integrating vertically, sometimes even buying plantations in growing countries, and certainly sending their agents into the coffee interior to purchase directly from producers (Goetzinger 1921: 3; Zimmerman 1969: 123). The most successful in integrating segments of the chain before World War II was the A&P chain store empire. The company imported, roasted, canned, branded, and retailed millions of bags of coffee in thousands of its own shops (Ukers 1935). This in-house strand ran parallel to its many competitors, who relied on numerous private outside links to the chain. A&P's own canned coffee was the prototype for the supermarkets' house brands that emerged after World War II. Command of "shelf space" and increasing concentration of supermarket companies allowed the brands to assert ever-greater governance over the coffee commodity chain, as the power of independent merchants, small-scale roasters, and shippers declined.

As a result, value—in the sense of market-priced processes—was increasingly added, as the housewife's unremunerated role in making coffee declined. This caused an ever-greater share of the monetary value of coffee to be added in consuming countries. An ever-smaller number of companies took advantage of marketing economies to go regional and finally, after World War II, national. They governed the chain.

John Talbot has calculated that the value-added in consuming countries grew from 47 percent of the final price in 1975–1976 to 79 percent by 2000–2001 (Talbot 2004: 167, 169). Consequently the coffee-consuming countries can rightfully be thought of as "producing" countries as well. Hence, I refer to coffee-cultivating countries as "growers" rather than "producers" to avoid confusion.

Because roaster profits came from using coffee as a raw material, rather than as an object of speculation as it had been for many merchants, roasters favored stable, predictable prices. They accepted state-run price controls beginning in 1906 in Brazil, which led eventually to a series of International Coffee Agreements (ICAs) from 1962 to 1989. Although the European coffee trade was slower to turn to large-mass roasters and retail sales of packaged coffee, brands such as Pelican Rouge and Kaiser captured large markets in the early twentieth century. European states also signed on to the ICAs as their share of world coffee imports grew to a dominating position after World War II.

The expansion of large roasting companies with their superior technology, greater efficiency, more reliable and cheaper product, and marketing sophistication led to ever-more concentration. By the 1950s the five largest roasters in the United States roasted over one-third of all coffee and held 78 percent of all stocks. Traders grew to satisfy the growing demand of roasters. According to the Federal Trade Commission, the top ten importers were responsible for over half the total of coffee imported into the United States.

Ten exporting houses in Brazil sent out between 67 and 90 percent of the crops until the 1920s, and continued to control over half after that. Because Brazil was exporting between 40 and 80 percent of the world's coffee until the 1950s, and these exporting houses operated in other producing areas as well, this meant a few houses dominated world exports.

State Intervention and Market Expansion

Government intervention, which characterized the world coffee market more than any other commodity for most of the twentieth century, brought some governance of the chain back to the producing countries. Beginning in 1906 some of Brazil's provinces held stocks off the world market to "valorize" them. This led to a federal price support program, the Inter-American Coffee Agreement, and finally in 1962 the first International Coffee Agreement. Because the main objective of these cartels was to stabilize prices rather than corner the market, roasters in the consuming countries grudgingly joined. They were willing to accept paying somewhat higher prices in return for guaranteed production because most value was added in the consuming countries. The coffee bean itself was increasingly a low-cost raw material.

After initially strenuously opposing valorization, the governments of the consuming countries signed on to create the International Coffee Organization (ICO) in 1962 to enforce the ICA. The agreement created the organization. Their reasons were less economic than political, however. Coffee was a pawn in the Cold War. It was no coincidence that the United States came on board three years after the Cuban Revolution. Concern with social revolution in 1960s Latin America and Africa also convinced their national governments to push state-led economic development, undertake some land reform, and intervene in the market by creating coffee institutes and marketing boards. These public agencies provided credit and infrastructure for the trade. Governance of the chain was now largely in the hands of state agencies in the cultivating and consuming countries. Participating growing countries were given annual export quotas to maintain coffee's international price. Studies of the ICO tend to agree that it maintained relatively high coffee prices and permitted exporting countries to enjoy a substantial share of the final consumer price (Bates 1997; Daviron and Ponte 2005; Talbot 2004). Steady and relatively attractive prices to the farmers and guaranteed markets encouraged ever-greater production. A "green revolution" for coffee, developed in good part in the coffee-growing countries such as Brazil and Costa Rica, allowed new chemical techniques and mechanization to intensify productivity; unfortunately, overproduction resulted.

John Talbot observes that the ICO spanned "the transition from developmentalism to globalism" (Talbot 2004: 94–95). The former version of state capitalism provided conditions for rapid consolidation and vertical integration in the consuming countries while usually protecting smaller-scale coffee farmers in the global South. As coffee processing became increasingly industrialized, economies of scale grew, and an ever-larger share of the value was added in consuming countries. Roasting, transporting, weighing, and packaging were mechanized and centralized. New products were created: decaffeinated coffee and, after World War II, instant coffee, in which processing added increased value (Talbot 1997a: 183). The main exception to this trend was in the few coffee-growing countries that also greatly expanded domestic coffee consumption, such as Brazil and Costa Rica (Vega Jimenez 2004). The chain bifurcated with the best-quality beans going abroad and the lower-quality ones supplying the growing number of domestic consumers. A few cultivating countries such as Brazil, Ecuador, the Ivory Coast, Colombia, and India began producing and exporting instant coffee, though in all cases except Brazil the soluble coffee was produced by multinationals rather than domestic factories. The United States raised tariffs on this industrialized product to protect American instant coffee producers (Talbot 1997a).

Instant coffee consumption grew to the point that it provided a third of all coffee drunk in the United States in its peak year of 1978 (Pan American Coffee Bureau 1970: 7; Dicum and Luttinger, 1999: 131). In some other countries such as England and Mexico, it was the main coffee consumed. This new product had a major impact on the world coffee market. Drinkers of instant coffee were concerned with speed and convenience, not the quality of the brew. Consequently the small number of roasters who captured this capital-intensive market used low-priced beans, especially Robusta beans. African producers such as the Ivory Coast, and Asian growers, especially in Vietnam and Indonesia, flooded the world market with Robusta. The world coffee market, which had been overwhelmingly for Arabica to this point, now had two major raw materials and two major price-setting markets: the New York "C" for Arabica and London for Robusta.

This undercut the price of Arabica beans, lowered the overall quality of coffee consumed, and increased returns to ever-larger processors rather than to growers. It also reduced Latin American growers' place in the world market. From the virtual monopoly of world production that Brazil and other Latin American producers enjoyed at the beginning of the twentieth century, by 2007 Brazil had declined to 32 percent of world production (up from 22.2 percent in the early 1980s) and Latin America to 61 percent (International Coffee Organization 2007; Marcellino Martins and Johnston 1992: 349–350). Such geographic fragmentation of cultivation strengthened the governance of the ever-larger multinational trading and industrial producing companies by playing the growers off against each other.

Marketing played as important a role in the growth of bigness as did mechanization, because many of the large coffee companies such as Hills Brothers and Folgers began as grocers and then vertically integrated backward. Arbuckle's became by far the largest coffee roaster in the United States in the late nineteenth century because it sold beans in one-pound paper sacks and awarded gift premiums in exchange for returned labels. The rise of chain stores such as the Great Atlantic and Pacific Tea Company, which made coffee their most profitable good, allowed wholesaling concentration, although each grocery store chain still roasted its own green coffee blends. This changed in the 1950s with the arrival of the supermarket. Selling a vastly larger number of goods, the supermarket depended on small margins but large volume. The popularity of modern processes such as the percolator and Mr. Coffee as well as instant coffee drove down the quality of what was brewed. This facilitated the spread of a few very large companies with lower-quality canned, ground, and roasted coffee. Increasingly the chain became buyer-driven, in the sense that retailers came to have more power over the chain.

The nature of the buyer, however, changed. This was because the rise of the supermarket coincided with two other phenomena. Giant food conglomerates such as Nestlé, General Foods, Coca-Cola, Ralston Purina, and Kraft began to take advantage of their growing market power to buy up smaller successful coffee companies. These conglomerates, which today include Procter & Gamble, Philip Morris, and Sara Lee, had less interest in coffee as a family tradition than did earlier coffee roasters such as Chase and Sanborn, or Maxwell House, which are today merely subsidiaries of conglomerates. Consolidation proceeded to the extent that by the 1980s four companies controlled 80 percent of the U.S. coffee market. Worldwide, in 1998 five multinationals had a 69 percent share of the roasting and instant coffee markets (Daviron and Ponte 2005: 92). Thus, although by the 1980s coffee was the world's second most important internationally traded commodity in many years, and it was produced in over a hundred countries while being consumed in virtually every country, it was surprisingly oligopolized and oligopsonized.

A New World, Post-1989

The more-than-a-century-long trend toward national and then international vertical integration and consolidation of the ever-greater links in the coffee commodity chain confronted two major countervailing tendencies at century's end. First, the demise of the socialist Soviet Union and other centrally planned economies reinforced the power of capitalist states and multinational corporations. At the same time the specter of social revolution faded to the extent that many politicians felt they could ignore pleas for the redistribution of wealth in coffee-cultivating countries. On the ideological plane Austrian School laissez-faire economics were championed, particularly in the United States and Great Britain.

This new world led to the dissolution of the International Coffee Agreement in 1989, though the ICO continued in much weakened condition. State governance of the chain shrank even further when most coffee-growing countries dissolved their coffee institutes. They stressed profits and efficiency over social justice. Governments did not step in when world coffee prices fell by almost half after the ICA's demise. The result was ever-greater control of the chain by companies such as Nestlé and Procter & Gamble, which are among the world's largest diversified industrial conglomerates. The world's five largest roasters bought nearly half of the world's green coffee in 2002 (Fridell 2007: 117).

This has been countered by the other major trend—the specialty coffee movement, which began in the most affluent countries and has diffused to urban centers in developing countries. Specialty coffee houses have increased demand for quality, generated awareness regarding the origins of different coffees, and created value in what Daviron and Ponte (2005) call "in-house service quality attributes." The best known of these corporations is Starbucks, which has experienced remarkable growth, first in the United States and then globally. Starbucks has educated the palates of American coffee drinkers to darker roasts, often adulterated with milk, and accustomed consumers to paying much higher prices than they had for the "bottomless cups" of the coffee shops. They have segmented the world coffee market by introducing new standards of quality and often going directly to growers, who can gain by playing the speciality buyers against their traditional buyers. Although in total volume specialty coffee pales against the traditional industrialized brands, its higher prices means it occupies a substantial place in the U.S. and Canadian national coffee markets. Unfortunately for the cultivating countries, most of the money associated with this "latte revolution" reflects the cost of milk and sugar additives, rents, and coffee house profits, not necessarily increasing returns to coffee growers.

Another less-market-driven countervailing trend, what anthropologist Karl Polanyi would call a "double movement," came from organizations such as Max Havelaar, Oxfam, and Fair Trade. They were not so concerned with coffee as a profitable commodity produced for enrichment, but with its symbolic role as a means for furthering social justice, peasant autonomy, and ecological equilibrium. This has become known as "sustainable development" (Renard 1999a; Daviron and Ponte 2005; Martínez-Torres 2006; Fridell 2007). Growing out of solidarity movements with Nicaraguan Sandinistas; religious groups concerned with impoverished peoples such as those who created Oxfam; supporters of indigenous peoples; anti-corporate globalization organizations; and ecologically sensitive groups, this effort has established alternative trade organizations and retail shops. They offer prices directly to growers based not just on the world price but also on considerations such as whether the coffee is organic, the shade bird-friendly, the cooperative democratically run, and the cultivation ecologically sensitive. They are mostly directed to small-scale owner-producers, not agrarian proletarians. The price has a "symbolic" portion that is paid to support a political or social ideal rather than strictly for the coffee (Daviron and Ponte 2005). Some of these purchases can be seen as manifestations of individual consumer politics as much as market-based decisions. They constitute novel and maybe promising strands of the coffee commodity chain, but are a very small part of it.

Conclusions

We have charted the historically evolving nature of the coffee commodity chain, which only began once coffee became a commodity in Yemen. It was an international trader-driven chain initially, with religious and military participants also playing important parts. After two centuries of the chain being centered in the Middle East and the Indian Ocean, Europeans entered, first as traders and then as cultivators. They spread coffee growing to the Americas, where it became transformed. Brazilian cultivators changed the nature of the world coffee market. Far from being passive victims of an anonymous world market, Brazilians were pricemakers and were intimately involved in the creation of market institutions. Yet U.S. and Western European merchants, roasters, retailers, and consumers also played dynamic roles. By historicizing the commodity chain, we see the agency in the two connected worlds. There is resistance to, as well as accommodation of, global trends of commoditization. All of the historical meanings of coffee coexist and compete. Markets are segmented, with coffee varying from an exotic luxury status symbol to a work-intensifying drug; a leisure beverage; a marker of Western modernity, fashion, and youth culture; and a building block for developing states and economies.

Over time, the nature of the international market shifted notably. Latin American producers played a key part in transforming coffee from an elite leisure beverage that served as a sign of distinction to a mass convenience drink. Governance went from farmers to local merchants, to importers, to roasters, to multinational corporations, and, for most of the twentieth century, to states. Although the market's dynamism came largely from private initiatives, state intervention was necessary to institutionalize and standardize practices once the market's size outstripped merchants' ability to operate it. The huge and rapid expansion of the international coffee market resulted from three linked phenomena: the ability of growers to meet growing demand without raising prices—initially by super-exploiting natural resources and labor rather than technological improvements, later by developing new cultivars and modernizing processing and transporting; technical refinements by processors and marketers in consuming countries; and, finally, consumers' shifting tastes and cultures.

This process, though, has brought into question some of our most cherished categories. Are coffee growers really the only "producers" when processing of the coffea cherry and roasting and grinding add most of the market value? At what point do we define what is "coffee"? Could we not just as aptly call many of the giant roasters and manufacturers of other coffee drinks such as bottled "frappucino" and instant coffee "coffee producers"? Similarly, why do we assume that "consumers" are only the overseas final users? Latin Americans have come to drink an ever-larger share of the coffee they grow, so it has become proportionately less of an export crop (Topik forthcoming). Brazil is today the world's second largest consumer of coffee and, on a per capita basis, Costa Rica is a leader.

In addition to being historically and culturally sensitive, the commodity chain approach should recognize the segmented nature of the market and its various niches. For example, both Brazil and Costa Rica could succeed in the world market at the same time, despite very different production, processing, and marketing systems as well as different products. Rather than just compete, their coffees sometimes cooperate in blends.

A historical examination of the coffee commodity chain demonstrates that even within the same commodity, a range of production systems, market strategies, and power relations coexisted since the late eighteenth century. The plethora of markets derived from botanical and mechanical difference, but also from the different lore that consumers attached to different provenances, which are only partially reflected in palpable taste. That is, product differentiation has resulted from variations in botany, climate, production techniques, historical traditions, marketing, and consumer reception. Over time, not only new cultivars but new coffee products developed. In Japan, for example, there are separate strands of the coffee chain depending on whether the consumer drinks upscale Blue Mountain Jamaican coffee in an elegant café, sips Brazilian or Colombian coffee brewed at home or in the office, or buys from a vending machine a can of blended coffee made with beans from Vietnam or Indonesia.

It is true that the coffee grower receives only pennies from the three-dollar Starbucks cup of coffee he or she purchases (Dicum and Luttinger 1999: 1909). However, the coffea cherry passed through many transformations and many hands from farm to cup. One hears few complaints about the small share of a Dior gown the cotton farmer receives. Coffee has been singled out as a peculiarly important actor in political and ethical disputes because it has so long been embroiled in political economic feuds. Today it is in the front lines of North-South debates about the political, economic, and ethical dynamics and consequences of globalization.

One of the few commodities that was already important to long-distance luxury trade in the early modern period, coffee continues to be one of the world's most valuable trade goods. But one should not reify the "coffee market," nor treat it mechanically. Rather than a continuous, homogeneous institution, the international chain has been marked by radical disjunctures and essential transformations and segmentations as production systems have varied and changed markedly. Coffee continues to enjoy great international importance because the nature of its appeal to consumers has shifted to conform to remarkable changes in the societies of the dominant buyers over the past four centuries. The "social life" of coffee—its meaning to producers and consumers—has changed also. Thus the unity and continuity of the term *coffee* is quite misleading, and hence analysis of the coffee commodity chain must be sensitive to great variation.

3 Trading Up the Commodity Chain?

The Impact of Extractive and Labor-Intensive
Manufacturing Trade on World-System Inequalities

David A. Smith and Matthew C. Mahutga

*G*LOBALIZATION IS A CURRENT BUZZWORD, BOTH IN POPULAR culture and in social science. Among the familiar themes discussed in the globalization literature are worldwide cultural convergence, growing international institutional isomorphism, and the gradual (inevitable?) spread of neoliberal economic models. But a more critical perspective, epitomized by the political economy of the world-system approach, stresses the pervasive impact of contemporary global capitalism, claiming that the structure and dynamics of the world-economy systematically creates sets of "winners" and "losers," through mechanisms ranging from "unequal exchange" (Emmanuel 1972; Bunker 1984) to unequal terms of trade and foreign capital penetration (Bornschier and Chase-Dunn 1985) to the uneven distribution of value-added in an international division of labor (Wallerstein 1979; Hopkins and Wallerstein 1986).

In this chapter we will develop a conceptual framework for exploring global networks of international commodity exchange from a world-system perspective. We will begin by linking certain types of commodity trade with the idea of unequal exchange, and move from there toward an image of global commodity chains (GCCs). Although much of the GCC literature focuses on consumer products, manufacturing, and the marketing of finished goods, we will emphasize the importance of incorporating the extraction of raw materials at the beginning of the commodity chain and discuss how this expands and deepens this framework. We will then proceed to a discussion of the empirical findings resulting from a network analysis of international commodity trade and consider the implications of these findings for debates regarding global inequality.

Theoretical Background

The progenitors of world-system theory stressed comparative and world-historic analysis and produced rich descriptive tomes about the origins, organization, and operation of the world-economy over decades and centuries (Wallerstein 1974; Chirot 1977; Frank 1978, 1979). These descriptions are qualitative and historical and seem very remote from formal sociological studies of social networks. But there is a relational or network imagery in their conceptualization of global capitalism (Tilly 1984). Growing out of a "dependency" framework that emphasized the idea of a dyadic "metropolis"-"satellite" relationship and stressed how the former underdeveloped the later (Frank 1969b), the world-system approach developed a more comprehensive notion of a global economic *system* (Wallerstein 1974, 1979). Viewed from the vantage point of poorer countries or regions, dependency remains paramount, and external relations condition economic growth and other types of development. But the real key is understanding "the consequences of occupying a given structural position within the world-system as a whole" (Evans 1979a: 15). Whereas the Latin American *dependentistas* tended to get stuck in an oversimplified version of the development of underdevelopment thesis, the world-system perspective takes scholarship beyond core and periphery. First, it allows for an intermediary stratum of "semi-peripheral" countries as "a necessary element in the world economy" (Wallerstein 1974: 349). Second, it raises the possibility of mobility in the international system through "dependent development" (Cardoso 1973; Evans 1979a).

Thus structural inequality is a central concept for world-system analysis. It involves some key generic assumptions. The first is that the proper unit of analysis is not the nation state or some other smaller unit, but rather the whole global economic-political system within which nation states are embedded. The second is that the role or position that different nations occupy within the world-system tells us much about the dynamics of social change within those units (Chase-Dunn 1989). Although it certainly is true that internal elements such as domestic politics play an important role in the fate of states (Evans and Stephens 1988), the claim is that the structural pattern of world-system role or position sets the initial parameters that constrain and condition the way class and political processes work themselves out (for a schematic model, see chapter 1 in Smith 1996).

So how do we go about measuring these roles and positions and the larger structural pattern that they constitute? One promising technique is social network analysis. Beginning with a seminal article by Snyder and Kick (1979) that used "blockmodeling" to gauge the empirical status of the world-system model of core-semi-periphery-periphery, there have been a series of efforts to do precisely this (see also Steiber 1979; Nemeth and Smith 1985; Smith and White 1992). Network analysis is only useful if there are good conceptualizations about the importance of particular types of relations. World-system theorists long posited that certain kinds of commodity trade will be critical in determining stratum membership in a multitiered world-economy. Specifically, the exchange of finished products versus raw materials was seen as a key mechanism of unequal exchange (Frank 1969a; Galtung 1971; Emmanuel 1972). In particular, these scholars claimed that core-periphery exploitation, while embedded in wage differentials, is transmitted via trade of low-value goods from the periphery in exchange for higher-value ones from the core (Emmanuel 1972; Amin 1980).

Although this early scholarship on unequal exchange provides some useful benchmark notions about the importance of the trade of primary products versus manufactures, there is good reason to believe that the world has changed since the 1960s and 1970s. One of the underlying issues in contemporary debates about globalization centers on the nature of worldwide economic restructuring in the past two or three decades. In 1980 a pathbreaking book argued that a "new international division of labor" (NIDL) based on globalized production processes was emerging (Fröbel, Heinrichs, and Kreye 1980). Consistent with the main contours of this argument were descriptions of a new "global assemblyline" (Feuntes and Ehrenreich 1984) implying the deindustrialization of the high-wage core nations (Bluestone and Harrison 1982) through capital flight to low-wage semi-peripheral or peripheral areas (Ross and Trachte 1990).

Of course, this suggests a very *different* pattern of periphery-core commodity trade, with low-wage manufactured goods, in particular, tending to flow from the former to the latter. It is under this changing NIDL that we see the rise of a number of newly industrializing countries (NICs). Manufacturing for export was hailed as the secret to rapid economic growth of countries such as South Korea and Taiwan in the so-called East Asian economic miracle (Gereffi and Wyman 1990; World Bank 1993). But we need to closely examine the *nature* of the manufacturing activities occurring in particular economies and the specific *linkages* between manufacturing enterprises; global markets; and local, state, and transnational capital. Some of the NICs (particularly in East Asia) have successfully engaged in "industrial upgrading" in which there is a shift from commodities such as textiles, apparel, and footwear to "higher value-added items that employ sophisticated technology and require a more extensively developed, tightly integrated local industrial base" (Gereffi 1992: 92). This might include production of computers, semiconductors, numerically controlled machine tools, VCRs, televisions, and so on. However, many peripheral countries remain primarily export platforms for simple low-technology, labor-intensive goods made by low-wage, unskilled workers.

This focus on an increasingly integrated global economy, in which countries fill distinct export niches and industrial upgrading seems to be the only viable option, leads Gereffi to argue that global commodity chains (GCCs) should be the key analytical construct (Gereffi 1990, Gereffi and Korzeniewicz 1990). There are parallels between the idea of GCCs and the value chains of economist Michael Porter (1990) or the production chains of geographer Peter Dicken (1992). But Gereffi grounds his initial conceptualization in world-system analysis, drawing on Hopkins and Wallerstein's (1986: 159) definition of a commodity chain as "a network of labor and production processes whose end result is a finished commodity." Elaborating further, "A GCC consists of sets of interorganizational networks clustered around one commodity or product, linking households, enterprises and states to one another within the world-economy. . . . [it is] the sequential stages of input acquisition, manufacturing, distribution, marketing and consumption" (Gereffi, Korzeniewicz, and Korzeniewicz 1994: 2).

A thorough GCC analysis of particular commodity chains requires some detailed knowledge of the *specific* qualities of the commodity itself. This has predisposed many researchers to do grounded case studies of the sort described elsewhere in this volume (see Chapter 2, by Topik, and Chapter 10, by Munro and Schurman). But we can also try to take a more overarching view. In network terms, these commodity chains can be conceived as consisting of a number of "nodes" that constitute the pivot points in transformation sequences: extraction and supply of raw materials, the stages of industrial processing, export of goods, and final marketing (Gereffi and Korzeniewicz 1990). Each node is connected to other nodes of related activity, and the local, regional, and world economies are seen as ever more intricate, web-like structures of these GCCs, creating spatially bounded structures of varying scales.

Some commodity chains are simple: production of a soft drink can involves extraction of bauxite from a mine; a smelting sequence that produces first alumina, then aluminum; and the fabrication of the container itself. But others are complex. In an early illustration of the utility of commodity chain analysis, Hopkins and Wallerstein (1986) detailed the raw materials and processes of industrial transformation necessary to build an eighteenth-century wooden sailing ship. It involved the procurement of several key raw materials that make up the hull, mast, sail, ropes, and so on, and then production sequences of varying complexity and length to make the components, leading to final assembly in a shipyard and distribution to various end users. Of course, the commodity chain (now assuredly "global") for something like a modern automobile is even more intricate.

Most recent research on production networks and commodity chains tends to focus on consumer goods sold in retail stores (Gereffi 1994, Bair and Gereffi 2001; Appelbaum and Smith 2001). Shining the spotlight on these final stages of particular GCCs and their relationship to the manufacturing links in these chains has been extremely fruitful, as scholars have learned a great deal about the promise and perils of industrial upgrading strategies for firms and countries.

Although the GCC models almost always nod toward the importance of raw material inputs at the sources of the chains, there is very little systematic attention to this in most research.[1] But analysts such as Stephen Bunker remind us that raw materials are extremely crucial, not only as inputs to all finished goods but also for basic energy production and infrastructural construction in contemporary society (Bunker and Ciccantell 2005). And their modes of extraction in peripheral areas of the global system also promote a form of unequal exchange and what Bunker has referred to as "progressive underdevelopment" (Bunker 1984, 1985).

Bunker's exploration of these issues began in years of field research in the vast, resource-rich Amazon basin. He explained how various modes of extraction are compatible or incompatible with the procurement of other raw materials from the same eco-regions, the need for state support and infrastructural development in frontier areas, and the swirling power politics that accompany all this (Bunker 1985). Although Bunker never explicitly used the term *commodity chains,* he came close at times in referring to "global chains of extraction and production" (Bunker and Ciccantell 2005: xx). And the focus, as in the GCC approach, is the "tangible commodities whose material differences typify the more abstract mechanisms by which the material properties of a commodity determine the way it is incorporated into global markets" (Bunker and Ciccantell 2005: 58). Although those of us who live in so-called advanced industrial societies are familiar with manufacturing and its attendant social relationships, we have much less exposure to agriculture, mining, forestry, and associated activities and their social impacts on land, people, and economic interests where extraction takes place.

The focus in Bunker's work is on the beginning of the commodity chain, but there are some intriguing parallels between the Bunkeresque approach and the GCC perspective. Both stress close, grounded analysis of specific commodities in particular places; Bunker's emphasis here recalls the argument by Gereffi and others (1994: 2) that commodity chains are "situationally specific, socially constructed, and locally integrated." Both bodies of work remind us that production or extraction occurs in particular places, so geographic location, clustering of ancillary activities, and importance of the logistics of transportation require attention. And there are also some striking similarities between extractive economies and low-wage manufacturing sites. Bunker's portrayal of the relative powerlessness of peripheral raw-material-producing areas, the way that control, technology, and power are wielded from distant corporate offices in the core, and the manner in which extractive enclaves are played off against each other by metropolitan interests, exhibit strong analogies to subcontracted factories incorporated into far-flung buyer-driven commodity chains in the consumer goods networks described in the GCC literature. There is a strong image of core control and peripheral dependence in both accounts.

This chapter asserts that we should combine the insights of a focus on modes of extraction with the GCC approach. Put differently, we need to develop a GCC approach that "starts at the beginning" (Smith 2005). There are several advantages to "bringing in Bunker." First, a key challenge is to understand why particular types of activities occur at particular locations. Trying to unravel the issue of shifting industrial location is a central question in studies of current global economic restructuring. Bunker stresses the natural endowment of geographic regions, the configuration of watercourses, and physical topography as critical for extractive advantages. Though not all of these matter for manufacturing, some clearly do: in their recent book, Bunker and Ciccantell (2005) show that the rise of Amsterdam was closely linked to the city's location on major rivers, which gave it access to high-quality lumber from the European interior that was used in the city's world-leading shipyards. There are also issues linked to transportation and other infrastructure that are critical for distributing and selling the vast majority of goods made in today's globalized economy (Bonacich 2005). Thus more attention to them by GCC scholars is warranted.

Second, the modes of extraction approach can contribute more to our understanding of technological change and what David Harvey (1989) calls time-space compression. Bunker argues that, to a great extent, extractive economies *drive* the process of technological innovation that creates a "smaller world" based on advanced transport and communication systems. The reason is fairly straightforward: with time, primary products that used to be easily harvested get progressively more difficult to extract. Surface deposits of minerals are used up, so heavy equipment and new techniques need to be developed to, literally, dig deeper. This requires technological innovation. And, beyond this, many raw materials are bulky, heavy, and costly to move, which promotes innovations in transportation (bigger, more powerful ships; railroads through jungles and mountains; and so on).

The GCC perspective's lack of attention to transportation is particularly problematic. For example, some scholars note the rise of East Asian manufacturing and its reliance on the vast consumer markets of the United States (Gereffi 1999; Gereffi and Hamilton, Chapter 7, this volume). This is only possible because of major improvements in port facilities and containerized oceanic shipping, which purveys consumer manufactures from places such as China or Indonesia to the U.S. West Coast. Indeed, the global assembly line relies on worldwide communications (especially improvements in telecommunications) and shipping to function. So Bunker and Ciccantell's focus on the evolution of globalized shipping, which was closely tied to bulk transportation of primary goods, is crucial not only to raw material procurement but also to the delivery of finished products analyzed in the GCC literature.

The vastness of large-scale extraction and its ancillary transportation infrastructures also presents a challenge to those who blithely point to globalization and "the decline of the state" (Strange 1996; Rodrik 1997). Although "flexible" light manufacturing might seem to fit some sort of neoliberal vision, massive mining complexes, huge agribusiness estates, and giant port and rail networks involve high levels of state subsidization, administration, and regulation. The need to not lose sight of the importance of politics and states is yet another insight that an extractive focus brings to the GCC framework.

Getting to the Networks: Examining International Commodity Trade

We are proposing a new, more comprehensive GCC framework that incorporates more attention to a range of commodity exports, including raw materials. The key issue that this approach addresses is, how and where does surplus or profit accrue at the various points where these commodity chains touch down? Examining GCCs in this way provides us with a new perspective to explore issues of national development. This leads to a second question: What are the prospects for upgrading to nodes in these chains that might increase the value-added and profits associated with local activities? Of course, one way to explore these issues would be the fine-grained case studies that Gereffi, Bunker, and their colleagues have pioneered. But we propose to use multiple network analysis of various types of international commodity trade between 1965 and 2000 to begin to explore issues of global inequality and development in a more comprehensive way.

Our research builds on a foundation of previous work exploring world-system structure and dynamics. Some of the earliest network analyses of international trade yielded empirical confirmation of the core-periphery hierarchy (Snyder and Kick 1979; Nemeth and Smith 1985; Smith and White 1992). These and other studies also found a positive relationship between structural position in the world-system and economic growth (Snyder and Kick 1979; Nemeth and Smith 1985; Kick, Davis, Lehtinen, and Burnes 2000; Kick and Davis 2001). They further demonstrated empirically that a country's structural position in trade networks is related to its specific economic role in the international division of labor (Nemeth and Smith 1985; Smith and White 1992).

More recent findings suggest that the structure of the world economy still conforms to this overall core-semi-periphery-periphery layering. Contrary to claims that globalization is primarily characterizable by the homogenous spread of "industry" to historically poor countries, the main dimension of core-periphery hierarchy continues to be differentiated by relatively advanced industry at the upper end of the hierarchy versus less advanced industry at

(1) High Tech or Heavy Manufacturing

(58) Plastic materials, regenerated Cellulose and artificial resins

(69) Manufactures of metal

(71) Machinery—nonelectrical

(2) Sophisticated Extractive

(25) Pulp and waste paper

(34) Gas, natural and manufactured

(64) Paper, paperboard, and manufactures thereof

(3) Simple Extractive

(04) Cereal and cereal preparations

(22) Oil seeds, oil nuts, and oil kernels

(41) Animal oils and fats

(4) Low Wage or Light Manufactures

(83) Travel bags, handbags, and similar containers

(84) Clothing

(85) Footwear

(5) Animal Products and By-Products

(01) Meat and meat preparations

(02) Dairy products and birds' eggs

(29) Crude animal and vegetable materials

FIGURE 3.1. UN commodity categories classified by type of processing
SOURCE: United Nations 1963.

the lower end. Confirming world-system expectations, upward mobility is exceedingly rare, even during recent decades that others describe as a period of massive change. Indeed, there are also changing mobility patterns over time. During the last two decades of the twentieth century there appeared to be *less* upward mobility than occurred in the 1960s and 1970s, suggesting that "globalization," rather than spreading wealth and facilitating development, may be creating barriers for nations that are at the lower rungs of the global economy (Mahutga 2006).

The research that we report on here results from a longitudinal analysis of trade that is disaggregated by commodity type (United Nations 1963) and uses the concept of regular equivalence (White and Reitz 1983; White 1984) to quantify the similarity or dissimilarity between the trade profiles of individual countries.[2] Figure 3.1 provides a list of the three commodities that constitute each of the five bundles.

Implications for Global Inequality and Differential Development

One of our central interests (and a major debate in contemporary social science) involves the degree of inequality in today's world, whether it is growing or declining, and the mechanisms that lie behind pressure for convergence or polarization. There seems to be broad consensus that within country, material inequality is on the rise, particularly in core countries, due to the impacts of neoliberalism (outsourcing of manufacturing, the decline of labor unions, reduced state spending, and so on). There is sharp disagreement whether there is increasing global income polarization. Korzeniewicz and Moran (1997, 2000) find robust evidence of greater inequality, but their findings are vociferously rejected by Firebaugh (1999, 2000a, 2003). But in keeping with the focus of this chapter and book, here we want briefly to summarize some issues of structural inequality as they relate to our commodity-chain-based model of changing world-system structure.

Our analytical strategy applies classic ideas and techniques from the role-position literature within the social networks canon. At the risk of oversimplification, the goal of role-position analyses is to start with a set of relational data N, usually an N X N socio-matrix, and attempt to simplify N into a B X B matrix B, where B_i is a group of actors from N that relate to all other actors in a similar way. The classic approach is to define an equivalence relation with which to sort out N into B. The approach we use here is regular equivalence, which receives detailed attention elsewhere (Alderson and Beckfield 2004; Faust 1988; Mahutga 2006; Wasserman and Faust 1994). Conceptually, "the notion of regular equivalence formalizes the observation that actors who occupy the same social position relate in the same ways with other actors who are themselves in the same positions" (Wasserman and Faust 1994: 473).

Technically, applying the standard optimal regular equivalence algorithm to our set of five trade relationships generates an N X N matrix R in which R_{ij} represents the level of regular equivalence between i and j, which scales from zero to one. The new matrix R then becomes the basis for the assignment of actors into regular equivalence classes. In general, the continuous solution of the R matrix (that is, actors are generally "more or less" equivalent, rather than completely equivalent) requires further analyses to find "cutpoints" defining approximately regular equivalent groups. To delineate groups of countries that are relatively equivalent, we use a hierarchical clustering algorithm that maximizes the within-group similarity (or minimizes the between-group similarity), where similarity is the measure of regular equivalence between each country (Borgatti 1994). Although these results produce an interpretable set of equivalence classes, the continuous reality implied by the definition of equivalence also suggests a continuous scaling of the R matrix. Thus we superimpose the hierarchical clustering results onto a correspondence analysis (Weller and Romney 1990), which provides a quantification and graphical display of the similarity between countries and groups in a low-dimensional space (Figures 3.2–3.4). Our correspondence analysis is classic, as described in Weller and Romney 1990.

As the legend in each figure indicates, the figures read from right to left with core countries on the right, and peripheral countries on the left. The correspondence analysis suggests a more or less one-dimensional solution because the first dimension explains 91, 94, and 96 percent of the variation in regular equivalence between countries in 1965, 1980, and 2000, respectively. Thus the main horizontal dimension on the X axis can be interpreted as a continuous measure of "coreness" (Borgatti and Everett 1999; Mahutga 2005), whereas the symbols demonstrate the extent to which countries along that

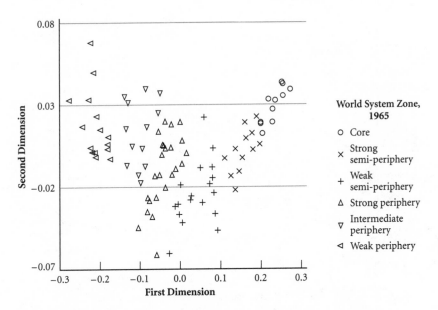

FIGURE 3.2. Single-link hierarchical clustering of regular equivalencies superimposed on correspondence analysis of regular equivalences, 1965

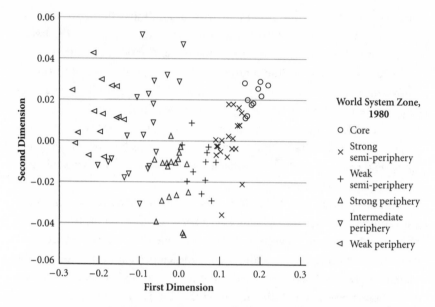

FIGURE 3.3. Single-link hierarchical clustering of regular equivalencies superimposed on correspondence analysis of regular equivalences, 1980

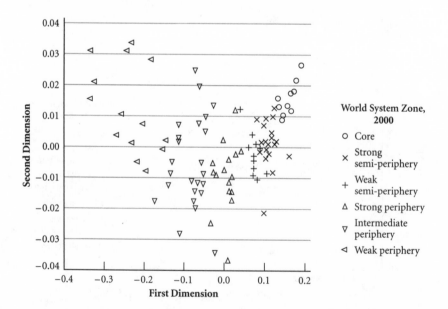

FIGURE 3.4. Single-link hierarchical clustering of regular equivalencies superimposed on correspondence analysis of regular equivalences, 2000

continuum are clusterable into regular equivalence classes. Thus the group in the upper right-hand side of Figure 3.2 (circles) contains the United States, Japan, and the larger Western European countries, while the group to the extreme left contains less-developed countries from Africa, the Middle East, and Asia.

Consistent with these empirical results, we labeled the groups from right to left as 1 = Core, 2 = Strong semi-periphery, 3 = Weak semi-periphery, 4 = Strong periphery, 5 = Weak periphery, and 6 = Weakest periphery. These labels communicate what is, in reality, a latent continuous core-periphery structure in these trade data. In other words, the Weak semi-periphery is more "core like" than is the Strong periphery, whereas the Strong periphery is more "core like" than is the Weak periphery. There are many types of analyses that could be carried out to convey this underlying empiric (for example, block modeling, examining commodity-specific trade profiles, in-group versus out-group preference, and so on), but none are more persuasive than the one-dimensional solution of the correspondence analysis—literally a continuous measure of "coreness" (see, for example, Borgatti and Everett 1999; Boyd, Fitzgerald, Mahutga, and Smith 2006; Mahutga 2005). Countries plotted on the origin of the Euclidian space in Figures 3.2 through 3.4 represent the average pattern of equivalence with all others. The origin thus provides a natural cut-off between what might be considered the "upper tier" and the "lower tier" economies. The three groups to the right of the origin constitute our core and semi-peripheral countries, while those to the left of the origin represent our peripheral countries, with their group titles representing an increasing dissimilarity from the core-like pattern of trade ties demonstrated by our core group.

As Figure 3.5 demonstrates, if we simply sum the countries in each of the blocks that our present analysis yields, we find that there is a "shrinking middle"—that is to say, more nations occupied the "strong semi-periphery" and "weak periphery" in 1980 than in 1965, and there were still more in 2000. These two zones of the world economy grew at the expense of the middling categories of "weak semi-periphery" and "strong periphery." This suggests a degree of polarization by world-system zone membership, evinced by the development of a bimodal distribution of countries along the core-periphery hierarchy.

We can take a more methodologically sophisticated look at this by assessing the degree to which various strata in the hierarchy have either increased

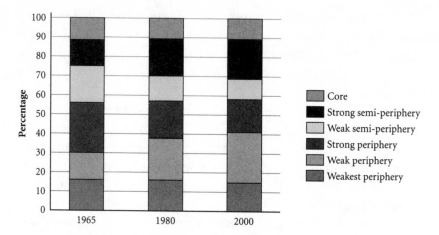

FIGURE 3.5. The shrinking middle: World-system zonal share of national economies

or decreased their distance from the core over time. Because the dimensions delineated from our correspondence analysis (Figures 3.2 through 3.4) are orthogonal by construction, we can evoke the familiar Pythagorean Theorem and measure the Euclidean distance of each country from the leading core country (United States) in each time period. Subsequently, we construct a simple measure of mobility for each country with (distance at time 2 − distance at time 1)/distance at time 1. Finally, we report the average mobility for each zone. Table 3.1 yields results broadly consistent with Figure 3.4. The periphery is increasingly distant from the core, with the weakest segments of the periphery doing the worst (downward mobility). However, two semi-peripheral groups are closing the gap between themselves and the core in the late twentieth century.[3] This general pattern is consistent with key claims by world-system theorists about an inherent tendency of the world-system to polarize between core and periphery (Chirot 1977; Wallerstein 1979), and also supports arguments regarding the existence of "dependent development" in the semi-periphery (Evans 1979a).

These patterns of structural mobility are interesting, but they tell us nothing about any "development gap" in the world-economy. For that we need to look at how the various strata fare in terms of economic measures. For simplicity's sake, we have chosen per capita growth in gross domestic product as our measure. Table 3.2 portrays the average GDP per capita growth by world-system zone. As this table demonstrates, globalization has produced

TABLE 3.1. Mobility toward or away from core by semi-periphery and periphery

Zone	1965–1980	1980–2000
Strong Semi-Periphery		
Mean	0.059	−0.033
Std. Dev.	0.395	0.385
Weak Semi-Periphery		
Mean	0.126	0.204
Std. Dev.	0.183	0.201
Strong Periphery		
Mean	−0.056	0.003
Std. Dev.	0.198	0.156
Weak Periphery		
Mean	−0.034	−0.005
Std. Dev.	0.144	0.144
Weakest Periphery		
Mean	−0.083	−0.12
Std. Dev.	0.087	0.152

TABLE 3.2. GDP per capita growth by world-system zone, 1965–2000[a]

Zone	1965–1980	1980–2000
Core	3.09	1.85
Strong semi-periphery	3.74	2.71
Weak semi-periphery	3.71	2.21
Strong periphery	2.17	1.10
Weak periphery	1.50	−0.67
Weakest periphery	1.13	−0.10

NOTE: [a]GDP per capita is measured at the foreign exchange rate and obtained from the World Development Indicators (World Bank 2006).

both winners *and* losers in the world economy. On one hand, the core has experienced declining growth rates since the "golden age" of economic growth ended in the late 1960s and early 1970s (Webber and Rigby 1996). On the other hand, the semi-periphery has experienced well-above-average levels of economic growth since 1965. Because the semi-periphery is also the most populous world-system zone, its above-average level of economic growth explains why several recent studies find that total world inequality (that is, the sum of between- and within-country inequality) is actually decreasing (Bhatta 2002; Firebaugh 1999, 2000a, 2000b, 2003; Firebaugh and Goesling 2004; Goesling 2001; Melchior and Telle 2001; Schultz 1998). Most important for the present study, the periphery grows much more slowly than both the core and the two semi-peripheries in both time periods, and actually demonstrates negative growth from 1980 to 2000. Thus, although the core and semi-periphery seem to be converging, these two groups are also diverging from the peripheral group on our measure of world-system position, as well as GDP growth per capita.

Although space precludes the kind of discussion needed to fully clarify all the issues involved in the debate on total world inequality, we would like to suggest that at the moment, arguments about trends in world income inequality are at an empirical impasse. The most up-to-date analyses suggest that inequality has likely been stable, if not increasing slightly since 1980, and that the two sides of previous debates (see Firebaugh 2000a; Korzeniewicz and Moran 2000) each contained biases that explain their divergent empirical findings (Dowrick and Akmal 2005). However, we would also like to point out the obvious fact that even if total world inequality were decreasing, it would still be possible to observe polarization—that is, a growing rift between the fastest and slowest growing countries—something that previous studies were unable to detect (Moran 2003). As Table 3.2 shows, even though the semi-periphery is growing faster than the core, the periphery is indeed growing much more slowly, and even had negative growth during the period that many associate with the onset of "globalization," suggesting that polarization is definitely taking place, whether total world inequality is increasing or decreasing.

The pattern of overall polarization that we identify may be empirically interesting, but we are especially keen to understand the mechanisms generating it. One way to do that is to see if our peripheral world-economic blocks are engaged in different sorts of production (returning, in a general way, to the issue of commodity production and trade that was our initial entrée into these networks). Table 3.3 shows that there are distinct sectoral patterns of growth in manufacturing and extraction across the semi-peripheral and peripheral zones. Manufacturing grew in all three zones in both periods (the exception is stagnation during the 1965–1980 era in the weak semi-periphery). The rapid growth in both manufacturing and extraction in the weak periphery during the earlier period coincides with the beginning of "capital flight" from the core into the periphery. Manufacturing exports from both the strong and weak peripheries grew very rapidly in relation to GDP (and at an astonishing rate approaching 250 percent in the weak periphery) between 1965 and 1980. This suggests an explosion of industrial relocation during this period of the type posited by the NIDL thesis, with a great deal of this occurring in the weak periphery.

But the strongest pattern that we see in this table—best summarized in the ratio of manufacturing to extractive growth—is in the much higher rate of industrial growth in both the strong and weak semi-peripheries in the later (1980–2000) period of "globalization"—a period during which two of our peripheral blocks actually experienced negative economic growth. From 1980 to 2000, the growth rate in manufacturing was much slower and more uniform across the three peripheral zones than in the semi-periphery. More important is the observed correlation between the ratio of manufacturing to extraction and economic growth. Our rapidly growing semi-periphery is, on average,

TABLE 3.3. Growth in peripheral extractive and low-wage manufacturing exports as percentage of GDP[a]

Zone	Average Growth by Block (percent)		Ratio of Manufacturing to Extraction Growth	
	1965–1980	1980–2000	1965–1980	1980–2000
Strong Semi-Periphery				
Manufacturing	6.56	22.19	2.62	10.31
Extraction	2.50	2.15		
Weak Semi-Periphery				
Manufacturing	−0.09	54.54	−0.11	5.52
Extraction	0.79	9.88		
Strong Periphery				
Manufacturing	29.95	7.37	20.67	0.63
Extraction	1.45	11.67		
Weak Periphery				
Manufacturing	245.96	9.93	2.00	5.37
Extraction	123.00	1.85		
Weakest Periphery				
Manufacturing	5.63	9.00	6.87	3.17
Extraction	0.82	2.84		

NOTE: [a]GDP figures were obtained from the World Development Indicators (World Bank 2006).

growing in light manufacturing at a ratio ranging from 10:1 to 5.5:1, whereas our slowest growing (and even falling) peripheral ratios range from 5.3:1 to 1:.63. Although low-wage manufacturing may not be the best road to development, it seems better than relying on raw material extraction for the fact that resources become depleted (Bunker 1984, 1985). We should suggest a note of caution, however. As with all higher levels of aggregation, this analysis does not exhaust the possible explanations for the stagnation and even decline we observed in the previous three analyses. Furthermore, Table 3.3 seems a better explanation for the most recent period than it does for the earlier one. Thus it is somewhat difficult to tell with certainty how much variation in upward mobility and economic growth we can explain with this analysis. That being said, this at least raises questions amenable to hypothesis testing of various types in the future.

Conclusion

The main theme emerging from our empirical analysis is one of structural polarization in the networks of the global economy during the final decades of the twentieth century. This is consistent with various contributions to the literature on global restructuring which suggest that the worldwide spread of industry has been very uneven, and that the consequences of industrialization in the places it occurs are much less likely to lead to sustainable economic growth and development than in decades past. Today the spread of manufacturing to peripheral areas of the world-system is often associated with low wages in those regions, perpetuating a "race to the bottom" rather than industrial upgrading, in sharp contrast to old developmentalist-modernization theory assumptions that assumed a strong positive link between "industrialization" and economic development (Rostow 1960). Along with the growing structural gaps in our network analysis of global patterns, we also see income polarization between upper strata (core-semi-periphery) and lower ones (the periphery), and this income inequality maps on to the structural divergence.

Although we see polarization in our structural analysis, there seem to be two types of "peripheralization" going on. First, there is one based on the spread of light, labor-intensive manufacturing. This is the fairly well understood and by now familiar pattern anticipated by those who argued that global restructuring creates a new international division of labor or global assembly line (Fröbel and others 1980; Feuntes and Ehrenreich 1984; Ross and Trachte 1990). But we also see a second form of peripheralization. This one is suggested by the work of Stephen Bunker and appears in our data as an increase in the importance of extractive exports, as some peripheral areas become increasingly specialized in raw material production. Like the light manufacturing regimes highlighted in the NIDL literature, these peripheral extractive economies can be very exploitative, underpinning a particularly pernicious form of unequal exchange (Bunker 1984, 1985; Bunker and Ciccantell 2005).

If we are seeing two types of peripheralization in non-core regions of the world-economy, we can speculate about some possible trends in these areas. First, we might expect to see an uneven increase in proletarianization and manufacturing in the semi-periphery and parts of the periphery. This process would be very episodic and even reversible in the poorer peripheral areas because of the tendency for capital to seek cheaper labor sites when wage costs show even the slightest tendency to rise in some of the lower-cost consumer product sectors. However, with some further proletarianization we are likely to see a spread of labor organizing and unrest and an increase in environmental degradation. In some particularly important sites for industrial relocation, such as China, we may see changes in civil society that increase pressure for democratic reform of authoritarian political systems. If proletarianization is maintained, this would also favor the slowing population growth associated with the "demographic transition" (Davis 1945).

We might see rather different scenarios in peripheral resource frontiers where raw material extraction leads to exploitation and unequal exchange. Here there may be a rapid rise in competition for increasingly scarce resources and a type of environmental destruction that is characteristic of areas where heavy mining and mono-export agriculture predominate. With a growing share of world population stranded in these zones of the world-economy, we might see a lot of people without much hope for the future, and perhaps a rise in radical ideologies, civil unrest, and violence.

This chapter reported findings from a network analysis of the world-system using international commodity trade data. But we also believe that this sort of research should be augmented by more detailed, historically grounded studies that probe deeper into particular cases, countries, and industries. Strategic selection of particular sectors or countries based on the network analytic patterns revealed in our work would be a good way to meld the quantitative and qualitative analytic strategies. Research on the dynamics of particular forms of extraction in specific resource frontiers on the periphery is especially needed. Similarly, studies of industrial relocation and the changing geography of production in various manufacturing sectors, and the struggle between the dynamics of upgrading and the race to the bottom, provide nice complements to the sort of research we have presented here. This chapter also points to some further cross-national research of the effects of world-system dynamics on labor organization and power, economic growth and income inequality, and commodity chains and industrial upgrading. Indeed, there is much work to be done to fully explore some of the empirical patterns previewed in this chapter.

4 Protection Networks and Commodity Chains in the Capitalist World-Economy

Immanuel Wallerstein

THE PRIMARY FEATURE OF ALMOST EVERY COMMODITY CHAIN is that it crosses national frontiers. Indeed, when Terence Hopkins and I launched the concept in the 1970s, our original primary purpose was to show that most production within the capitalist world-economy that placed items for consumption on the market was the result of a long chain that did in fact cross frontiers, and that this had been so throughout the entire history of the capitalist world-economy from the long sixteenth century to today. This was as opposed to the idea that most such chains were entirely encapsulated within national boundaries.[1]

There is one inevitable consequence of this simple fact. All chains are, as a result, subject to interference by state authorities, because states have the sovereign right within the interstate system to establish rules about what crosses their frontiers. They may permit or forbid crossing of persons, merchandise, or capital in general. They may distinguish between the crossings that come from or go to particular countries. They may set limits to amounts that may cross frontiers. They may charge fees on goods (usually called tariffs) that cross frontiers. They may pressure other governments to make conditions that are in the interests of the state placing the pressure, or in the interests of particular producers in the country of the state placing the pressure.

If a state makes no conditions whatsoever on the crossing of its frontiers, we say that it is observing laissez-faire or permitting free trade. If it does make conditions, we say that it is engaged in protectionism. There is probably no state that has ever been entirely open and made no conditions whatsoever. And there have been only a few states who have ever closed their frontiers almost entirely, and then only for limited periods. So the actual practice of states lies somewhere in between these two hypothetical positions. We can talk of frontiers that are relatively open and frontiers that are relatively closed or protected.

We also know that there are ideologies of free trade and of protectionism; that is, that there are intellectuals who preach the virtues of each, and there are states that formally accept some of these ideological statements and act on them, and also assert that their foreign policy is to encourage other states in one direction or the other. This matter is today the major subject of the debates within the World Trade Organization (WTO). What I would like to explore in this essay is who has been most likely to take one ideological position or the other, and what the consequence is for producers or states acting on one ideological position or the other.

It is clear that, in a perfectly free market—one in which no state ever makes rules about the rights of producers to sell products as they wish, and where they wish—those producers of any given product who can, for whatever reason, produce it at the lowest total cost at the locus of proposed sale will be able to propose a lower price than their competitors, and thus presumably be more likely to attract buyers. So, in a perfectly free market, there are, at any given moment, winners and losers among the producers. And those who would lose consistently would eventually be forced out of business.

However, it is crucial to remember that no producer is, or ever has been, primarily interested in being more competitive than others producing the same item, that is, producing the item at lower total cost than all others. Producers are interested rather in maximizing profit, which depends on the differential between the price at which they can sell the item and the total cost of its production. Producers who are not competitive in terms of the cost of production can still be, and quite often are, those who garner the most profit. This depends on their being able to obtain relative monopolies, either in the world market or in particular local markets. And these relative monopolies are dependent on state actions of various kinds. Capital accumulation is not about free enterprise but about monopolies.

Furthermore, we know that buyers do not always purchase the item that is priced lowest, even if we hold quality constant. A buyer may prefer his or her customary seller, for what are often erroneously defined as economically irrational reasons. Actually, buyers may be subordinating short-term advantage to middle-term advantages—for example, greater reliability of a particular seller, or unwillingness to be at the long-run mercy of the particular seller who offers the lowest price. But if the price differential is significant, most buyers will give way over time to short-term economic self-interest, and the "efficient" seller of the moment will win out. This is indeed the main ideological argument for laissez-faire, that it benefits the buyer.

In general, the so-called efficient producers obviously favor open frontiers and put their political weight within countries to get governments to do what they can to achieve this. Indeed, whole countries may find that, overall, open frontiers favor the interests of at least the majority of their producers, and hence decide to push for free trade. We see this, at the present time, in the general policy of the U.S. government, which argues in favor of free trade in multiple arenas—for example in the WTO, in regional trade pacts such as NAFTA, and bilaterally with individual states.

The problem, as the U.S. government presently realizes, is that other countries may have "comparative advantage" (to use the Ricardian concept) in certain goods, and expect the United States, or any country to which they might open their frontiers, to reciprocate by opening its frontiers in turn to the goods of the other countries. To take the most obvious examples, many countries in the South can today produce many agricultural products and many varieties of textiles at lower cost than U.S., or for that matter, Western European, producers.

Were the United States (and Western Europe) to permit the import without conditions of these products, the result would be that agricultural and textile producers in the United States and Western Europe would find it difficult, sometimes impossible, to compete in the home market, and would therefore go out of business or at least be forced to reduce production. And this would hurt not only the owners of these production units but those employed in them. As a consequence, there results considerable political pressure on the United States and Western European governments not to open their frontiers in this way, or at least to limit seriously the degree to which they open them. But, in this case, we are faced with a situation in which the United States and Western Europe (more generically, the countries of the North) would be asking the countries of the South to open their frontiers without adequate reciprocity. And, even given the disproportionate political power of the states of the North and of the South, the latter tend to be very resistant to such a lopsided arrangement, which is quite understandable.

If there are barriers to crossing borders, there are ways to get around them—for example, by transferring the location of a key part of the commodity chain within the frontiers of the target country of final sale. Another way is to launder parts of the chain (in the same way that one launders money) so that they appear to be products of one country when they are in fact products of another, and in that way circumvent laws that require that a certain percentage of the final product be produced in the country of final sale, or at least in a restricted list of countries.

Because there are so many ways to play games with commodity chains, we have situations in which one set of producers in a country of final sale wants laws that are directly contrary to those preferred by another set of producers in the same country. The political pressures at this point go in opposite directions. In addition, to the extent that there are significant electoral contests in a given country, pressure from the workers within production units can play an important political role, and these pressures too, of course, can also go in opposite directions.

Furthermore, as is obvious, wherever there is a commodity chain, it is possible for units of the chain to be linked to each other under the aegis of a single owner. This is called vertical integration and has a number of advantages. In the first place, it guarantees supply between the lower (or earlier) unit and the higher unit in the chain. This may occasionally be crucial in situations of uncertain supply, whether because of scarcity or because of potential political constraints. In the second place, it may enable a given producer to obtain a quasi-monopoly at some point in the commodity chain and hence guarantee that the owner of this nexus can obtain a particularly large share of the overall surplus value generated within a chain.

In the third place, and perhaps most important, it may enable a producer to minimize tax transfers to particular states by playing games with the sales price of items going between two elements in the chain, both of which are owned by the same company but located in different political jurisdictions. In the continual struggle between states and their need for tax revenues and producers and their desire to reduce their tax burden, the transnational nature of the commodity chain is one of the best weapons at the disposal of the producers. I would go so far as to say that, without it, the likelihood of serious accumulation of capital would be radically reduced.

In consequence, one cannot make sense of decisions by particular producers in a commodity chain without first taking into account the geopolitical
situation, the worldwide struggles of social movements, and the fluctuations
in the governing geocultural norms. Take, for example, one of the clichés of
the 1980s, which is still regularly reproduced: TINA—there is no alternative,
that is, no alternative in the face of a new phenomenon called "globalization."
This is, of course, on its face, utter nonsense. There are always alternatives.
Indeed, this last statement, that there are always alternatives, is one of the
few sociological assertions that seems to me self-evident. Furthermore, as I
have long argued, what is called globalization is in no way new, if by new one
means something that is less than fifty years old (Wallerstein 2000b).

Let us therefore analyze what we mean by TINA. It was a slogan launched
by Mrs. Thatcher and reflected an ideological push of certain countries and
capitalist forces to persuade intellectuals, media, social movements, and ultimately governments to abandon their previous belief in developmentalism.
Developmentalism, a doctrine propagated by almost everyone in the period
1950–1970, is the belief that all countries can "develop" and attain the standard
of living of the presently richest countries by appropriate government action.
This doctrine was as absurd as the neoliberal slogan of TINA (Wallerstein
1988). I do not intend here to trace the history of the two successive rhetorical
traps (see Wallerstein 2005). I merely wish to underscore the degree to which
what is rhetoric has had a great impact on actual governmental decisions, and
has in turn had a great impact on the practices and decisions of actual producers in actual commodity chains.

In the gamut of possibilities for governments to choose between the ex-
tremes of total protectionism and total openness of frontiers, developmentalism pushed governments toward the protectionist option and globalization
toward the openness option. Of course, we have to distinguish among states,
because states in the North and those in the South made, had to make, different choices within the framework of each of the rhetorics. Nor can we leave out
the pressures exerted by the geopolitics of military confrontation. It is quite
clear that the United States tolerated many protectionist decisions of Western
Europe, Japan, South Korea, and Taiwan as part of its effort to strengthen its
political and military position within the framework of something we call the
Cold War. And of course, the Soviet Union did the same with its allies.

The same remains true in the framework of what since 9/11 has been called
the "war on terror." In 2005, the United States government placed much pressure

on Western Europe not to lift the arms ban on China and not to sell certain items to Iran, to take the most obvious examples. Considerations of competitiveness in the relevant commodity chains were entirely ignored, as they were in the massive expenditures of the U.S. government in Iraq. In the global economy of 2005, such pressures accounted for a great deal more of the value-added, and its distortions, than anything that has to do with TINA.

Then there is the small question of currency rates of exchange. The prices of U.S. goods in the world market are fundamentally affected by the state of the U.S. dollar, a function in turn of budgetary decisions of the U.S. government, both the executive and legislative branches. And these budgetary decisions are dictated by a whole series of considerations, one of the least of which is maximizing the competitiveness of U.S. producers. Although in theory the rates of exchange of any currency are determined by world market conditions, who believes in such a fairy tale? They are determined by political power, and the jostling that goes on constantly is decided by real power. No doubt the power is exercised in part in terms of creating favorable economic benefits in the middle run, but first of all, only in part, and second with only middling prospects of success.

Remember also the small issue of environmentalism. There are first of all some strong aspects of the environment that constrain the market, in the short run, in the middle run, in the long run. Climate, for example. As a result, we have governments making decisions as to whether they should or should not increase costs to producers (by taxation or by requiring them to internalize certain costs). And different governments, as we know, are making different decisions. These decisions are affected by the pressures of producers but also by those of social movements, and even of consumers. This has absolutely nothing to do with competitiveness, in the simple sense that the ecological problems we are encountering are in part, probably in large part, the result of producers seeking to maximize their profits by ignoring the ecological damage they have been causing. The Kyoto Accords may have far more impact on the ability of given firms to succeed in the market than instituting the latest improvement in organizational management. But the producers do not directly decide on the measures incorporated in the Kyoto Accords.

There is much discussion these days of the fact that workers in the North are claiming unfair loss of jobs as a result of the poorer working conditions in the countries of the South, conditions that enable producers in the South to pay lower wages. They often call for worldwide labor standards or worldwide wage minimums. They assume that such measures would increase the costs to producers in the South, thus making them less competitive, and hence allowing producers in the North to continue to employ their present workforces. This is perhaps analytically correct. And it may even be morally or politically justified or wise or desirable. The point, however, is that it has nothing to do with TINA, or with competitiveness in some absolute sense. These are political positions, exercised via the states. And they are justly called protectionism.

The alternative of protectionism is one that virtually every government in the world today is currently exercising. The only ones who exercise it minimally are those who are too weak politically to exercise it. Of course, there is protectionism and protectionism, as there is free trade and free trade. But we get nowhere in our political analyses by accepting the slogans. And we get nowhere in our analyses of the world-economy if we fail to include such central issues. The Federal Reserve Bank of the United States claims to make its crucial decisions on the basis of the real underlying trends of the economy. So do the OPEC oil ministers. But it is they, as much as anyone, who are creating many of the so-called real underlying trends. And they do so in terms of some narrow self-interest that constitutes political options.

Studying commodity chains is for the political economist something like observing the operations of the human body by means of multiple tests for the physician or looking through the Hubble telescope for the cosmologist. We are measuring indirectly and imperfectly a total phenomenon that we cannot see directly no matter what we do. The point however is to figure out how this total phenomenon operates, what are its rules, what are its trends, what are its coming and inevitable disequilibria and bifurcations. It requires imagination and audacity along with rigor and patience. The only thing we have to fear is looking too narrowly.

PART II
GETTING AT GOVERNANCE: POWER AND COORDINATION IN GLOBAL CHAINS

5 The Comparative Advantages of Tropical Commodity Chain Analysis

John M. Talbot

M UCH OF THE THEORETICAL AND CONCEPTUAL APPARATUS that we use in commodity chain research today is derived from studies of manufacturing chains. These studies have greatly advanced our understanding of commodity chains, but their findings may not always be applicable to other types of chains. There is now a substantial and growing body of literature on agricultural chains, and specifically on tropical commodity chains.[1] This chapter provides an overview of this literature, with a focus on the ways in which its findings can add to an understanding of commodity chains that has been derived primarily from the study of manufacturing chains. In the process, I identify the "comparative advantages" of tropical commodity chain analysis, that is, those aspects of commodity chains as organizational forms and as units of analysis that the study of tropical commodity chains is particularly well-suited to address. It will also suggest some future directions for commodity chain analysis.

Arguably, the most significant comparative advantage of tropical commodity chains is their North-South orientation. Because of the nature of these crops, they can only be profitably produced in the tropics, that is, the global South. They are consumed mainly in the North, however. Further, many of the major tropical commodities were key items in the old colonial trade, and therefore the means through which the areas that became the South were originally incorporated into the world economy. Analysis of the structures of tropical commodity chains thus provides insights into the nature of relationships between the core and periphery, and into the structure of international inequality and how it has been maintained over long historical periods. Of course, tropical commodity chains are not the only ones linking North and South, and analyses of other types of chains can also help us to understand core-periphery structures. However, I would argue that these structures cannot be completely understood without consideration of the tropical commodity chains. Therefore, in this discussion I will focus primarily on tropical and other similar agricultural chains.

I will organize this discussion under five general subtopics:

1. The rootedness of tropical chains and the analysis of their environmental impacts
2. The necessity of analyzing the entire chain and its implications for governance structures
3. The importance of including actors other than transnational corporations (TNCs), such as states, social movements, and nongovernmental organizations (NGOs), in considering the governance structures of chains
4. The importance of following the money along the chain
5. The value of comparative analysis for identifying the ways in which differences in the structures of chains influence the distribution of benefits along them[2]

Rootedness

Tropical commodity chains are literally *rooted* in specific locations within the tropics because the crops thrive in particular ecological niches. We can trace the chains back to these locations and analyze their social, cultural, economic, and environmental impacts. It is tempting to contrast this rootedness of tropical chains with the rootlessness of chains for manufactured goods such as apparel and autos; however, as I discuss further on, the apparent rootlessness of manufacturing chains is a result of the failure of scholars to consider the entire chain in their analyses. All commodity chains, then, are rooted, in the sense I am discussing here, in some extractive activity taking place in specific geographic locations. Their intermediate processing and manufacturing stages may be relatively rootless, depending on the nature of the commodity involved and the ways in which the different stages are linked. But generally, only agricultural commodity chain analysts have incorporated these extractive activities and the locations in which they take place into their analyses[3] (compare Smith and Mahutga, Chapter 3 in this volume).

The rootedness of tropical and other agricultural chains has driven the many efforts to connect production and consumption in commodity chains. For example, analyses of the fresh fruit and vegetable (FFV) chains linking African producers and European markets have shown how the use of fresh "exotic" fruits and vegetables as a means to draw higher-income consumers into British supermarkets has led to a consolidation of growers and shippers in African producing regions such as Kenya and Zimbabwe (Dolan and Humphrey 2000). Working in the opposite direction, Gellert (2003) has shown how strategic alliances between the Indonesian state and (crony) capital, and between Indonesian and Japanese capital, allowed Indonesian timber and plywood producers to dominate the Japanese market for a decade.

Another aspect of rootedness is the way in which the characteristics of the commodity influence the structure of the chain. For the tropical commodities, the nature of the initial processing that is needed immediately after harvesting affects the scale of these processing operations and who controls them. For example, coffee and cocoa can be processed in small batches with rudimentary technology, whereas sugar and tea processing use machinery that requires a large and continuous input in order to operate efficiently. Although all of these commodities were originally established as plantation crops by the colonial powers, economies of scale determined how production evolved after independence. Therefore coffee and cocoa now tend to be grown by smallholders, and sugar and tea have tended to remain plantation crops controlled by foreign owners. In either case, state intervention can alter these influences. Thus state support in the form of roads and local collection stations was crucial to the rise of smallholder tea cultivation in Kenya, whereas state action to maintain control over land and indigenous people was key to the maintenance of a plantation system in Guatemalan coffee production (Talbot 2002, 2004; Paige 1987).

For many tropical and other agricultural commodities, these initial processing stages are relatively rooted, in that they cannot be moved too far from where the crop is grown. Other stages that are further removed from the growing stage, such as the roasting of coffee and the refining of sugar, are relatively rootless. In contrast, even the initial processing stages of many mineral commodity chains are relatively rootless, because bauxite or iron ore can be taken out of the ground and shipped elsewhere for its initial processing.

One of the most important potential outcomes of this focus on the roots of commodity chains is the analysis of environmental impacts. For instance, in my analysis of the coffee commodity chain, I have shown how the consolidation of the coffee TNCs in the 1980s led to demand for increasingly large volumes of consistent-quality coffee. This demand was met by efforts in coffee-producing countries (particularly in Latin America) to increase production through technification—the adoption of green-revolution-type high-yielding varieties. Accompanying technification was an increase in intensity and scale of cultivation and an increased use of chemical fertilizers and pesticides that had severe environmental impacts: clearing of shade trees that provided critical bird habitats and increased organic runoff into lakes and streams (Talbot 2004). However, few commodity chain analysts have integrated environmental impacts into their analyses.

Efforts to make connections between production and consumption, and to incorporate environmental factors into the analysis, are apparent in the growing literature on organic and fair trade, or more generally, sustainable production (for example, Murray and Raynolds 2000; Raynolds 2002, 2004; Renard 1999b; Levi and Linton 2003; Taylor 2005). Most of these analyses have focused on the tropical commodities, primarily coffee and bananas. This is related to the North-South orientation of these chains, and therefore the ability of tropical commodity chains (and especially Northern control of such chains) to act as potent symbols of neocolonial domination. As more affluent consumers in the North become concerned about the social and environmental impacts of their consumption, they are drawn into these "ethical" chains as a way to counteract the more destructive aspects of the global food system (see Chapter 9, by Guthman, in this volume).

However, these analyses do not connect variations in the degrees of environmental damage caused with variations in the structures of the commodity chains. Although they contrast the environmental damage caused by conventional chains with the lower environmental impacts of sustainable chains, they do not show how these differential environmental impacts result from differences in chain structures. In my analysis of the coffee commodity chain (Talbot 2004), I have discussed the technification of coffee production, particularly in Latin America. This process was driven, in part, by the state coffee agencies that controlled the production end of the chain and attempted to increase the crop yields (and thus revenues) by applying "modern," scientific methods of cultivation. This changed the input-output structure to one that was more environmentally damaging, but one that also meshed better with the demand for increasing volumes of consistent-quality coffee by the consolidated TNCs.

Therefore the first comparative advantage of tropical commodity chain analysis is that it includes the extractive beginnings of the chain. It thus is particularly well-suited to analyzing how the nature of the commodity influences the structure of the chain, and how the structure of the chain determines its environmental impacts. Although there has been some work in the first of these areas, the second has been relatively neglected.

Analyzing the Entire Chain

There are good reasons why analyses of manufacturing chains tend to exclude the extractive beginnings of the chains (Raikes, Jensen, and Ponte 2000). The apparel or auto chains are complex enough as they are; to go back to the production of the various fibers, buttons, and zippers in the apparel chain or to the various metals, rubber, and glass involved in the auto chain would add another, even more complex, layer to the story. In effect, it would involve the analysis of another whole set of commodity chains. However, this characteristic of manufacturing chain analysis has had significant repercussions for the large literature that has grown up regarding the governance of commodity chains.

Gereffi's (1994) original distinction between producer-driven and buyer-driven chains turned out to be extremely useful for understanding governance in manufacturing chains. However, it created problems for analysts working with tropical chains. I wrestled with how to apply these two categories in my work on the coffee chain, for example. The coffee chain seemed to have aspects of both producer-driven and buyer-driven governance. On the one hand, the coffee TNCs acted as the large apparel firms in the buyer-driven chains. They concentrated on designing and marketing their products and controlling their markets through branding and advertising. They used global sourcing strategies to manage their risk and obtain supplies of coffee at the lowest prices, while maintaining the consistent tastes of their proprietary blends. On the other hand, the coffee TNCs did engage directly in manufacturing their products, using capital-intensive and technologically sophisticated methods (for example, computer-controlled, large-scale roasting and freeze-dried instant coffee production). Although they contracted out the production of the components they needed for their manufacturing operation (the different varieties of coffee to be blended), the contract suppliers in this case were large international trading houses (compare Ponte 2002). Other analysts grappled with similar problems when trying to apply the producer-driven versus buyer-driven governance schema to various kinds of nonmanufacturing commodity chains (for example, Clancy 1998; Raikes and Gibbon 2000; Raikes, Jensen, and Ponte 2000; Gellert 2003).

Gibbon (2001a, 2001b) introduced a third type of governance structure to deal with some of these difficulties: the international trader-driven chain. This type accurately described the governance of many tropical chains, as the same large trading houses have typically dealt with a range of tropical commodities, such as coffee, cocoa, and sugar (but not tea or bananas). However, the additional clarity provided by the introduction of this third type of governance structure came at a cost; it neglected the portion of the chain beyond the traders—namely, the stages of final production and sale to consumers. By the 1990s, the major TNC roasters, not the international traders, were clearly driving the coffee chain, and the former had the power to influence the behavior of the latter (Ponte 2002). Similarly, although the cocoa trader-grinders occupied a more important position in the cocoa chain than did the traders in the coffee chain, the major chocolate manufacturers still exerted a major influence over the structure of the chain (Fold 2001, 2002). So as a description of the overall governance structures of tropical commodity chains, the international trader-driven designation had serious shortcomings.

In fact, the problem with Gibbon's proposed international trader-driven governance structure highlights the overall weakness of the original producer-driven versus buyer-driven dichotomy: none of these governance structures characterize the entire chain. These analysts were able to posit a typology of governance structures that purportedly encompassed whole commodity chains only because they had restricted their focus to particular parts of those chains. Gereffi excluded the extractive beginnings of his manufacturing chains, and Gibbon excluded the marketing and retail activities at the end of his primary commodity chains. In other words, both analyzed their respective commodity chains with reference to an overarching governance structure that supposedly defined the chain in its entirety, but in reality applied only to a particular segment.

Gereffi's recent work has acknowledged some of these difficulties. Gereffi, Humphrey, and Sturgeon (2005) argue that the producer-driven versus buyer-driven dichotomy fails to capture newer forms of network governance that have recently arisen (see also Chapter 1, by Bair, and Chapter 6, by Sturgeon). They elaborate a typology of five governance structures ranging from market to hierarchy, with three different types of network governance in between. However, on closer inspection, these types of governance seem to apply primarily to one transaction linking two successive nodes in the chain, rather than being forms of governance characterizing larger segments of the chain (Gibbon 2003a). This focus on individual links of the chain is an important contribution because it allows for the recognition of multiple forms of governance (and the role of multiple governing agents, as I explain further on) along a chain, but it is too micro-oriented and does not address the problem identified earlier regarding the need to understand the relationship between the different governance structures that often coexist and sometimes conflict along a single chain. Thus we are still in need of a better typology that can simultaneously capture the governance structures characterizing larger segments of (and not just individual links in) a chain without oversimplifying the complexity of governance forms that can be found in a chain (Gibbon 2003a).

I would suggest that the way to approach this problem is to use a strategy similar to that of Gereffi, Humphrey, and Sturgeon (2005) and begin to identify the key underlying variables that determine differing governance structures. Because the nature of the commodity may influence the governance structure, as a preliminary step we will need to distinguish between agricultural, mineral, manufacturing, and services chains. We may need further subdivisions of these broad types as well. Then we should differentiate between different types of governing agents, such as vertically integrated firms, branding and marketing firms, states, and NGOs. In addition, we might identify the different types of rules or conventions relevant to the governance of a chain, and ascertain whether governance is "tight" or "loose" (Gibbon 2001b), or as Ponte (2002) puts it, the chain's "level of drivenness." This approach would allow us to build up a more encompassing typology of governance structures to facilitate analyses of new commodity chains. Finally, the preceding discussion has pointed to another important variable that must be considered when analyzing governance, which is the breadth of a particular governance structure across the length of the chain (in other words, how long the segment is that is covered by it).

Therefore the second comparative advantage of tropical commodity chain analysis is that it encompasses the entire commodity chain. It thus is more likely to encounter different segments of a chain with different governance structures. This provides opportunities not only to develop a more complete typology of governance structures but also to analyze how different governance structures interact and are accommodated to one another at the points along the chain where they intersect. Here again, although work is progressing in the former area, the latter is relatively neglected.

Actors Other Than TNCs

If we are going to analyze entire commodity chains and recognize that different segments of a chain may have different governance structures, then we should also recognize that different types of governing agents may be involved as well. Gereffi's (1994, 1995) original distinction between producer-driven and buyer-driven chains focused on the roles of lead firms, which were typically transnational corporations (TNCs). Other actors were relegated to the institutional framework in Gereffi's formulation, viewed as players whose influence was limited to setting the conditions under which the TNCs decided how to structure the chains. This focus probably makes sense for most manufacturing chains, but is not appropriate for tropical and other agricultural commodity chains. As Raynolds (2004) has pointed out, agri-food chains have historically been among the most heavily (state-) regulated chains in the world economy.[4]

The insight that different segments of a chain can have different governance structures leads directly to the insight that different segments can be governed by different actors. In the case of many tropical commodities, state agencies and marketing boards were the major governing agents for the extractive ends of the chains, at least during the period of international regulation stretching roughly from the 1950s to 1990 (Gibbon 2001b). These agencies set and monitored the quality standards for growers and processors, helped growers to meet the standards through agricultural extension services, and, through their pricing policies, determined the distribution of benefits within this segment of the chain. Through their participation in international bodies regulating the trade (International Coffee Organization, International Cocoa Organization, and so on), and through their international marketing arms, they were able to influence the world market prices for their commodities. As I pointed out in my analysis of coffee (Talbot 2004), the point at which the producing state-governed segment of the chain met the TNC roaster- and trader-governed segment became the major focal point for North-South conflict over the regulation of the coffee commodity chain and the distribution of benefits along it.

Other tropical commodity chain analysts have also emphasized the key role of the state in commodity chain governance, particularly within peripheral countries. For example, Gellert (2003) shows that action by the Indonesian state was crucial to the formation of a successful plywood export industry, first by banning the export of raw logs, second by sponsoring the creation of a plywood industry association, and third by helping to discipline the producers to follow the association's rules. Rammohan and Sundaresan (2003) demonstrate how the differing policies of two Indian states created differing structures in the coir commodity chain. The nonintervention of Tamil Nadu state into coir processing facilitated the development of a large-scale, capital-intensive coir fiber industry in the 1970s. However, in Kerala, a traditional center of coir production, a more interventionist state had prevented the development of large-scale mechanized coir fiber factories in the 1950s and 1960s in order to protect employment of coir workers. The analysis by Rammohan and Sundaresan also shows how even seemingly unrelated state policies can influence the rules governing a chain. Land reform in Kerala undermined the power of large landlords who had controlled the supply of coconut husks and the access to backwater sites used for retting (the first stage of coir processing). This loosened patron-client ties and controls that the landlords had exerted over coir workers and allowed the rapid unionization of the industry. Finally, when technological upgrading of the Kerala industry was undertaken in the 1990s, it also was state-led.

Analyses of organic and fair trade chains have pointed out the key roles played by social movements and NGOs in chain governance. For example, Raynolds (2004) describes the standard-setting role of the International Federation of Organic Agriculture Movements (IFOAM) in organic food chains. Adherence to these organic standards is certified by IFOAM-accredited certification agencies, although this role is increasingly being taken over by states. Levi and Linton (2003) describe the very similar governance structure of the fair trade coffee chain, in which the standards are set by the Fairtrade Labeling Organization (FLO), but certification in this case is carried out by the FLO member organizations. Interestingly, although states have been involving themselves in enforcing the organic standards, they have stayed away from fair trade (with its implicit claim that so-called "free" trade is unfair).

The examples of organic and fair trade chains also raise another issue about the scope of commodity chains requiring further clarification. Chains may be segmented vertically, as discussed earlier, but they may also be segmented horizontally. For example, fair trade coffee, specialty coffee, and industrial coffee all have analytically separable chains with different structures and types of governance; however, they are all part of the larger coffee commodity chain. To add even more complexity, the industrial coffee chain has a fork in it after the green coffee stage; one branch leads to roasted and ground (R&G) coffee and the other leads to instant coffee. These branches have different structures implying different outcomes and developmental prospects for producing countries.

Commodity chain analysts, myself included, have been very imprecise in our application of the term *commodity chain* to all of these different types of units, but more precision is needed. I have sometimes used the term *strand* to refer to these horizontal segments, whereas Sturgeon (2001) introduced the term *thread*. However, Sturgeon's usage seems to imply that all threads of the chain have similar structures and governing agents, whereas this is not true for fair trade, specialty, and industrial coffees. I would suggest that we use Sturgeon's term *thread* as he has defined it (but without the assumption that all threads are necessarily similar in structure, in which case R&G and instant would be threads), and introduce the term *strand* to denote horizontal segments that are more distinct, as exemplified by the differing governance structures characterizing fair trade, specialty, and industrial coffees. At the same time, I do not think it would be accurate to consider these strands of the coffee chain as separate chains because their structures and forms of governance are mutually conditioning, meaning that the study of how different strands relate to each other and to the larger commodity chain of which they are a part is one important task for chain analysts.

Therefore, in developing a typology of governance structures for chains, we need to pay attention to the nature of the governing agents and recognize that TNCs are not the only possible governing agents, given that states and other social actors may also play important governing roles (Raikes, Jensen, and Ponte 2000). We should recognize that chains can be segmented both vertically and horizontally, and that different segments may have different types of governing agents and governance structures. Furthermore, we should acknowledge the possibility that different types of agents can play different types of governing roles within the same segment of a chain, leading to possible conflict between these agents (Kaplinsky 2000b). Tropical commodity chains, because of the variety of governing agents and governance structures that characterize them, have a key role to play in this project.

Following the Money

One of the most important questions in commodity chain analysis is, Who benefits? The structures of chains, their geographical distribution, and their forms of governance all have implications for the distribution of benefits along the chain. The distribution of benefits, in turn, has implications for economic development, the extraction of surplus, and international inequality. As I have argued earlier, one of the most important advantages of tropical commodity chains is their North-South linkage, which makes them ideal for studying these questions. The relatively simple structures of these chains, compared to those for manufactures, also facilitate this type of analysis.

Conceptually, we can think of commodities as flowing from the extractive end to the consumption end of the chain, and money as flowing back in the opposite direction. The actors that exercise governance over segments of the chain set rules that influence how commodities and money flow through their respective segments, and thereby, how the money is distributed within those segments. Participants in the chain segment cooperate or come into conflict with other participants and governing agents in attempts to alter this distribution. Governing agents and other participants may also attempt to influence how commodities and money flow through adjoining segments of the chain, creating conflict and cooperation across chain segments, particularly at points along the chain where different governance structures intersect. Most commodity chain analyses to date have concentrated on analyzing the flows of commodities. However, measuring the flows of money along the chain, how much is allocated to different nodes, and how this amount is divided between compensation to factors of production and profits, is one of the most important tasks of commodity chain analysis. Changes over time in these distributions of benefits are key indicators of changes in the structures of chains and of shifts in power along them.

I was fortunate in my analyses of the coffee chain to have access to a relatively long time series of good data on prices at key points along the chain, which enabled me to do this kind of analysis.[5] I was able to show how the distribution of benefits along the chain changed over time, in response to changes in the structure and governance of the chain. In particular, I showed that producers' collective action and the resulting international regulation of the chain led to increased levels and stability of benefits flowing back to the producing countries. Once the coffee TNCs had consolidated their control over the consuming markets and international regulation had collapsed, the shift of benefits away from producing countries and to the TNCs was massive and rapid (Talbot 1997b, 2004).

Because of the availability of data, the analysis of the distribution of benefits has gone farthest in coffee (for example, Fitter and Kaplinsky 2001b). There are a few other tropical commodity chain analyses that attempt to estimate the distribution of benefits along the chain (for example, Roche 1998 for bananas), but they are generally snapshots at one point in time. It is not possible from these estimates to link changes in structure and governance to shifts in benefits. We need more longitudinal analyses of the distribution of benefits, and this means undertaking the task of constructing time series of prices for other commodity chains. These data are difficult to obtain, particularly for chains in which vertically integrated TNCs are involved, but they are necessary for our understanding of the dynamics of commodity chains (Raikes, Jensen, and Ponte 2000).

Therefore the third comparative advantage of tropical commodity chain analysis is that it is easier to follow the money in these chains than it is in manufacturing chains. Tropical and other agricultural chains should be used to build up our conceptual and methodological capabilities for analyzing the flows and distribution of money along chains, which can then be applied to manufacturing and other more complex chains. Much work remains to be done in this area.

Comparative Analysis

Most commodity chain analyses thus far have been case studies of one chain. We have learned a lot from these studies, but the case study approach can only take us so far. The conclusions drawn from case studies are always tentative. We can never be sure that the analysis has identified the key factors that account for the structure of the chain or the distribution of benefits along it, and why these might change over time. The conclusions may be idiosyncratic, based on the peculiarity of one case, with little or no general applicability. That is why we need to move to comparative analyses of commodity chains. By comparing chains, we can begin to see how differences in the structures of chains cause different outcomes. Most people working in the field of chain research recognize this need (such as Sturgeon 2001), most notably the value chains group at the Institute of Development Studies at Sussex. However, case studies of one chain are difficult enough, and comparative studies are at least doubly so. Nonetheless, some comparative studies are beginning to appear. A brief look at a few examples shows the advantages of comparative analysis.

In my comparative analysis of coffee, cocoa, and tea (Talbot 2002), I was able to identify two structural features of chains that influenced possibilities for upgrading: the economies of scale in the initial processing stages, and the relative point along the chain at which the intermediate product first becomes storable and transportable. Economies of scale in initial processing determined whether locally controlled smallholder production or foreign-controlled plantation production predominated. When the latter predominated, actors in the producing countries had to struggle to gain control over local production before they could upgrade, making upgrading more difficult. The closer to the consumption end of the chain that a storable intermediate product first appeared, the easier it was for actors in developing countries to control the stages up to that point, and therefore, the easier was the task of upgrading. Within these parameters, relative successes or failures of upgrading attempts in different countries depended on effectively aggressive state action, the existence of a capable local capitalist class, and the size of the domestic market for the final product.

Daviron and Gibbon (2002) compared cotton, coffee, and cocoa to show that the extent to which a chain is characterized by a buyer-driven governance structure depends on the degree of TNC control over the final consuming market for that product. For both coffee and cocoa, when consolidation among TNCs has occurred, the chains have become more buyer-driven; in the case of cotton, when such consolidation has not occurred there has not been a noticeable trend in this direction. Degree of buyer-drivenness in turn, in combination with the distribution of capacities for collective action and technical

innovation, helps to determine the locus of control over product differentiation. In cocoa, with high buyer-drivenness, the TNC grinders have captured
control over product differentiation with technical innovations that allow
them to generate diverse intermediate products independent of the origins of
the cocoa (with the exception of Ghanian cocoa). In cotton, with much lower
levels of buyer-drivenness, Zimbabwe was able to establish itself as a producer
of high-quality cotton and thereby differentiate itself from other cotton growers by preserving its national quality control system following liberalization.
Finally, in coffee, with high buyer-drivenness, the development of specialty
coffees has allowed producing countries to retain more control over product
differentiation (for example, through the creation of "single estate" coffees
such as La Minita Terrazu), although roasters have gained control over differentiation for bulk, industrial coffees, which depend on blends of coffees from
several different origins. Control over product differentiation matters because
it allows actors to target particular niche markets and receive higher prices,
thereby appropriating larger shares of the money flowing along the chain, in
the form of what Kaplinsky (1998) calls "product and marketing rents."

In contrast, Freidberg's (2003b) study of fresh vegetable production in
Zambia and Burkina Faso shows that similar buyers do not necessarily drive
chains to the same degree or in the same way. Her study highlights the importance of differences in colonial history and in cultural attitudes about
food and food production for the structures and governance of commodity
chains. In Zambia, the agricultural sector is dominated by large-scale white
settler farms. The fresh vegetable export sector is controlled by two large vertically integrated export firms, which supplement their own production by
buying from white contract farmers. The chain looks very much like the one
described by Dolan and Humphrey (2000) for Kenya, strongly driven by the
British supermarkets with their rigid "industrial" quality standards, overseen
by agents of the supermarkets who visit the export firms to inspect their production practices.

However, the fresh green bean chain connecting Burkina Faso and France
varies considerably from this model. Although supermarket chains dominate
both the British and French retail food markets, the French supermarkets
have a different relationship to their African suppliers. French shoppers are
not as enamored of food in plastic packaging as are their British counterparts;
their standards of quality rely more on relations of trust developed over time

between the direct producers and the traders who bring the product to the consumer. French supermarkets purchase loose beans in bulk and leave the importing to French import firms with long histories of working in Africa, who supply a diverse range of clients besides the supermarkets and are therefore adept at juggling a variety of quality standards. Further, the legacies of French colonialism and rural development projects have left Burkina Faso with an agricultural sector dominated by peasant smallholders, so it is from among them that the French importers must seek out trustworthy suppliers. In addition, the exporters are local capitalists who act as professional post-colonial middlemen in a variety of ways. Thus, although the products and the structures of the consuming markets are similar, the British strand is highly buyer-driven, whereas it is difficult to identify a driving agent in the French strand with an analogous "gate-keeping" function, in terms of making access to the chain contingent on meeting rigorous standards of the sort imposed by British supermarkets.

Finally, Taylor's (2005) comparison of Fair Trade coffee with Forest Stewardship Council (FSC) certified wood shows the different outcomes associated with different strategies for constructing alternative strands of commodity chains. In the latter case, major retailers were involved in the development of the "Forest Stewardship" standards, which focus on the social and environmental impacts of wood production rather than on the impacts of the trade in wood products. In the case of Fair Trade coffee, NGOs were the initiators, and they focused on the impacts of trade on the social and economic conditions of the producers. As a result, Fair Trade coffee has returned more benefits to developing country producers, whereas FSC certification has served as more of a risk-management strategy for major retailers, and much of the wood certified under this scheme comes from Northern forests.

In these cases, comparison has sharpened the analysis. It has helped to identify those factors that cause differences in the structures and governance of commodity chains and the way in which these differences affect the distribution of benefits along the chain. Case studies of any one of these chains individually would probably not have produced such definitive and important conclusions. Therefore we need to undertake more systematic comparative studies to increase our understanding of the dynamics of commodity chains. However, this call for more comparative research is accompanied by a caution against codifying a *particular approach* to comparative analysis, of the kind

Sturgeon (2001) has proposed, for example. Comparative commodity chain analysis is a relatively new area of research, and there are thousands of chains that have not yet been analyzed. The risk of codification at this point is that it will focus researchers' attention on factors or characteristics of chains that seem important at the moment, on the basis of the relatively small sample of chains analyzed thus far, and thereby result in a neglect of other factors or characteristics that may be important in yet unanalyzed chains. At this point, it would be best to let each researcher, building on the base provided by the existing literature, make his or her own decisions regarding how to approach a comparative analysis.

Conclusion

This review has suggested three comparative advantages of tropical commodity chain analysis. First, it includes the extractive beginnings of chains. Therefore it is well-suited to analyzing the ways in which the nature of a commodity influences the structure of its chain, and to analyzing the connections between the structure of the chain and its environmental impacts. Second, and related to the first advantage, it encompasses analysis of the entire chain, often including segments with different governance structures and governing agents. Thus it can play a key role in the development of a typology of governance structures, and in the analysis of how different governance structures interact along a chain. Third, the relatively simple structures of tropical commodity chains make them ideal sites for studying flows of money and the distribution of benefits along commodity chains. Some work has been done in a few of these areas, but others are relatively untouched. I would suggest that tropical commodity chain analyses focused on exploiting these advantages will best advance the field of commodity chain research.

In addition to pointing out the benefits of tropical commodity chain analysis, this review has suggested three more general areas in which further work is needed to advance this field. First, we need to be more precise in defining the units that we are analyzing. To date, scholars have been applying the term *commodity chain* loosely to a variety of different units and subunits, including chains, segments, strands, and threads. To avoid confusion, particularly when pursuing comparative research, we need to develop a classificatory scheme that allows us to separate different types of units of analysis, while at the same time having a clearer picture of how they are interconnected. This scheme should be open-ended, because there are probably more types of units than have been considered here. In part, the problem of defining more precisely what constitutes a commodity chain involves defining more precisely what can be considered a commodity for the purposes of chain analysis. For instance, the category of fresh fruits and vegetables is probably too broad for talking about an FFV chain; however, to talk about a fresh green bean chain is probably too narrow a usage of the term.

Second, we need to develop a more comprehensive typology of governing agents and governance structures. Governing agents include not only TNCs but also states, social movements, and NGOs; again, there are probably other types of social actors involved in governance as well. Types of governing agents may well be correlated with types of governance structures. To develop a better typology of governance structures, I have suggested that we need to begin to identify the underlying variables that generate different types of governance structures. As we do this, we also need to be explicit about the types of units and subunits of the chain that these governance structures cover, and focus on the types of conflict and cooperation that arise at the points where different governance structures intersect. For instance, although the cotton and apparel commodity chains have been analyzed separately, it would be more productive to analyze them as two segments of the same chain, to see how the different governing agents interact, and how their governance structures mesh.

Third, we need more comparative analysis. Comparative analysis can allow us to identify differences in the characteristics of commodity chains that determine the diversity of outcomes experienced by participants in these commodity chains. Comparative analysis should also help us to better understand how and why structures of chains, their governing logics, and the distribution of money along them change over time. Tropical commodity chain analysis may not enjoy a comparative advantage in these areas, but it certainly has a role to play in all of them. We need to bring to bear analyses of as many different types of commodity chains as possible on these questions, so that the conceptual and methodological tools that we develop are broadly applicable, and not specific to only one type of commodity chain.

6 From Commodity Chains to Value Chains

Interdisciplinary Theory Building in an Age of Globalization

Timothy J. Sturgeon

RECENT CHANGES IN THE GLOBAL ECONOMY, ESPECIALLY THE rise of East Asia as an economic force, have rendered static notions of permanent dependency and underdevelopment obsolete.[1] Regions, countries, and individual localities *can* improve their relative position in the global economy. The much-debated question is, How? Sound macroeconomic policy, sector-specific industrial development policies, technological borrowing, and firm-level responses to the demands of overseas buyers have all been put forward as explanations and prescriptions for rapid industrial upgrading and economic development in East Asia and elsewhere. Proponents of these different views have debated each other to a standstill, or have simply chosen to talk past each other. Could it be that there is no single explanation for why places advance, or fail to advance, in the global economy, and that unitary explanations will always fall short?

The specificities of technology, industry, society, and historical moment all have the potential of being decisive in shaping individual and aggregate outcomes for places, firms, and workers. As a result, the variety that can be observed in the global economy is effectively infinite. Given the great complexity that exists in economic systems, any theory that is meant to explain and predict outcomes for entire industries, countries, regions, or the global economy as a whole should be treated as highly suspect, at best. Because multiple forces of change are always at play, theory, if used in a totalizing manner, can obscure as much as it reveals. But complexity should not lead to the abandonment of theory, or to the development of theories that are so inclusive and flexible that they fail to provide any traction.

It is better, in my view, to develop discrete theoretical areas to deal with specific questions. A theory with a modest and clearly defined explanatory scope, one that identifies one or a few important causal mechanisms that can be used to *partially* explain and predict outcomes, can have great utility. What is important is to recognize the limits inherent in such partial theories and to actively seek compatibility and linkages with complimentary frameworks. Not least, this "modular" approach to theory building is useful for researchers because it directs them to a manageable set of questions that can be tested in the field or applied to specific policy problems. But because of the great variety of causal forces at work in the global economy, it is incumbent upon those who develop and apply fractional theories to policy and strategy to be cautious, and to actively consider alternative explanations and approaches.

The need for serviceable theory is great. The global economy has entered a new phase of deeper, more immediate integration that is exposing national and local economies to the winds of economic change as never before. These winds can fill the sails of domestic firms and industries, blow them away, or, perhaps even worse, bypass them entirely. The geographer Peter Dicken (1992) argues that it is the *functional integration* of internationally dispersed activities that differentiates the current era of "globalization" from an earlier era of "internationalization," which was characterized by the simple geographic spread of economic activities across national boundaries. Functional integration has come with tighter coordination within an expanding set of multinational firms (Zanfei 2000), but also with the rise of firms in the West—retailers and branded merchandisers with little or no internal production (Gereffi 1994; Feenstra and Hamilton 2006) and de-verticalizing "manufacturers" that have shed internal capacity—that have come to rely on an emergent set of global and East Asian regional contract manufacturers for production (Borrus, Ernst, and Haggard 2000; Sturgeon 2002).

Nor is the situation static. It is worth highlighting two recent developments that are enabling even greater functional integration in the global economy: (1) rapidly increasing industrial capabilities in developing countries, especially in China and India; and (2) new computer-mediated approaches to real-time integration of distant activities. These new features facilitate international trade in many intermediate goods and services that have not previously been sent across borders. As a result, opportunities have opened up for firms to engage with the global economy—as buyers, suppliers, sellers, distributors, contractors, and service providers—in ways that were impossible even a few years ago. These changes have created new challenges and risks, as well as opportunities. Because activities are being integrated in the global economy at a very granular level, pressure has increased for firms and individual workers that may have been insulated from global competition in the past. The result is accelerating change and an increased sense of economic insecurity, even among the "winners" in the global economy.

Policymakers responsible for responding to the pressures of global integration are desperate for conceptual frameworks and theoretical constructs that can help to guide their work, which often includes making difficult trade-offs in the context of extremely complex and rapidly changing situations. The so-called "Washington Consensus," the view that countries simply need to get their macroeconomic house in order and be open to international trade and investment to advance in the global economy, provides little guidance to policymakers and nongovernmental activists dealing with the concerns of workers, communities, and industries that are in the midst of wrenching change or that remain completely severed from the global economy. The need for pragmatism motivates theories characterized by simplicity, easy applicability in the face of variety, and resonance with real-world situations.

In the fall of 2000, a group of academic researchers with deep experience in field-based observation of cross-border production in a range of industries began to meet in a series of workshops to develop a theory of governance for what we eventually chose to call "global value chains" (GVCs).[2] The participants hailed from a variety of countries and disciplines, including sociology, economics, geography, regional planning, political science, management, and development studies. This joint work continued to be developed through 2004 in the context of four multiday workshops, several smaller meetings, and an ongoing dialogue and collaborative writing effort by core members of the group.

An important goal was to develop a theory that could help policymakers explain and predict governance patterns in cross-border production networks. With such tools in hand, our thinking went, interventions aimed at upgrading the position of local workers, firms, and industries within global-scale production systems could be more finely crafted and effective. Each workshop included policymakers and activists from nongovernmental organizations who voiced their concerns and provided feedback on the utility of our ideas as they developed in various iterations. Because of the policy orientation of this work, our goal was to create a relatively simple theoretical model that was robust, relevant, and easily applicable to real-world situations. At the same time, we recognized the need to ground the theory in the existing academic literature to help build consensus among researchers. Our strategy was to set a virtuous cycle in motion in which a growing, relatively coherent body of scholarly research would build academic legitimacy that would in turn embolden practitioners to apply nonstandard concepts in the field to help solve real-world policy problems.

The first output from this work was contained in a special issue of the *Institute for Development Studies Bulletin* (32:2) titled "The Value of Value Chains: Spreading the Gains from Globalisation," which appeared in July 2001. This volume comprises articles written by several of the core participants of what came to be known as the "Global Value Chains Initiative." The articles summarize the nascent ideas developed by the group in the areas of GVC terminology, chain governance, and industrial upgrading. The volume also includes several articles that applied some of the new thinking to case studies. The work on firm-level governance was our initial focus, but other strands of work developed, and continue to be developed today, including theoretical work on standards, industrial upgrading, labor, the development of GVC metrics, and a robust stream of field research. Out of this work has come numerous peer-reviewed publications, a large body of policy-related consulting reports, the development of methodological handbooks for policy practitioners, and a Website to provide a single point of access to GVC-related work.[3] One strand of this initial theoretical work, on firm-level network governance, culminated in an article that I wrote with Gary Gereffi and John Humphrey titled "The Governance of Global Value Chains," which appeared in the *Review of International Political Economy* in March 2005.

The limits of space in our original 2005 article, and the insights gained from subsequent reactions we have had to it, motivate this effort to situate, elaborate, and further explain the theoretical framework we developed. First, I discuss the motivations for supplementing the "buyer-driven" and "producer-driven" modes of global commodity chain governance developed by Gary Gereffi in the 1990s with an industry-neutral, non-empirical framework. Second, I briefly present the features of the GVC governance framework as they appeared in the 2005 article, and discuss its interdisciplinary theoretical underpinnings in more detail than was possible in the original article. Third, I discuss the problem of variation in GVC governance. Fourth, I situate the GVC governance framework in a larger field of GVC-related theory, including but not limited to power and institutions.

From Global Commodity Chains to Global Value Chains

In developing our theory of GVC governance we drew on a variety of previous work that we felt was relevant to our project. I will discuss these various theoretical influences later in the chapter, but first I will explain how the concept evolved from its most direct progenitor, the "global commodity chains" (GCC) framework as developed by Gary Gereffi (1994, 1999). Gereffi's framework lays out four key structures that shape GCCs (input-output, geographic, governance, and institutional) but one, the governance structure, has received the most attention, both from Gereffi and his immediate coauthors and from the many others that have made use of his framework.

As Jennifer Bair explains in her introduction to this volume, the GCC concept was first developed by Hopkins and Wallerstein (1977, 1986), who highlighted the power of the state in shaping global production systems, exercised in large part in the form of tariffs and local content rules affected at the point where goods crossed borders (see also Wallerstein, Chapter 4 in this volume). Gereffi (1994) revived the GCC concept by refocusing it on the strategies and actions of firms, in part because of the restricted ability of states to set tariffs and local content rules in the context of trade liberalization. But trade openness does not in itself create industrial capabilities. Liberalization has enabled the growth of international trade, but without the push from advanced-economy firms seeking to tap capabilities and markets in developing countries, the cross-border flows of goods and services would surely be more modest, in terms of both total volume and technological content, than they are today. Because firms from advanced economies have done so much to create capabilities in developing countries, they continue to control and guide many of the key industrial resources in the global economy, even those that they do not own.

The "governance" function within Gereffi's GCC framework captured variation in the way that firms organized their cross-border production arrangements. Specifically, the GCC framework contained a key distinction between global chains that are "driven" by one of two kinds of lead firms: buyers and producers. Gereffi's producer-driven variant can be equated with the internal and external networks emanating from large multinational manufacturing firms, such as General Motors and IBM. Multinational firms have long been a focus of research and debate among scholars of the global economy (for example, Vernon 1966, 1971, 1979; Caves 1996). This work examined and debated the methods, timing, and motivations of multinational firms and the degree to which they acted as conduits for the transfer of capabilities from developed to developing countries. Gereffi's framework focused attention on a new set of Western-based actors and the roles they play in driving capability development, especially in East Asia (see also Gereffi and Hamilton, Chapter 7 in this volume). The buyer-driven GCC variant focused attention on the powerful role that large retailers, such as JCPenny, Sears, and later Wal-Mart, as well as highly successful branded merchandisers, such as Nike and Liz Claiborne, have come to play in the governance of global production and distribution.

"Global buyers" do more than place orders; they actively help to create, shape, and coordinate the global value chains that supply their products, sometimes directly from "overseas buying offices" and sometimes through intermediaries, which include a wide range of actors, most notably trading companies based in Hong Kong, Korea, and Japan. Although they typically own few, if any, of their own factories, the volume of their purchases affords global buyers a huge amount of power over their suppliers, which they sometimes use to specify in great detail what, how, when, where, and by whom the goods they sell are produced. But even when explicit coordination is not present, extreme market power has allowed global buyers to extract price concessions from their main suppliers. Suppliers have responded by locating more of their factories in low-cost locations and working hard to extract price concessions from their own workers and upstream suppliers.[4]

Why are commodity chains buyer- or producer-driven? Gereffi did not explore this question in detail, but instead let the empirical evidence speak for itself: capital- and technology-intensive industries such as electronics and autos tend to be governed by producers, whereas labor-intensive industries such as apparel and consumer goods tend to be governed by buyers. But how is the level of capital intensity in an industry related to its governance form? Because innovation in buyer-driven GCCs lies more in product design and marketing than in manufacturing know-how, it is relatively easy for lead firms to outsource the manufacturing of labor-intensive products. In the more technology- and capital-intensive items made in producer-driven chains, technology and production expertise were core competencies that needed to be developed and deployed inhouse, or in closely affiliated "captive" suppliers that could be blocked from sharing them with competitors.

In our group, we discussed how these variables played out in the context of recent field research findings in both buyer- and producer-driven chains, and found it to be increasingly difficult to assign these characteristics to specific industries in a static way, as the GCC framework does. The intense interest in Gereffi's framework, and especially the "buyer-driven" commodity chain type, underscored the appetite for an industry-independent, firm-level theory of production network governance. The shift in focus from the state to the actors in the chain and their interrelationships, and especially to the relative power that some firms are able to exert on the actions and capabilities of their affiliates and trading partners, was immediately accepted and put to use by both practitioners and researchers because it reflected and helped to explain several of the most novel features of the global economy.

Nevertheless, as we discussed our own recent research findings, as well as the findings of others (Feenstra 1998; Arndt and Kierzkowski 2001), we detected a shift in the organization of global production toward external networks. An outsourcing wave was breaking over producer-driven chains, and as a result "manufacturers" in producer-driven chains were becoming more buyer-like. De-verticalization was being driven not only by the rise of powerful retailers but later, in the 1990s, by a broader effort on the part of branded manufacturing firms to increase shareholder value by shifting fixed assets (such as factories) and risk to suppliers—both to an emergent set of "global suppliers" based in the United States and Europe (Fold 2001; Sturgeon 2002; Humphrey 2003) and to local suppliers in East Asia that could meet, or be taught to meet, the required specifications and to use the right process technologies and procedures (Gereffi 1999; Lee and Chen 2000).

Furthermore, what could and could not be transferred to suppliers proved to be a moving target as better codification schemes developed and the capabilities in the supply base improved over time. The new digital tools supporting global-scale functional integration were being deployed in a wide range of industries, labor- and capital-intensive alike. For us, it was clear that changes in the governance of cross-border production arrangements that were being observed in the field demanded more network types than buyer-driven. Specifically, we perceived four new features in the governance of global-scale economic activity that stimulated us to reconceptualize the key variables in cross-border chain governance:

1. Improvements in information technology and industry-level standards that enable the codification of complex information were easing the way for network forms of organization in technology-intensive industries (Baldwin and Clark 2000; Balconi 2002).

2. Flexible capital equipment was enabling technology- and capital-intensive production equipment to be pooled in the same way that labor-intensive production can be pooled, again easing the way for network forms of organization in technology-intensive industries (Brusoni and Principe 2001; Langlois 2003).

3. Sophisticated supply-chain management tools were pushing labor-intensive industries up the technology curve (Abernathy, Dunlop, Hammond, and Weil 1999).

4. Increased outsourcing by manufacturing firms and increased involvement in product definition by retailers (private label) were blurring any clear distinction between buyers and producers.

To sum up, the buyer- and producer-driven GCC typology was based on a static, empirically situated view of technology and barriers to entry, but both are dynamic because of technological change and firm- and industry-level learning (Henderson, Dicken, Hess, Coe, and Yeung 2002; Ponte and Gibbon 2005). As we adopted a more dynamic view of chain governance two things became clear: (1) there was a clear shift away from the vertically integrated, producer-driven variant in a range of industries; and (2) the buyer-driven type could not characterize all of the network types being observed in the field. We also chose to replace the term *commodity* with *value* because of popular connotations of the word *commodity* with undifferentiated products, especially primary products such as crude oil and bulk agricultural goods, and because the term *value* both captured the concept of "value added," which fit well with the chain metaphor we were using, and focused attention on the main source of economic development: the application of human effort, often amplified by machines, to generate returns on invested capital.

The (Firm-Level) Governance of Global Value Chains

In moving beyond the empirically based typology of chain governance developed in the GCC stream, our goal was to construct a dynamic, operational theory that could account for observed changes and anticipate future developments. Our first step was to ask three questions of case material collected from a range of global industries: (1) What activities are bundled in one node of the chain or split among various nodes? (2) How are knowledge, information, and material passed from one node to the next? and (3) Where are the nodes located? One of our greatest challenges was to overcome the specific language that most case studies use to discuss these features (see Sturgeon 2001 for an early attempt to develop industry-neutral terminology). From this comparison, we were able to identify five generic ways that firms coordinate, or "govern," the linkages between value chain activities: (1) simple *market* linkages, governed by price; (2) *modular* linkages, in which complex information regarding the transaction is codified and often digitized before being

Key Variable / Governance Type	Complexity of transactions	Ability to codify transactions	Capabilities in the supply base	Degree of explicit coordination and power asymmetry
Market	Low	High	High	Low
Modular	High	High	High	
Relational	High	Low	High	
Captive	High	High	Low	
Hierarchy	High	Low	Low	High

FIGURE 6.1. The global value chain governance framework

NOTE: There are eight possible combinations of the three variables. Five of them generate global value chain types. The combination of low complexity of transactions and low ability to codify is unlikely to occur. This excludes two combinations. If the complexity of the transaction is low and the ability to codify is high, then low supplier capability would lead to exclusion from the value chain. This is an important outcome, but it does not generate a governance type per se.
SOURCE: Gereffi, Humphrey, and Sturgeon 2005, as adapted by Dicken 2007, p. 158.

passed to highly competent suppliers; (3) *relational* linkages, in which tacit information is exchanged between buyers and highly competent suppliers; (4) *captive* linkages, in which less competent suppliers are provided with detailed instructions; and (5) linkages within the same firm, governed by management *hierarchy*. We found that these five linkage patterns could be associated with predictable combinations of three distinct variables: the *complexity* of information exchanged between value chain tasks, the *codifiability* of that information, and the *capabilities* resident in the supply base (Figure 6.1).

This "GVC governance" framework helped us to explain why some value chain activities are firmly rooted in place and some are more easily relocated. Specifically, modular GVC linkages raise the potential for tight coordination of distant activities, even when complexity is high, whereas relational linkages typically require co-location to support the exchange of tacit information, driving co-location, agglomeration, and industrial clustering. Furthermore, we found that changes in one or more of the three variables altered value chain governance patterns in predictable ways. For example, if a new technology rendered an established codification scheme obsolete, or was overwhelmed by increasing complexity, modular value chains became more relational. If competent suppliers could not be found, then captive networks and even vertical integration became more prevalent. Conversely, rising supplier competence tended to push captive governance toward the relational type, and better codification schemes prepared the ground for modular governance.

The Theoretical Underpinnings of the GVC Governance Framework

As already mentioned, our approach to constructing a theory of GVC governance was to draw from the existing literature on inter-firm governance and industrial organization to the extent possible. Several important categories of governance have been developed and debated in the literature over the course of many decades. The first question, asked by Ronald Coase (1937), was why the market did not govern all transactions. In other words, why were some business activities bundled within firms? Williamson (1975) built a theoretical framework around the answer provided by Coase, that there were sometimes costs to transacting that could be reduced when activities were brought inside of the firm to be governed, not by relative prices but directly by the firm's internal management "hierarchy." The key variable in transaction cost economics is *asset specificity:* relationship-specific investments that tend to lock business partners into their relationships, creating opportunities for either party to take advantage of the other. The dynamic outcome is that the buying firm would eventually internalize the function, to avoid being taken advantage of, because asset specificity tends to increase over the life of an inter-firm relationship (Williamson 1981). Williamson eventually noted the prevalence of network forms of organization in which there is some form of explicit coordination beyond simple market transactions but which fall short of vertical integration, and acknowledged networks as an intermediate organizational form (Williamson 1985).

Granovetter (1985) disagreed with the opportunistic view of human nature underpinning transaction cost economics. His view is that economic activity is embedded in social relationships, not the other way round, and that trust and even goodwill can and often do build up in the interpersonal relationships that inevitably underlie inter-firm relations. The "relational" view of economic life suggests that inter-firm relationships can be sustained in the face of asset specificity. The stream of work that explored this question (Johanson and Matsson 1987; Lorenz 1988; Jarillo 1988; Powell 1987, 1990) drew on the work of Granovetter, as well as on the example of Italian "industrial districts" provided by Piore and Sabel (1984), to argue for a distinct "network" form of industrial organization, based on trust, long-term relationships, social and spatial proximity, and the desire for repeat business on the part of suppliers.

Geographers, for their part, have long argued that social and spatial proximity could substitute for vertical integration (Scott 1988a; Storper 1995). For many, Adler (2001) provided the final word in this debate, mapping out three types of industrial organization: market, communitarian-trust, and hierarchy. As Bair points out in the introduction to this volume, the GVC framework, by internalizing the insights of economic sociologists such as Granovetter in the "relational" GVC governance form, created a connection to economic sociology that the GCC literature has not. At the same time, the centrality of the concept of asset specificity links the GVC framework to the work of heterodox economists. Although the relational and Hobbesian views of economic life have typically been framed in mutually exclusive terms, the GVC governance framework incorporates a range of solutions to the problem of asset specificity.

At the same time, a stream of literature centered on the concept of capabilities, largely from the field of strategic management, was influential in our thinking about GVC governance. This literature assumes that firms compete on the basis of internal "resources" that take time to develop (Penrose

1959). Because firm-level competencies can be scarce and difficult to replicate, it may be impossible for lead firms to internalize functions or find substitute suppliers in time to compete effectively. Related ideas have been developed by a series of scholars from the evolutionary economics school, launched by Nelson and Winter (1982), to the "resource view of the firm" developed by Barney (1991) to examinations of firm-level "dynamic capabilities" (Teece, Pisano, and Shuen 1997) to more recent work on "industry architectures," meant to reconcile the transaction cost and capabilities explanations for industry organization (Jacobides and Winter 2005). The capabilities literature identifies access to expertise and competencies as ample motivation for forging and maintaining external relationships, even when asset specificity is significant. This pragmatic view of industry organization provides an antidote to the mechanistic, immediate, frictionless view of organizational change contained in the transactions cost framework.[5]

Our approach was to combine the key insights from these different streams of literature. First, we recognized asset specificity as a potential hazard in inter-firm relationships. This resonated with our field research, where we learned that managers commonly valued the ability to switch suppliers when conditions dictated. But we also found that many companies had developed a tolerance for sustained relationships with other firms in the face of asset specificity. Finally, we observed firms exchanging extremely complex information in codified form, often using advanced information technology, and learned that lead firms could choose among an elite but growing set of suppliers and contract manufacturers that had sufficient capability to receive the information and act on it appropriately. In all, we perceived three network forms situated between markets and hierarchies. The first, and most "hierarchy like," was for lead firms to dominate their supplier's business to the point where they were unlikely to act in opportunistic ways (the captive governance form). The second was for buyers and suppliers to maintain relationships in the face of asset specificity, either by building up mutual trust or by simply tolerating it out of necessity because of the barriers to easy internalization created by learning or scale (the relational governance form). The third was for buyers and suppliers to reduce asset specificity by passing information in codified form, according to open standards, while keeping tacit knowledge contained within each firm (the modular form).

A view of where the "network" form of industrial organization resides in the industrial organization and GCC-GVC literatures is provided by Figure 6.2,

Transaction Costs	Networks	Global Commodity Chains	Global Value Chains	
Market	Market or price	[Assumed]	Market	
	Intermediate; network; community; trust	Buyer-driven	Modular	*Network Organizational Forms*
			Relational	
		Producer-driven	Captive	
Hierarchy	Hierarchy; authority		Hierarchy	
Vertical integration as asset specificity increases	Static variation	Static variation	Predictable shifts in network form as complexity, codifiability, and supplier competence change	*Variation in Organizational Form*
Coase, 1937 Williamson, 1975, 1981	Williamson, 1985 Powell, 1990 Adler, 2001	Gereffi, 1994	Gereffi, Humphrey, and Sturgeon, 2005	*Key References*

FIGURE 6.2. The evolution of network organizational forms

which shows the three GVC governance forms as a tripartite elaboration of the single inter-firm governance form variously described as intermediate, network, community-trust, and buyer-driven by different streams of literature. The variation in transaction cost economics is dynamic, but unidirectional, tilted toward vertical integration because of the tendency for asset specificity to build up in inter-firm relationships over time (Williamson 1981). Williamson's (1985) acknowledgment of an "intermediate" form between markets and hierarchies, along with subsequent literature on "network" and "communitarian-trust" forms of industrial organization (Powell 1990; Adler 2001) did much to establish a third, distinct mode of industrial organization.[6] In the GCC framework (Gereffi 1994), producer-driven chains comprise vertically integrated firms and their captive suppliers, governed largely by management hierarchy, or something close to it, whereas buyer-driven GCCs comprise linkages between independent firms, a generic network form in which coordination mechanisms are not specified, where retailers and branded merchandisers happen to wield a great deal of power. The variation in the network and GCC literature is static: different forms of industry organization are assigned to specific industries but no mechanism is provided to explain the transformation of one form into another.

The GVC governance framework contained in our 2005 article, and outlined again here, is not a grand theory of globalization or economic development but a more modest theory of linkages, or, perhaps better, a theory that seeks to explain and predict how nodes of value-adding activity are linked in the spatial economy. These linkages may be within the same firm or between firms, although the element of direct managerial control that holds sway within firms imbues intra-firm linkages (hierarchy) with a distinct character. Linkages may be forged within the same building, across town, or across great distances. The word *global* in global value chains simply signals our interest in value chains that include an element of vast distance. Regional, national, and local value chains are nested firmly within global value chains, as we perceive them, and GVC governance theory operates equally well at any and all of these spatial scales.

Variation in GVC Governance

Whereas the three variables in the GVC governance framework are drawn from case research, the five governance patterns are ideal types. We recognize that the organizational character and economic geography of entire industries, or even of a single value chain, cannot be read from the characteristics of value chain linkages. First, the characteristics of a single link in the value chain cannot substitute for an in-depth analysis of how governance patterns in different parts of the chain are variegated and mixed, or how they change over time. Any value chain, and the larger networks of production and consumption it contributes to, contains thousands, if not millions, of individual transactions, depending on the time period considered. Of course, because products and services typically contain inputs with very different technical characteristics, not all transactions in a chain have the same character (Ponte and Gibbon 2005). Just as chains are composed of multiple linkages, so too can they contain multiple governance forms. In other words, characterizing larger amalgams of transactions according to one of the five ideal GVC governance types requires an assumption that all linkages within a chain or industry have the same character. Such value chains do not exist in the real world.

Second, because firms can be slow to adjust, and because of institutional differences that structure the norms of buyer-supplier relations, value chains can retain old linkage mechanisms even as the variables of complexity, codifiability, and supplier competence change. As I will discuss in the following section, how fast and far firms and industries go in responding to changing GVC variables (to tap the potential for relocation and outsourcing contained in the modular form, for example) is influenced by institutional factors and relative firm power. Changes in the technical factors of GVC governance help to set the parameters of value chain coordination; they enable change but do not determine it.

As a result, what we observe in the field is a mixing of GVC governance forms within industries, value chains, firms, and even single establishments. For example, a lead firm will typically forge market relationships for standardized goods; modular linkages in complex transactions when standards for exchanging codified information exist and are widely known; relational linkages with select partners when complex inputs are impossible to specify in advance and knowledge is not easily internalized; and captive relationships when smaller suppliers can be provided with sufficient knowledge to provide needed inputs and, at the same time, dominated in order to keep that knowledge from spreading to competitors. And, of course, firms must manage the value chain activities, and the linkages, that exist within their own organizations. How these ideal types are constructed, mixed, and managed in practice is a key element of corporate strategy. In the realm of policy, as in corporate strategy, the ideal types generated by theory must be held up against and applied in real-world situations. Given the complexity of industries and wide variation in governance patterns in different stages of the value chain and geographic locations, it can often be misleading to characterize entire industries according to a single, empirically prevalent GVC governance type. The problem of how to extrapolate the characteristics of individual transactions to the sectoral level is one that has yet to be solved, but recent progress has been made.

Jacobides, Knudsen, and Augier (2006: 1201) offer "industry architectures" as historical, path-dependant "templates that emerge in a sector and circumscribe the division of labor among a set of co-specialized firms." Extrapolating from Teece's (1986) model of capability development in dyadic inter-firm relationships, they argue convincingly that industry architectures evolve from the dynamic, co-evolutionary interplay between complementarity and factor mobility. For example, governance patterns established by early, successful movers can attain high levels of prevalence and stability through a combination of path dependence and network effects. But here again we are asked to define governance patterns in industries empirically, and although research on the evolutionary dynamics of value chain governance in specific industries remains a critical and necessary step, we are left with few generic reference points, no industry-neutral explanatory variables or descriptive terms that allow for easy comparability and aggregation of results, and therefore a weak pathway to any generic, first-pass solutions to common policy or strategy dilemmas.

Ponte and Gibbon (2005: 3) suggest dealing with the problem of defining industry-level GVC patterns by separating the concepts of *chain coordination*, to characterize the immediate coordination of linkages between specific segments of the chain, and *chain governance*, to denote the processes that structure the chain by limiting membership and establishing prevailing coordination mechanisms (such as rules, grading systems, standards). In this view chains can be "governed" according to a single set of rules yet contain a variety of coordination mechanisms. But the rules that "govern" industries are also myriad, variegated, and dynamic, and so require a concerted research effort to grasp in specific sectors. Ponte and Gibbon provide no framework for describing and explaining such differences, but this is an important area of

GVC theory building that I would gather under the heading of "institutional effects" (see next section).

A way to assign GVC governance characteristics to larger amalgams of transactions, albeit imperfectly, is to view the initial link between lead firms and their largest, first-tier suppliers (if they exist) as structuring the governance of the chain as a whole. For example, if a lead firm has modular linkages with its first-tier suppliers, which eases supplier switching even when transactions are complex, second- and third-tier suppliers will be forced to cope with the high degree of organizational and geographic flexibility that lead firms are able to extract from the system, even if they have relational or captive linkages with their immediate customers.[7] In other words, the linkages that powerful firms forge with the most important suppliers go a long way toward setting the governance character of the entire chain.

Three Pillars of Global Value Chain Analysis: Bringing Power and Institutions Back In

The broad thrust of GVC analysis contains more than the theory of firm-level governance just outlined. As I mentioned earlier, there are numerous ongoing streams of research and theory-building going on under the GVC or closely related rubrics. This includes work on global value chains in the primary and agro-commodity sectors, theoretically focused on the role of public and private standards in determining the distribution of gains from trade among different actors in the chain (Fold 2002; Gibbon 2003b; Gibbon and Ponte 2005; Ponte and Gibbon 2005). As the Talbot and Topik chapters in this volume show (Chapters 5 and 2), the GCC stream remains very robust, focused largely on how institutions, especially standards and grading systems, tend to tilt power away from small producers in global chains producing agricultural products, where the traditional connotation of the word *commodity* is less problematic. Work is also continuing on how labor (especially female labor) is utilized differentially in GVCs (Barrientos, Dolan, and Tallontire 2003; Barrientos and Kritzinger 2004; Raworth and Kidder, Chapter 8, this volume), and on the prospects for small firms, and clusters of small firms, to leverage GVCs for industrial upgrading (Humphrey and Schmitz 2002; Schmitz 2004). Rafael Kaplinsky and his coauthors have examined determinants of upgrading and measurement issues in a variety of industries in an effort to understand how rents are distributed and appropriated in GVCs (Kaplinsky, Morris, and Readman 2002; Kaplinsky 2005, 2006).

Despite differences in terminology and emphasis, recent scholarship on "global production networks" (Henderson and others 2002; Dicken 2005; Yeung, Liu, and Dicken 2006; Yueng forthcoming) shares the GVC literature's baseline assumption that various types of international, inter-firm networks have become central features of a wide range of contemporary industries, including agriculture, manufacturing, and services. In my view, the chain metaphor is simply a heuristic tool for focusing research on complex and dynamic global industries. It provides enough richness to ground our analysis of global industries, but not so much that the analysis gets bogged down in excessive difference and variation, or is forced into overly narrow spatial, analytic, or sectoral frames in response to the overwhelming complexity and variation that researchers inevitably encounter in the field. Although debates over the relative merits of terms and metaphors, such as global commodity chains, global value chains, global production networks, and chain governance will certainly continue, it is safe to say that this work shares a focus on the organizational and spatial structure and dynamics of industries, the strategies and behavior of major firms and their suppliers, and the need to identify scalable conceptual tools that help researchers move easily from local to global levels of analysis. These commonalities, in my view, define a core research agenda that cuts across these chain and network paradigms.

If theory building is best pursued in a segmented fashion, what are the main areas that deserve attention? A thoughtful and comprehensive list developed by Henderson and others (2002: 447) includes the spatial organization of firm-level networks, power-in-the-chain, institutions, labor, and the determinants of value capture. Going back to Gereffi's (1994) fourfold framework of input-output, geography, governance, and institutions, we can summarize recent progress, at least in part, as follows. The first two elements of Gereffi's framework, input-output and geography, are descriptive. They provide GVC researchers with their initial marching orders: to map the organizational and spatial division of labor in the chain that is under examination. This will inevitably include an overlapping set of discrete value chain activities contained within, or spread across organizations and locations. This is an extremely useful starting point for asking questions about the dynamic economic geography of industries.[8]

The last two elements of Gereffi's framework, governance and institutions, are causal. They contain explanations for observed organizational and spatial features of GVCs, and highlight the forces external to the chain that structure (enable and limit) what actors in the chain do. The notion of "drivenness" contained in Gereffi's original framework usefully focuses attention on power in the chain. Even if clear distinctions between buyers and producers, or the association of these forms with specific industries, have been superseded by events, the identification of powerful actors in the chain and an examination of the sources of this power and the ways that it is used remain a central project of GVC theory-building.

If we split Gereffi's category of "governance" into two distinct areas of inquiry, power and the determinants of firm-level coordination, and include institutions as a third category, we are left with three "pillars" of GVC analysis, broadly defined: (1) the character of linkages between tasks, or stages, in the chain of value-added activities (explained in part by a theory of GVC *governance*); (2) how power is distributed and exerted among firms and other actors in the chain; and (3) the role that institutions play in structuring business relationships and industrial location. These three elements, individually and even more so in combination, can contribute to robust explanations of why observed inter-firm relationships and geographic patterns have evolved in an industry, or part of an industry, and even provide insight into how they might evolve in the future. Because I have already summarized the GVC governance framework, I will touch briefly on power and institutions in the remainder of this section.

Power in the Chain

As Perrow (1981) argues, power is an integral part of economic life. The effects of power, or lack of power, can be discerned at every level of analysis. Institutional actors, including states and multilateral institutions such as the World Trade Organization (WTO), shape GVCs through the enforcement, or lack of enforcement, of laws and the terms of international agreements. Consumers have power through the purchasing choices they make, when they turn the products and services they buy to unintended purposes (Leslie and Reimer 1999), and even more so when their wishes are amplified by advocacy groups and through class action litigation. Workers also have power, especially when they are represented by labor unions with the ability to call work stoppages at the level of the enterprise, industry, or broader economy.

At the firm level, power is accumulated, held, and wielded in different ways and in different amounts by various actors in the chain. GVC analysis commonly divides an industry into two broad types of firms: *lead firms* and *suppliers*. Lead firms, at the very least, set product strategy, place orders, and take financial responsibility for the goods and services that their supply chains churn out. As Gereffi envisioned, lead firms can be *buyers*, with little or no production of their own, or *producers*. Lead firms, because they have the agency (within limits) to choose and replace suppliers, wield *purchasing power*. Although it is not always exercised, purchasing power allows a lead firm to explicitly coordinate the activities of its supply chain and to pressure suppliers to lower costs, increase quality, adopt specific equipment, employ specific business processes, purchase inputs from specific vendors, and invest in specific locations.

A second category of firm-level power in GVCs is *supplier power*. Extreme forms of supplier power have been variously refered to as "platform leadership" (Gower and Cusumano 2002) and "Wintelism" (Borrus and Zysman 1997). Market and technological dominance afford platform leaders the power to set standards. True platform leadership in the supply base is rare, but there are notable examples in which suppliers either dominate the chain or share power with lead firms, forming what Fold (2002) calls "bi-polar" GVCs.[9] Supplier power based on platform leadership, even if it is extremely strong, is typically not associated with explicit coordination of buyers or other "downstream" value chain actors. For example, Intel issues several thick specification books with each of its new microprocessors that allow its customers to incorporate Intel semiconductors in their product designs. But Intel does not dictate where those final products will be made, in what number, or among which firms work will be divided.

More typical is a softer form of supplier power, *competence power*, stemming from technical and service capabilities that are difficult to replace (Penrose 1959; Palpacuer 2000). Suppliers wield competence power when their products and services are seen as nearly indispensable for the lead firms they serve. Lead firms can use their purchasing power to place limits on supplier power, often with a large measure of success, because even the most competent and important suppliers base their success on winning future orders. Retaining the ability to switch suppliers, even among a very small group of two to four, appears to be adequate in most instances to keep supply power in check.[10]

Although it is tempting to refer to platform leaders as "lead firms," because even their customers have to accommodate to the standards they set, it is analytically useful to retain the distinction between lead firms and suppliers that are platform leaders, because the power that accrues to lead firms from placing orders (purchasing power) has a source (risk taking) that is distinct from the extreme technological competence required to set industry-level standards.

Although an examination of power in GVCs is a distinct realm of analysis, a point of overlap with GVC governance theory relates to the relative power of firm-level actors in the chain. In modular value chains, suppliers take responsibility for their bundle of activities (purchasing, process development, production, and so on), and though their largest customers typically monitor them closely, the fact that their capacity is easily switched to other customers provides them with more freedom of action than that of suppliers that are more deeply embedded with their customers. When supplier capacity is generic, suppliers can and do spread risk across a large and diverse pool of buyers. In relational value chains, the tacit knowledge that suppliers bring to the table provides them with some leverage, but the thick linkages they must forge with buyers may be hard to replicate with other buyers in time to avoid severe hardship. If we view the power conferred on lead firms by their buying role as decisive, over time, this lock-in with customers creates a higher level of power asymmetry in GVCs with a high concentration of relational linkages than in GVCs with many modular and market linkages. Of course, as transaction cost theory stresses, the opposite scenario is also possible, in which relational linkages, asset specificity, and the deep competencies of suppliers make it all but impossible for lead firms to replace them. The key point is that asset specificity can shift power toward either party in the transaction. How these dynamics play out in specific situations is a central question of GVC research.

Institutions

Institutions have been defined in a very broad way. On one side of the spectrum, we can think of institutions as bureaucratic organizations with payrolls and physical addresses, including government agencies and nongovernmental organizations such as multilateral agencies, industry trade groups, labor unions, and advocacy groups. On the other side, we can think of institutions as the rules that govern society, either bureaucratically, as codified in legal canons and regulatory systems, or existing more amorphously, though perhaps no less powerfully, in the realm of societal norms and expectations

(North 1990). Firms and industries clearly adapt in response to institutional pressures (Meyer and Rowan 1977). By setting the rules that firms must operate within, "institutions . . . [shape] the creation and functions of units in market and the relations between them" (Stinchcombe 1997: 2). The rules set by institutions are derived, to a greater or lesser degree, by the beliefs, values, meanings, and priorities embedded in the societies that create them, fund them, and staff them. As a result, limits are placed on actions, and firms or managers that surpass those limits run the risk of sanction, creating pressure for firms to operate according to the norms and expectations of the societies in which they operate (Yeung, forthcoming).

The impact of institutions on the geography and character of GVCs can be profound, as Bair (2005) stresses. For example, the enlargement of the European Union, the establishment of the North American Free Trade Area (NAFTA), and China's accession to the WTO have had a large effect on the economic geography of many industries, including the location of direct investment and the relationship between production systems and their target markets (Bair and Gereffi 2001; Bair 2002). At the firm level, routines of interaction between suppliers and lead firms can be deeply rooted in domestic and even local institutions and culture, and often structure (enable or limit) firm-level GVC governance in an ongoing manner (Sturgeon 2007). Because industries have developed within different institutional contexts, for example in Europe, Japan, and North America, it is not surprising that firms and industries respond to common pressures differently at home (Helper 1991). It is more surprising, perhaps, that these specificities continue to exert influence even as the largest firms have developed global operational footprints (Berger and MIT Industrial Performance Center 2005).

Again, there are major points of intersection between the three pillars of GVC-related theory. For example, the increasingly stringent standards (such as for product quality and consumer protection) and competitive differentiation in previously undifferentiated product categories (such as fresh fruit and vegetables) introduced new levels of explicit coordination (via modular linkages and vertical integration) in horticultural GVCs that had previously been market-based (Dolan and Humphrey 2000). Another example has to do with the standards for exchanging information, limiting behavior, and ensuring quality in GVCs. Creating such institutions, or "conventions," is almost always a contentious process (Ponte and Gibbon 2005), with outcomes clearly related to power in the chain. Countries with large markets, such as China, can more easily set local content rules than can smaller countries. Firms with a large market share or an unassailable technological advantage have the power to set standards and requirements for other value chain actors. For example, the process of developing industry-level codification schemes needed to support value chain modularity can be blocked in industries in which power is concentrated in a handful of huge lead firms, such as the automotive and commercial aircraft industries (Sturgeon, Van Biesebroeck, and Gereffi 2007; Kimura 2007).

Conclusions

Because the stakes are so high, we must take global integration seriously, and develop ways of thinking that place novel and emergent features of the global economy in the foreground. In simpler times it made sense to focus on the roles of comparative advantage and the market- and capability-seeking activities of multinational corporations in motivating and structuring international trade and investment. These concepts have proved to be extremely robust and are still valuable, but they do not emphasize the fragmentation of the value chain or the fluid, real-time integration of capabilities in advanced economies with the rapidly rising capabilities in places that were all but outside of the capitalist global economy only two decades ago, such as China, India, Russia, and Vietnam. In fact, they emphasize the opposite: national export specialization in undifferentiated commodities, on one hand, and finished products, on the other, and the extension of existing national advantage, via multinational affiliates, to places where industrial capabilities lag far behind. The rise of GVCs does not render this view of global competition completely anachronistic, but it is safe to say that the picture has grown much more complex.

In an attempt to bring some order to this complexity, the GVC governance framework revisits the terrain between markets and hierarchies, exploding the network form into three distinct modes of inter-firm governance: modular, relational, and captive. The framework identifies the problem of asset specificity as an important, but not sole or unidirectional driver of firm-level decision making, and elevates three variables that dynamically shape the content and character of inter-firm linkages: complexity, codifiability, and supplier competence. The focus is not only on the organizational patterns and power dynamics that are generated by different variable combinations, but also on the geographic possibilities (for example, clustering versus dispersal of industries, rapid versus gradual relocation of work) that are enabled by each governance form.

As a theory of linkages, the GVC governance framework is not intended to provide a complete theory of economic development, but a transaction-, firm- and industry-centric theory of governance among the firm- and establishment-level actors in the chain. As such it cannot provide a full accounting of the characteristics and consequences of GVCs. It can, however, provide a bottom-up, research-driven method that accounts for the governance characteristics that tend to arise in global value chains *absent other factors and influences.* As Peter Doeringer has suggested,[11] if the pattern of global value chain governance in an industry does not fit the theory, then an alternative force, such as a strong institutional mechanism or an extremely concentrated industry structure, is likely to be at work. In this way, GVC governance theory can provide researchers with a relatively simple set of baseline research questions and policymakers with a first-pass tool for analysis. Moreover, the larger GVC framework can provide a neutral conceptual space for comparing research results across industries and geography.

Our goal in developing a theory of GVC governance was to tidy up a relatively small corner of the theoretical room, with the hope that others would accept—and work to improve—our solution, and go on to build compatible frameworks dealing with other aspects of globalization. This theoretical partitioning is especially important if the goal is to develop dynamic frameworks that can predict and account for change, because with moving parts, complexity goes up. Together with the shaping power that institutions have on an industry's organization and geography, and the various forms of power that are exerted among firms and at the industry level, we can use GVC governance theory to begin to develop a relatively comprehensive view of the forces driving change in the organization and economic geography of specific sectors. But more work remains to be done, not only in the realm of power and institutions but also in the more pragmatic and policy-oriented areas of GVC metrics, industrial upgrading, and work organization.

Although it is important to develop various aspects of GVCs as distinct theoretical realms, it is equally important to actively nurture points of intersection. For example, the variables of complexity, codifiability, and competence all have powerful influence at the intersection of work organization and technological change (Levy and Murnane 2004). How the influence of social and spatial proximity plays out in the face of ongoing efforts to codify complex information and knowledge will help to determine not only the prevalence of the relational and modular GVC governance forms but also the prospects for location-specific industrial agglomerations (Scott 2006), systems of innovation (Lundvall 1992; Lundvall, Johnson, Andersen, and Dalum 2002), and varieties of capitalism (Hall and Soskice 2001). No theoretical framework can, or should, try to accommodate everything. In an age of globalization, theory building needs to be approached in an additive, modular fashion, with an eye toward compatibility with methods and frameworks that both broaden the scope of analysis and add detail in specific areas. In this way, the multiple streams of GVC-related theory can be built into a broad, cohesive framework for understanding global industries and responding to the risks and opportunities they pose.

It is important to bear in mind how nascent this theory-building project remains. Julia Lane has likened the current state of qualitative industry research to the study of the natural world in the sixteenth and seventeenth centuries.[12] In this era, curious researchers made detailed notes and drawings of what they could see of the vastness and variety around them, but there were few mechanisms for compiling the findings of individual researchers into larger pools of knowledge that could reveal broad patterns. Comparison of results came haphazardly with personal communication between scholars and in the few forums, such as the British Royal Society, where research could be presented and results debated and compared. In this way classification systems gradually came into being and some of the mechanisms at work in nature were revealed.

Similarly, scholars of global industries have now had several decades to present, publish, and debate their research results. These findings show that the process of global integration is expressed differently in different industries and places. The precise patterns and effects of global integration depend in some large part on the technical and business characteristics that prevail in specific industries, the relative power of firm and nonfirm actors in the chain, and the social and institutional characteristics of the places in which the tendrils of GVCs are embedded. Although field research on industry-specific GVCs remains as important as ever, the accumulation of case studies has created the conditions needed for the development of generic, industry-neutral theories to explain observed patterns and to predict outcomes associated with them. More effort is shifting to the construction of classification schemes and conceptual models that can stand in for the mechanisms that work to create the variety observed in the field. Yet we remain very close to the starting line. The field of GVC-related theory building is wide open.

7 Global Commodity Chains, Market Makers, and the Rise of Demand-Responsive Economies

Gary G. Hamilton and Gary Gereffi[1]

I N THIS CHAPTER, WE CALL ATTENTION TO THE DISJUNCTURE within economic sociology at the macro level of analysis and examine one aspect, namely the cleavage between the conventional approach, which emphasizes structures and institutions, and the global commodity chain (GCC) approach, which focuses on organizational processes.[2] We argue that it is possible to reconcile these approaches if, and only if, the historical dynamics of globalization are taken seriously and incorporated into economic sociology.

There is truth to the aphorism that you go where you look. Economic sociologists are a diverse group. They look in different directions and arrive at often contradictory conclusions. Some look at structure, particularly the structure of networks; others look at institutions, mainly political and social; and yet others look at organizational processes. Those adopting structuralist and institutional perspectives, the conventional core of economic sociology, find plenty of evidence supporting their claims that middle-level phenomena, such as social networks and economic policies of the state, are crucial factors shaping the organization of local and national economies. These same theorists often downplay or even ignore the effects of global economic processes on local and national levels of economic activity. As a consequence, concludes Richard Swedberg in his programmatic evaluation of the field, the conventional approaches in economic sociology have "shown little interest in connecting up to other research traditions that study the international economy. . . .

This trend represents a weakness in contemporary economic sociology, as does its absence from the debate on globalization" (2003: 69).

Those adopting the alternative GCC approach to economic sociology also have blinders. GCC theorists locate plenty of evidence supporting their claims that the dynamics of production and distribution underpin the organization of the global economy, or at least segments thereof. As a consequence of this focus, concludes Jennifer Bair in her evaluation of this literature, GCC theorists have "become increasingly oriented analytically towards the meso level of sectoral dynamics and/or the micro level of firm upgrading." She concludes that "closer attention to the larger institutional and structural environments in which commodity chains are embedded is needed in order to more fully inform our understanding of the social and development dynamics of contemporary capitalism at the global-local nexus" (Bair 2005: 154)

Indeed, many theorists of both the conventional and GCC approaches underplay the historical dynamics of their respective topics. Although using different analytic lenses and arriving at very different conclusions, they focus primarily on some aspect of economic organization, particularly inter- or intra-firm relationships, and use "meso-level" variables as proximate causes for the nature of, or changes in, economic organization. For most conventional theorists, the proximate causes of economic organization are sociological variables, usually some combination of network structure, social relations, economic policies, and bureaucratic efficiencies. In the case of GCC theorists, the proximate causes are industry variables: product characteristics, technology levels, inter-firm linkages, barriers to entry, and governance structures. Despite a similar concern with inter-firm networks, the two perspectives differ in the proximate causes, which in turn creates an apparent divergence between the two perspectives. We contend, however, that the divergence disappears once a longer-term vantage point is adopted.

The Disjuncture Within Economic Sociology

In the past decade, most economic sociologists focused on the significance of inter-firm networks and their institutional environments in understanding the organization of economic activities, but in very different ways. In this section, we will outline the conventional approach in order to contrast this with the GCC approach, which we describe in the following section.

Network research in economic sociology grew out of an interest in trying to verify and work out the implications of C. Wright Mills's thesis in *The Power Elite* (1956), but efforts (for example, Domhoff 1967; Mintz and Schwartz 1985) to develop a theory and methodology of networks languished until the early 1990s (Scott 1991). At that time, sociologists developed a number of approaches to renew sociological interest in the linkages between networks and economic organization. The most prominent reengagement with these ideas came from Mark Granovetter's work (1973, 1974), and especially from his influential article "Economic Action and Social Structure: The Problem of Embeddedness" (1985), in which he theorized the importance of social relationships in the formation of economic organization. Since its publication, Granovetter's theory of embeddedness has provided economic sociology with its most widely acclaimed programmatic statement.

The importance of this article is in Granovetter's contention that the embeddedness perspective offers an effective sociological counterpart to Oliver Williamson's microeconomic transaction cost theory. Williamson (1975, 1985) argues that economic organization (that is, intra-firm organization) grew out of efficient ways in which individual firms solve the transaction costs involved in doing business. Objecting to Williamson's economic individualism, Granovetter counters with the thesis that all economic actions are socially situated and grounded in ongoing networks of social relationships. "Social relations, rather than institutional arrangements or generalized morality," argues Granovetter, "are mainly responsible for the production of trust in economic life" (1985: 491). The networks of social relations constituted by trust, in turn, organize the economy.

In making this claim, Granovetter clearly recognizes the meso-level nature of his theory. "(T)he causal analysis adopted in the embeddedness argument is a rather proximate one. I have had little to say about what broad historical or macro-structural circumstances have led systems to display the social-structural circumstances they have, so I make no claims for this analysis to answer large-scale questions about the nature of modern society or the courses of economic and political change" (1985: 506). Granovetter, however, is not saying that embeddedness has nothing to do with the macro structures of economy and society. Quite the contrary, Granovetter is making a case for using the meso level as a way to create an "adequate link between macro- and micro-level theories." Therefore, he concludes, "The use of embeddedness analysis explicating proximate causes of patterns of macro-level interest is well illustrated by the markets and hierarchies question. The extent of vertical integration and the reasons for the persistence of small firms operating through the market are not only narrow concerns of industrial organization; they are of interest to all students of the institutions of advanced capitalism" (1985: 507).

The Meso-Orientation of Conventional Approaches

Understanding advanced modern economies through meso-level variables has been the hallmark of economic sociology. The most prominent theme running through much of this literature is an emphasis on the proximate causation between embeddedness and organizational outcomes. This theme is developed in two distinct ways, depending on the conceptualization of where economic activities are embedded: in network structure itself, or in social, economic, and political institutions culminating with the state.

Many researchers, using advanced network methodologies, link the formal structural properties of networks to diverse sets of economic outcomes (for example, Burt 1992, 2004; Podolny 1993, 2005; Uzzi and Spiro 2005; Wasserman and Faust 1994). Most of these theorists assume that immediate structural properties of networks (and not the long-term causes of networks) produce observed outcomes, such as higher profits, greater upward mobility, and more power and influence.[3] Despite their emphasis on outcomes for individual actors inside networks and not on the origins of the network themselves, there is also an assumption that activities of individual actors have effects on the macro level; namely, that the macro-level structures represent path-dependent accumulations of individual actions taken in the context of diverse structural configurations.

Another set of researchers focuses on the relational and institutional foundations in which economic networks are embedded. Some of these studies came before the publication of Granovetter's 1985 article, but they uniformly took on greater theoretical meaning after it appeared. These researchers examined business group networks (Hamilton and Biggart 1988; Gerlach 1992; Granovetter 1994, 2005; Stark 1996; Stark and Bruszt 1998; Biggart and Guillén 1999; Guillén 2001), ethnic business networks (Waldinger 1986; Waldinger, Aldrich, and Ward 1990; Light and Bonacich 1988; Light 2005), and gender networks (Biggart 1990; Brinton 2001). Unlike structuralist interpretations, these network studies show that the embeddedness of economic networks in social institutions produces economic outcomes. However, as in structuralist accounts, the researchers typically do not analyze the long-term or underlying causes of the networks themselves, but rather the shorter-term institutional factors that shape them, in one form or another, without actually causing them in the first place. For example, a number of the theorists cited above examine the effects of social (national, ethnic, or gender) relations on economic activity, and thereby assume, implicitly, that these social relations produce the economic activity, instead of merely shaping what would have occurred in some guise even in the absence of those social relations.

Although many conventional theorists look at the link between social institutions and economic organization, the more common focus in the institutional approach is the state. This variant of the institutional approach is less inspired by Granovetter's sociological thesis than by a new interest in industrial organization, an interest spawned in part by a number of diverse publications in related fields, including those by Williamson (1975), Chandler (1977, 1990), Piore and Sabel (1984), Newfarmer (1985), Harvey (1989), Scott (1988b), and Porter (1990). Sociologists began to rework the conclusions of these studies. Reacting to Chandler's (1977) efficiency explanation for American corporate structure, a number of sociologists (Perrow 1981, 2002; Roy 1997; Fligstein 1985, 1990; and Prechel 1990, 2000) countered with their own interpretations. Although differing somewhat from one another, all of these sociologists argued against an efficiency explanation and for an institutional explanation that included the political power of the state to determine corporate outcomes.

This interpretation initially paralleled, and then later merged with, a concurrent theme that a number of sociologists began to promote regarding the relative autonomy and administrative capacity of the state (for example, Skocpol 1979; Evans, Rueschemeyer, and Skocpol 1985; Evans 1995). In this reworking of an older Marxian conception of the state (Poulantzas 1969; Jessop 1982; Block 1987), political institutions specifically relating to the bureaucratic apparatus of the state were different and partially autonomous from the interests of the "ruling class." This abstract and, within the neo-Marxian literature, rather erudite thesis was brought to earth by a number of scholars focusing on Asia, who borrowed these ideas and empirically applied them to explain East Asian industrialization.

The first Asianist to do so was Chalmers Johnson (1982). In his book on MITI, he posited the idea of the "developmental state" and argued that Japanese industrialization could be explained largely by the state's active intervention in the economy. According to Johnson, well-trained and well-disciplined bureaucratic officials developed and implemented a rational plan creating Japan's globally competitive industrialization. Many other Asian scholars (for example, Cumings 1984, Gold 1986; Amsden 1989; Wade 1990; Woo 1991) soon elaborated the causative formulations of Johnson's thesis for other rapidly industrializing Asian economies, especially South Korea and Taiwan. Peter Evans, who first put forward the importance of the state regime in Brazil's economic development (1979b), conceded that East Asian states were "stronger" than Latin American states, and thus could industrialize faster and more successfully than those in Latin America (1987). He further argued that the presence of a "Weberian bureaucracy" was instrumental in establishing the Asian states' "embedded autonomy" (Evans 1995; Evans and Rauch 1999).

This literature emphasizing the signal importance of political institutions in causing economic organization was further reinforced by a separate and diverse literature from scholars examining primarily European economies (Boyer 1990; Hollingsworth, Schmitter, and Streeck 1994; Hollingsworth and Boyer 1997; Dobbins 1994; Fligstein 1996; Berger and Dore 1996; Whitley 1999; Quack, Morgan, and Whitley 2000; Hall and Soskice 2001), but also those of Asia (Whitley 1992) and the United States (Nelson 1994). Strands of this literature are variously known as regulation theory (for example, Boyer 1990), business systems (such as Whitley 1992, 1999), and varieties of capitalism (Hollingsworth and Boyer 1997; Hall and Soskice 2001), but taken as a whole, the literature concludes that the intertwined nature of national and subnational political and social institutions inexorably localizes the conduct of capitalism. Most (but not all) of these theorists would agree with Block and Evans's most recent conclusion: "(S)tate and economy are not analytically autonomous realms but are mutually constituting spheres of activity. . . . Our argument is that *market economies are embedded within a civil society that is both structured by, and in turn helps to structure, the state* [our emphasis]" (2005: 505–506).

Conventional approaches typically treat institutions as prior, proximate, and exterior forces that, collectively or singly, shape economic organization. Extending this line of reasoning, many institutional theorists end up concluding that the global economy is little more than an aggregation of national economies. For them, globalization mainly refers to processes encompassed by and contained within national economies. Some national economies are big and globally significant, such as that of the United States; others are small and relatively unimportant globally, such as Nepal's; but add them all up and you get the global economy.

Following this logic, such a leading economic sociologist as Neil Fligstein finds the literature on globalization unconvincing and suggests that the expansion in world trade "has neither created widespread changes in the organization of production nor undermined the power of governments" (2001: 222). Big governments and big firms, he argues, stabilize national economies and create international agreements that stabilize the global economy (Fligstein 2001, 2005). Not citing the GCC literature, Fligstein pays little attention to specific industries in his analysis of twenty-first-century capitalism and seems oblivious to what has occurred in Asia in the last half of the twentieth century, all of which, we believe, are crucial to global capitalism today.

Another indication of the divergence between economic sociology and globalization studies comes from none other than Richard Swedberg himself. As quoted earlier, Swedberg (2003) observes that the new economic sociology pays very little attention to globalization. Yet in the same book, despite his call for more attention to globalization in economic sociology, Swedberg's (2003) programmatic statement on the "principles of economic sociology" contains neither a chapter on globalization nor even a reference to global commodity chains—this despite the fact that Gereffi's work is well-known to him and is included in both editions of *The Handbook of Economic Sociology*, books co-edited by Swedberg.

In fact, so silent are most conventional theorists about global commodity chains that one might argue that their very silence is a choice to support explanations centered on the state or other institutions, and to deny that global processes matter in explaining economic organization. Victor Nee, a China specialist and prominent economic sociologist, is very explicit about his aversion to considering the impact of exogenous forces on the contemporary Chinese economy and society: "I have not put as much emphasis as others have on the international activities of Chinese firms. The focus has been on domestic market activities rather than on globalization per se. . . . my emphasis has been to develop an endogenous explanation for the rise of capitalism in China. . . . So if I slight the exogenous forces, it's intentional" (Nee 2007: 5). According to Nee, the fundamental challenge for economic sociologists is "to develop a theory of endogenous institutional change" (2007: 6), which leads him to ignore the role of global or transnational factors in explaining the extremely rapid growth occurring not only in China but in a multitude of developing economies.

In claiming that the state and economy are "mutually constituting spheres of activity" (Block and Evans 2005), state-centered economic sociologists are, in reality, only interested in one half of the dialectic they posit. In trying to provide a distinctly sociological explanation for economic organization, they have lost sight of all economic activities except for those reinforcing their theories. This stance amounts to a form of sociological imperialism, a stance used perhaps to counterbalance the imperialist attitude that they attribute to economists. However, in so doing, they also ignore a world of economic activities in which profits, prices, and efficiencies do matter to the businesspeople actually involved, a world of activity that is globally oriented and that has greatly changed in the course of the past half century.

Using Global Commodity Chain Analysis to Move Beyond Conventional Economic Sociology

As Jennifer Bair's introduction to this book demonstrates, a substantial and diverse group of interdisciplinary scholars have used the GCC approach to analyze the globalization of economic activity that has occurred in the past fifty years. Many of these researchers focus on inter-firm linkages in global production networks and the implications and effects of these networks on local, national, and regional economies in which the networks are located. As Bair correctly notes in the introduction and elsewhere (Bair 2005), most of this research is "oriented towards the micro- (individual firm) or meso- (sector) level, as opposed to the macro and holistic (levels)."

These previous GCC studies reach several general conclusions: first, that national economies are interconnected through firms doing business with one another, and that the *spread of these interconnections is global*; second, that whatever social or political relations might shape these interconnections, *firms are also linked through economic processes, which include manufacturing, distribution, merchandising, and retailing*; and third, these interconnections among *firms are organized and controlled, not directly by governments or ethnic groups, but rather by firms occupying points of leverage in the chain.*

In this chapter, we go beyond these conclusions to demonstrate macro-level consequences of the spread of GCCs. In particular we will show the connection between the global spread of GCCs and the development of what Feenstra and Hamilton (2006) call "demand-responsive economies."

Tracking Global Commodity Chains: International Trade and the Organization of Industries

Empirical GCC analysis is focused on industries and products. A good first step to demonstrate the global significance of commodity chains is through an analysis of international trade. The growth of world trade has received considerable attention in the globalization literature because of its direct relevance to employment, wages, and the expansion of free trade agreements around the world. However, a number of economists, especially in the trade field, argue that international trade reflects key new features in the global economy that underscore the salience of a GCC approach. For example, Paul Krugman (1995) has argued, like Sachs (1998) and Rodrik (1997), that the rapid growth of large volumes of manufactured exports from low-wage to high-wage nations is something new and important. The biggest change at the structural level is the rise of intra-industry trade in parts and components, especially those that are used as inputs for final assembly in other countries.

What has made the international trade of inputs possible is the "ability of producers to *slice up the value chain,* breaking a production process into many geographically separated steps" (Krugman 1995: 332). Feenstra (1998) takes this idea one step further, and explicitly connects the "integration of trade" with the "disintegration of production" in the global economy. The rising integration of world markets through trade has brought with it a disintegration of the production process of multinational firms because companies are finding it profitable to "outsource" (domestically or abroad) an increasing share of their non-core manufacturing and service activities.

The importance of looking at international trade from an "organization of industries" point of view can be seen in terms of contemporary U.S.-China relations. In 2007, the United States had a record bilateral trade deficit with China of $256.3 billion, which comprised $321.5 billion in imports and $65.3 billion in exports (U.S. Bureau of the Census, Foreign Trade Statistics). However, these figures are deceptive because China's exports of consumer products rely heavily on imported inputs from the United States and especially from other East Asian countries. Up to two-thirds of China's manufactured exports come from foreign-invested firms (Gereffi 2007), and four Asian economies

(Japan, South Korea, Taiwan, and Hong Kong) account for 70 percent of the total direct foreign investment in China (Lardy 2003).

China is the world's factory and the United States is its supermarket. China's role in many of these export-oriented industries has mainly been to assemble products of components made elsewhere. In the case of Apple's enormously popular iPod, researchers at the University of California, Irvine, calculated how the $299 retail value of the 30-gigabyte video iPod is distributed between Apple and all the companies that make the 450 parts that go into the iPod, which is assembled in China. The findings provide a rather startling insight into who captures most of the value from global production. Apple was the biggest winner ($80 of the retail value, for the conception, design, and branding of the product), and a Japanese manufacturer's (Toshiba's) hard drive was the most expensive component ($63). American companies and workers captured a total of $163 (about 55 percent of the retail value), whereas the cost of the final assembly done in China was just $4 per unit. Thus, "even though Chinese workers contribute only about 1% of the value of the iPod, the export of a finished iPod to the United States directly contributes about $150 to our bilateral trade deficit with the Chinese" (Varian 2007).

One of the major strengths of the GCC framework for examining contemporary issues such as U.S.-China trade is that it ties the concept of the value-added chain directly to the global organization of industries (see Gereffi and Korzeniewicz 1994; Gereffi 1999, 2005). This insight led to identification of global buyers (mainly retailers and brand marketers, or "manufacturers without factories") as key drivers in the formation of globally dispersed production and distribution networks, known as "buyer-driven" chains (Gereffi 1994). However, this same approach can be used to track the emergence of GCCs over time, as we will see in the following section.

Global Historical Trajectories and National Economic Organization

Many international trade economists analyze factors influencing the balance of trade throughout the world. However, they typically use a level of aggregation that makes detailed descriptions and causal attributions impossible. Indeed, they use trade data only as aggregate measures of rapid growth or as loose indications of outcomes produced by state planners.

In an innovative break with this tradition, Feenstra and Hamilton (2006) developed ways to use trade data as historical records to chart the formation and spread of GCCs from the 1970s on. The trade data they used was compiled by Feenstra for the International Trade and Investment Program at the National Bureau of Economic Research from a comprehensive database of all U.S. imports from 1972 to 2001. This is the most disaggregated trade data available anywhere.[4] What this database shows are "the footprints left behind on the path to [East Asian] industrialization" (Feenstra and Hamilton 2006: 239). The data represent a product-level record of growth and economic transformation, and are the best remaining evidence of the actual items that both led to the formation of GCCs and fueled Third-World industrialization. These data not only give analysts an ability to track the changes in the products being produced for export but also permit them to make inferences about the economies producing those products.

To illustrate how these data can be used, let us first establish two trends for consumer goods. We emphasize consumer nondurables for the simple reason that, aside from petroleum products, the largest categories of U.S. imports are consumer goods. Figure 7.1 displays imports as a percentage of total U.S. consumption in major categories of consumer goods (except for

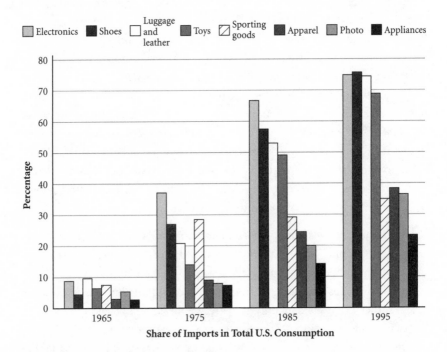

FIGURE 7.1. Import penetration in consumer goods
SOURCE: Robert C. Feenstra, 2001, "U.S. Imports and Exports: Data and Concordances," NBER Working Paper #9387, available online at http://www.internationaldata.org.

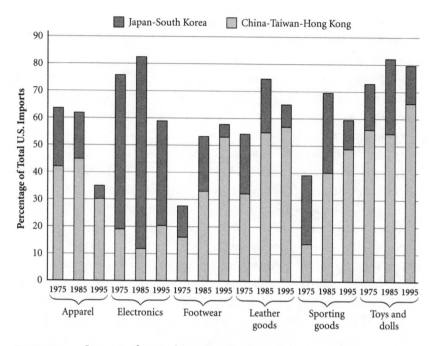

FIGURE 7.2. Imports of general merchandise from Asia
SOURCE: Robert C. Feenstra, 2001, "U.S. Imports and Exports: Data and Concordances," NBER Working Paper #9387, available online at http://www.internationaldata.org.

automobiles) at ten-year intervals from 1965 through 1995. In 1965, no consumer good import contributed 10 percent of total U.S. consumption in that category. In fact, the only U.S. import above 10 percent of total consumption in 1965 was an intermediate good, steel from Japan, most of which went into the booming U.S. automobile business in a period of labor unrest in U.S. steel mills. From this low point, consumption of imported goods in all the major categories of consumer goods rose rapidly. Now for the second trend: Figure 7.2 shows that the vast majority of these imported goods came from just a handful of East Asian countries: Japan, South Korea, Taiwan, Hong Kong, and after 1985, China.

These two trends suggest that the spread of GCCs rapidly increased after 1965 and that the largest density of GCCs developed in East Asia. These two implications, of course, have to be qualified, because they derive from a database that contains only U.S. imports. Nonetheless, this gives us access to GCCs in the world's largest market for consumer goods over multiple decades.

Using the database derived from records of the U.S. Customs Service, Feenstra and Hamilton (2006) examine in detail the development of GCCs in two prominent East Asian economies, South Korea and Taiwan. They show that during the initial period of industrialization, from 1965 to 1985, the primary goods exported from these two countries were mostly the result of buyer-driven commodity chains and contract manufacturing.

In summarizing these findings, it is well to keep two facts in mind. First, in the initial decade of rapid economic growth, roughly from 1965 to 1975, most of the growth in both economies was accounted for by the export sector. This is particularly true for Taiwan, whose population and total economy were roughly half the size of South Korea's, but whose export totals to the United States exceeded Korea's every year from 1965 to 2000. Second, in the late 1960s, exports to the United States suddenly leaped forward, making the United States by far the largest single market for exports from South Korea and Taiwan. Moreover, unlike South Korea's and Taiwan's exports to other countries such as Japan, which included many agricultural products, the exports to the United States overwhelmingly consisted of diverse manufactured goods. In fact, in the twenty years from 1965 to 1985, nearly 50 percent of the value for all manufactured goods exported from Taiwan and 40 percent from Korea went to the United States. In a nutshell, the growth of the South Korean and Taiwanese economies during this period primarily resulted from their manufactured exports to the United States.

Feenstra and Hamilton (2006) use the U.S. import database to examine the economic organization of both the exporting and the importing countries. For the United States, the main importing country, they ask, "How does one explain, in organizational terms, the rapid growth of imports of consumer goods?" For South Korea and Taiwan, two of the main exporting countries, they ask, "How does one explain, in organizational terms, the rapid growth of exported consumer goods?"

In answer to the first question, they demonstrate that the rapid growth in imports arose as a consequence of an economic transformation in the U.S. economy, a transformation they call, following Bluestone and his colleagues (1981), a "retail revolution." The full scope of this retail revolution is only now being examined in detail (Petrovic 2005; Hamilton, Petrovic, and Feenstra 2006; Hamilton, Senauer, and Petrovic forthcoming), but the broad outlines are clear enough. In the last half of the twentieth century, driven by the sudden spurt of shopping malls across the United States, the retail sector of the American economy greatly expanded and changed form. Chain stores came to dominate most sectors of retailing. These sectors also became highly concentrated, with a handful of the largest chains having a huge market share in each sector. An indication of these changes is that in 1955 there were only about five hundred shopping centers in the United States, most of which were quite modest in size. By the year 2000, that number had grown to fifty thousand, many of which were gargantuan. Before the 1970s, shopping centers and malls were largely American, with a few exclusive European exceptions. By the year 2000, shopping centers and malls had become a global phenomenon.

In response to the initial growth of these shopping centers, new breeds of chain stores emerged, namely specialty retailers, such as The Limited and Gap, and discount retailers, such as Wal-Mart and Target. It is no coincidence, in fact, that Wal-Mart, Kmart, Target, and Kohl's all started discount retailing in the same year, 1962. It was also no coincidence that all the leading specialty retailers, including Home Depot, Office Max, Best Buy, Circuit City, The Limited, and Gap, started their current businesses in the 1960s and 1970s. Another equally important part of the retail revolution was the rise of brand-name merchandisers, such as Nike, Dell, and a host of others—merchandisers that marketed brand-name goods, but owned few if any retail outlets or factories.[5] By the 1980s, brand-name merchandisers and specialty retailers dominated an increasing range of consumer goods, including footwear, garments, toys, bicycles, and non-Japanese consumer electronics.

In answer to the second question, Feenstra and Hamilton show that the retail revolution resulted not only from the rapid proliferation of organizational buyers but also from the emergence of new forms of offshore manufacturing—in other words, buyer-driven commodity chains (see Gereffi 1994). The new types of retailing and the new sources for manufacturing are two aspects of the same phenomenon. A third and related element is the comprehensive transformation in global logistics, which facilitated the linkages between U.S. and European retailers and Asian manufacturers (Bonacich and Wilson 2007). Trade data show that, in a matter of just a few years, these buyer-driven chains had become a key force that created both the emergence and the divergence of Asian economies, and whose underlying economic processes produced what Feenstra and Hamilton (2006) call "demand-responsive economies."

The Rise of Demand-Responsive Economies[6]

A demand-responsive economy is one that develops and becomes economically organized in direct response to the demand from intermediary actors in global commodity chains. This demand is created by orders from retailers and brand-name merchandisers—that is, the "big buyers," to use Gereffi's term (1994). Analysts conceptualize most economies as producer-driven. From this perspective, manufacturers secure the primary and intermediate inputs they need in production, and organize their distribution channels. Retailers and final consumers are the last steps in these commodity chains.

By contrast, demand-responsive economies are organized "backward" from final demand, which is estimated by retailers and merchandisers through point-of-sales information or other means, such as focus groups. Retailers and merchandisers use that information to design products and to locate manufacturers that can produce the goods at the quantity and quality levels required by the big buyers. The manufacturers, in turn, secure the inputs needed to produce the ordered goods. In the case of a long-term relationship between big buyers and Asian manufacturers, a market for intermediate parts and services also develops, which leads to an economy organized around contract manufacturing.

The conventional narrative about East Asian industrialization that virtually all analysts give is a supply-side story. We know that big buyers have been active in Asia since the late 1960s, but there has been very little research linking this fact with East Asian industrialization. Quite the contrary, the studies of capitalist development in Asia continue to debate the same three sets of supply-side causes that first appeared in the late 1970s and 1980s: (1) the macro-economic environment (market fundamentalism, "getting the prices right"); (2) the developmental state ("getting the prices wrong"); and (3) non-state institutions, such as the family and authority systems, and related cultural factors. The pros and cons of this debate about the origins of East Asian industrialization remain important even today because analysts seek a balanced assessment of causes in order to formulate policies that would ostensibly allow developing countries to "achieve sustainable high growth rates" (Ito 2001: 91) without repeating previous mistakes, such as occurred in the Asian financial crisis.

Throughout this debate, there is an unexamined article of faith that the causes for the Asian Miracle, as well as the causes for continuing changes in the Asian economies, are to be found solely in Asia, and that the story of Asian industrialization is strictly a supply-side narrative (World Bank 1993). The underlying assumption, shared by nearly all participants in the debate, is that the Asian Miracle is an Asian product. Their theories are country-centered, producer-driven accounts of how this Asian product was created in situ.

In each interpretation, the presumed set of causes (such as market failure, macro-economic management, state policy, institutional environment) forms a structure of constraints, incentives, and "organizing logics" (Biggart and Guillén 1999) that are external and temporally prior to economic activity and that, in turn, produce a specific set of organizational and performance outcomes within the economy. Although many of these standard explanations acknowledge the importance of what is ambiguously described as "globalization" or "global capitalism" or the "world economy," very few theorists of whatever bent incorporate globally significant economic or organizational factors in their causal explanations of local and national economic development.

The extraordinary thing about all of these interpretative accounts is how rarely any of them ever mention the demand-side of Asia's export orientation. Of course, theorists frequently cite export trade as "the engine of growth in East Asia" and emphasize the bilateral trade with the United States as being particularly significant for Asian economic growth (for example, Chow and Kellman 1993). But then, when they give causal explanations for these observations, they examine the producers of goods and, more frequently, the circumstances of production, rather than the buyers of goods and the circumstances relating to consumption. Even those strong-state theorists, such as Amsden (1989, 2001), Wade (1990), Evans (1995), and Kohli (2004), who are most critical of market explanations simply assume that market processes prevail at the demand end: somehow all those manufactured and exported products find overseas buyers. Robert Wade (1990: 148), who discusses the Taiwanese government's economic policies in meticulous detail, seems to speak for most theorists when he writes that the "marketing side of Taiwan's export growth . . . remains a mystery" (1990: 148).

In our view, the core theoretical issue concerning local- and national-level economic development in the contemporary world is not merely whether a supply-side or a demand-side perspective leads to a more accurate explanation. Instead, it is that producer-driven, supply-side narratives cannot account for the emergence and operation of global markets. These narratives remain rooted in the local and national economic, political, and social institutions, with each economy being conceptually isolated from every other economy as well as from global capitalism. By contrast, adding a demand-side perspective not only makes global markets a core topic needing explanation but also allows analysts to hypothesize that "market-making" processes, which include global retailers, play a causative role in Asia's industrialization (Petrovic and Hamilton 2006; Gereffi 1999).

The GCC approach helps to conceptualize these market-making processes. In ideal-typical producer-driven commodity chains, manufacturers not only control the process of production but also "make the consumer markets" for the products that they produce. Empirical examples of this market-making ability of producers are the automobile dealerships and credit facilities affiliated with specific manufacturers, both of which aim to make consumer buying easier and more appealing. In the heyday of American manufacturing, many industrial companies actively marketed their own products to final consumers through retailers directly affiliated with them (such as authorized dealerships) (Petrovic 2005).

In ideal-typical buyer-driven commodity chains, market-making processes are organized in a very different way from those in producer-driven chains. With buyer-driven chains, the retailers and merchandisers have increased leverage to organize both consumer markets and supplier markets. Moreover, they have incentives to keep both types of markets separate and distinct from each other. On the consumer side, retailers in the same sector compete with each other to win and maintain customers. To compete effectively, retailers and merchandisers need to locate their stores (even their virtual stores on the Web) for customers' convenience, to develop or otherwise obtain attractive products, to advertise and display their merchandise well, to establish a price structure that enhances sales and profit, and to provide product warranties and guarantees.

On the supplier side, retailers and merchandisers need to locate or develop one or, more likely, a set of manufacturers that can deliver the goods ordered in the quality, quantity, and price points required. Retailers and merchandisers are usually actively involved in developing new products and production specifications. Because retailers and merchandisers sell a range of goods, they typically deal with a significant number of suppliers, in effect creating markets, complete with price structures, for specified final products as well as component parts of those products. GCC researchers (Gereffi, Humphrey, and Sturgeon 2005) have shown that over time these supplier markets have evolved from loosely organized relational networks to globally organized firms engaging exclusively in contract manufacturing and actively bidding on big-buyer contracts.

U.S., European, and Japanese buyers played a fundamental role in creating supplier markets for differentiated consumer goods in South Korea and Taiwan (Feenstra and Hamilton 2006; Hamilton and Kao 2007). Developed in response to the intermediary demand created by big buyers, these supplier markets were a large enough component of the respective economies that they shaped the organization of the entire economy. The emergence and simultaneous organizational divergence of both economies can be charted directly by using a combination of primary data from each government's manufacturing census and highly disaggregated U.S. import data.

Figure 7.3 illustrates the emergence of suppliers in South Korea and Taiwan. In the early years of industrialization, until 1985, there was in both countries a rapid proliferation of the types of goods (at a seven-digit level) exported to the United States, and a less spectacular but still substantial growth in the number of categories of garments and footwear in that total. This figure reveals the rapid diversification of production that occurred in both countries. Although the total number of products exported to the United States dramatically increased in subsequent years, Feenstra and Hamilton (2006: 241–243) discovered that the total value of the U.S.-bound exports was highly concentrated in only a handful of products.

As shown in Figure 7.4, the highest concentration for both countries occurs in the earliest period, with nearly 50 percent of the value of Korea's exports to the United States and 25 percent of the value of Taiwan's exports contained in only ten products. As the number of different types of products increased rapidly in the late 1970s and early 1980s, the concentration lessened, but then increased again in the late 1980s and throughout the 1990s, as firms began to move labor-intensive production to China, Southeast Asia, and other locations.

The trade data also show that at the same time both economies were rapidly growing, the organization of the two economies was also diverging (Feenstra and Hamilton 2006: 245–251). Divergence begins at the outset of industrialization and becomes more articulated and dramatic as industrialization proceeds, and this divergence occurred across all product categories.

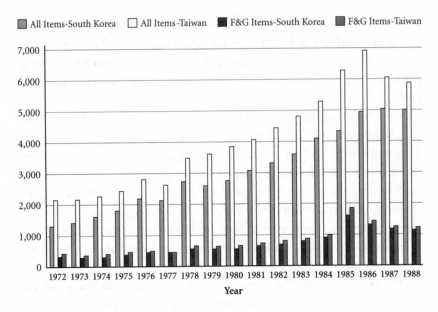

■ All Items-South Korea   □ All Items-Taiwan   ■ F&G Items-South Korea   ■ F&G Items-Taiwan

FIGURE 7.3. Number of seven-digit tariff categories of imports: Total, and footwear plus garment combined, 1972–1988
SOURCE: Robert C. Feenstra, 2001, "U.S. Imports and Exports: Data and Concordances," NBER Working Paper #9387, available online at http://www.internationaldata.org.

For instance, South Korea and Taiwan each produced footwear, but disaggregated trade data show that both countries specialized in very different types of shoes. Whereas Korean firms mass-produced a very limited range of leather athletic shoes for men and boys, Taiwanese firms batch-produced a wide range of rubber and plastic shoes, mainly for women and girls. With this division of labor, the two countries produced over 50 percent of all shoes imported into the United States in 1985.

The same pattern recurs in every other industrial sector. Both countries produced rubber and plastic (nonfootwear) products, but Korea quickly began to specialize in the mass production of tires for cars and trucks, whereas Taiwan produced an exceedingly wide range of miscellaneous products: toys, kitchen products, pipes, knobs, household furnishings, even Christmas tree ornaments. Both countries exported large amounts of household appliances, but Korean firms specialized in microwave ovens, whereas Taiwanese manufacturers exported a wide variety of products, including vacuum cleaners, hair dryers and curlers, and irons. After 1985, both countries exported products classified under the major heading "transportation equipment."

Whereas South Korea mass-produced automobiles, Taiwan became a major parts supplier, specializing in automobile part replacements. Also, after 1985, both countries produced large quantities of high-technology products. Most of the value of Korean exports, however, came from only a few products, primarily from a special category of mass-produced Dynamic Random Access Memory (DRAM) chips. Taiwan's high-technology firms produced a vast variety of products; the semiconductor segment of the high-technology industry specialized in batches of made-to-order foundry chips, specifically designed by big buyers.

Feenstra and Hamilton (2006: 253–298) argue that both the emergence and divergence of these two East Asian economies can be explained by *iterated* processes associated with GCCs. How do retailers and merchandisers develop a systematic approach to ordering products? How do they match the product they want with the firm that they contract to make it? It is important to emphasize here that these processes of matching products with manufacturers are core activities in export-oriented economies dominated by contract manufacturing. As all veteran observers of these economies know, these activities are ubiquitous (but largely ignored by researchers), in the form of world trade centers, trade fairs, business associations, advertisements in every hotel

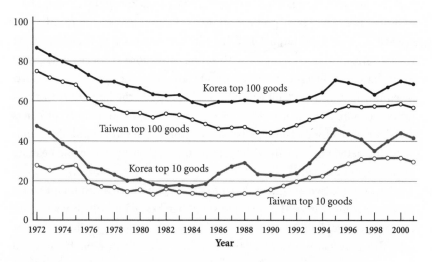

FIGURE 7.4. Share of top-ten and top-one-hundred categories of goods in total export value, South Korea and Taiwan, 1972–2001
NOTE: 1972–1988 based on the seven-digit TSUSA; 1989–2001 based on the ten-digit HS.
SOURCE: Robert C. Feenstra, 2001, "U.S. Imports and Exports: Data and Concordances," NBER Working Paper #9387, available online at http://www.internationaldata.org.

room, and showrooms in every factory. The processes involve the actual and repeated nature of matching intermediary buyers to Asian manufacturers: order by order, year by year.

As discussed theoretically by Schelling (1978), Mortensen (1988), and Krugman (1996), iterated matching at the individual level can lead to emergence outcomes at the macro level, outcomes that cannot be predicted in advance. Feenstra and Hamilton hypothesize that, in a competitive environment, iterated matching between intermediary buyers and manufacturers creates a feedback loop that reinforces the characteristics of the production system by rewarding successful competitors and the governance structure of successful firms and networks. The matching also drives a number of emergent background processes, most important being geographical agglomerations and the opening of economic niches that entrepreneurs can fill, thus creating a more systemically organized economy.

A full description of these demand-responsive processes is not possible within the space limitations of this chapter, but in a simplified form the logic is as follows. Both intermediary buyers and Asian manufacturers quickly become sophisticated players in the market-making game. Retailers and merchandisers learn of and increasingly go to those manufacturers capable of making particular kinds of products. Manufacturers known for certain kinds of products develop their production networks so that they can fulfill or exceed the buyers' expectations. For institutional reasons at the outset of rapid industrialization, Korea began with larger and more vertically integrated firms than those in Taiwan (Feenstra and Hamilton 2006: 169–211). Therefore, when buyers wanted a long run of a single product, the large Korean firms would be more likely to get the order, but for more fashion-oriented products for which only a limited number or an indefinite batch was needed, the manufacturing networks of small and medium-size firms in Taiwan would be more likely to get the order.

For example, when Nike ordered footwear from both Taiwan and South Korean manufacturers, they ordered small batches of high-quality and relatively expensive shoes from Taiwan and large runs of lower-quality shoes for mass distributors from South Korea (Levy 1991). Needing a rapid turnaround time, specialty retailers, such as The Limited, ordered 100 percent of their products from Taiwan (Gereffi and Pan 1994). Wanting to stock their shelves with inexpensive mass-produced microwave ovens, Kmart and Wal-Mart contracted South Korean manufacturers to produce high volumes of the same product. The initial competitive characteristics of each economy became amplified through the iterated orders, which in turn led local manufacturers to build production networks to fill existing orders and to obtain orders for new products that corresponded to that particular type of production network.

Our research over the past two decades has convinced us that rapidly increasing contract manufacturing is the primary driver of East Asia's economic transformation. This demand, however, led to the distinctive trajectories of growth that East Asian economies experienced. The exact mechanism for creating these divergent trajectories, as Feenstra and Hamilton (2006) show, grew out of the competitive struggle among local Asian manufacturers to respond to rapid increases in intermediary demand. The iterated and emergent process of matching buyers to manufacturers corresponds to the equally emergent patterns seen in the export trade statistics.

The actual process of matching buyers to manufacturers involved not only the products being purchased but also the system by which the products were made. Big orders of the same product were more likely to go to those locations specializing in volume production, regardless of the exact item being ordered. Likewise, smaller batch orders were more likely to end up with firms that did not need large orders to survive and that were flexible enough to produce many different small lots effectively and efficiently. This iterated matching process led to economies that became more specialized in their style of production and, accordingly, in the products they produced.

Moreover, under conditions of rapidly increasing demand, the activity of responding to orders (keeping orders coming in from previous buyers and finding new buyers, and possibly obtaining orders for new types of products) meant that owners needed constantly to enlarge, upgrade, or otherwise enhance their production capacity. For *chaebol* owners in South Korea, this necessity, brought on by the intense competition from only a few other *chaebol,* led to aggressive internalization strategies: strategies to enlarge production in existing firms, to establish new firms, to create a mechanism for internal financing, and to develop greater internal self-sufficiencies, all of which denied competitors any access to internal resources. These internalization strategies began very early in the period of rapid growth and encouraged owners to follow a "path of least resistance" in creating inter-firm networks over which they would have control, namely networks of firms personally owned by *chaebol* heads and their families, and managed by people personally dependent on, and loyal to, these owners.

Through such patrimonial systems of control (Feenstra and Hamilton 2006, Biggart 1990), a few owners and their personal staffs were able to control vast resources within their respective groups and to chart the direction of group expansion. In a relatively short period of time, this centralized control of *chaebol* owners and the competition among these relatively few large players pushed the entire South Korean economy along a trajectory of development toward oligopoly. By the early 1980s, this trajectory of development was in place and, for all practical purposes, could not be changed, short of a total catastrophe, which to some extent occurred during the 1997 Asian financial crisis, when about half of the fifty largest chaebol went into bankruptcy or otherwise dissolved, including one of the top four, Daewoo.

In Taiwan, the activity of responding to orders led to an equally rapid buildup of production networks. Even in the early days of growth, these networks were widely dispersed in rural as well as urban areas, and involved many relatively small and medium-size firms. In enlarging their production capacity, firm owners here too followed the path of least resistance. Instead of trying to expand the size of their firms, they expanded their subcontracting networks. That path was much easier than trying to obtain large amounts of capital needed for large firms from recalcitrant state-owned banks, or to fight the competition from others that would surely have arisen if individual entrepreneurs tried to go it alone. Building cooperative *guanxi* networks was a tried-and-true method to accomplish risky tasks and a method that could also be highly predictable. Once these production networks turned out to be successful in getting and keeping orders, they quickly proliferated. Joining such production networks became a clear strategy to get rich, and an astounding percentage of Taiwanese households pooled their resources, started their own firms, and, through their connections, joined one and sometimes several production networks.

The outcome of these activities was for entrepreneurs to search frantically for production and service niches in which they might have some relative advantage over others and, finding such a location, then to organize networks of colleagues to create a position of economic power that would discourage others from entering the same pursuit. In this competitive environment, almost any attempt to upgrade a family-owned business, however large, into a self-sufficient production system manufacturing goods for export would be doomed. Such an export strategy, if momentarily successful, would be quickly undermined by the aggressiveness and cheaper cost structures of satellite assembly systems.

This evidence, based as it is on new data, permits us to conclude that the Asian Miracle is not simply about Asia and its catching up with the West, but rather about the emergence of global markets for consumer products and global supply chains for those products. Demand-side factors need to be incorporated in order to have a balanced explanation of Asian industrialization, but it is equally certain that, when these factors are incorporated, the explanation substantially changes.

Conclusion

In this chapter, we seek to bridge the gap between the institutional, endogenous, and meso-level orientation in much of mainstream economic sociology, and the macro-level research tradition that focuses on the organization of economic activity in the global economy and its impact on the institutional features of both developed and developing societies. We draw heavily on research linking the United States and East Asia to illustrate key theoretical and empirical aspects of this new paradigm. Our main thesis is as follows. First, the so-called Asian Miracle is an aspect of the globalization of markets for differentiated consumer products that has been fueled by the retail revolution, initially in the United States and later in Europe and elsewhere. Second, the emergence of these global markets was made possible by the formation of demand-driven "backward linkages" that made manufacturing into organizational extensions of retailing and merchandising, that is, into buyer-driven commodity chains. Third, these backward connections between global intermediaries and local manufacturers became organized and institutionalized in very different ways in different places, leading to radically different outcomes in all of the first-mover Asian economies.

We believe that this type of market-making explanation for the emergence and divergence of Asian economies is a paradigm-changing theory. It is a theory that encompasses not only individual Asian economies but also the global integration and change in economies over time. If these hypotheses are correct, then economic organization, in general, and in South Korea and Taiwan, in particular, is best explained by the organizational dynamics of "doing things together" (Becker 1995). In this explanation, neither the state nor macro-economic conditions nor transaction costs play fully independent causal roles.

The perspective developed here encourages us to ask for a reassessment of the answers given by most students of Asian economic development. We cannot provide a full account here. However, we can offer a preliminary reassessment on which future research might be based.

In our view, state officials always look at economies for which they are trying to develop and implement policies as going concerns. For the most part, they tacitly accept and take for granted the cultural milieu as well as the organizational features of the societies and economies of which they are a part. Perceiving economies as complex objects in motion, state planners spend most of their time trying to figure out what is going on. They collect statistics, they consult experts, they read world economic trends to see which industrial sectors are worthy of support and which ones are not. They also listen to local businessmen, some in official gatherings and others in private within their circle of families, friends, and colleagues. Although their world of activity is as complex and as confusing as any other in the society, state planners also have an added dimension of needing to plan and to take some sort of action. They need to do what is possible, and if politics is the art of the possible, this means to refine what is already present and to cultivate what is already growing.

Much of the literature on the developmental state overstates the rationality and expertise of these government officials and exaggerates the accuracy and impact of their policies. Although state policies and programs may enhance an economy's ability to grow and change, the effects of state actions are often much more limited than is represented in the literature on the developmental state. In terms of Asian industrialization, it is clear that decisions made in reference to the economy were, in fact, often solutions to noneconomic problems (such as nationalism in times of martial law) that were made after it was apparent that the intended goals of the policies would be reached without the actual policies being implemented. The five-year plans developed in both South Korea and Taiwan are cases in point.

This is not to say that the state has no role in economic development. Quite the contrary, even if state actions are often lagging effects (as opposed to a leading cause) of economic growth, they can help to sustain or rationalize existing trends. Capitalist economic organization involves complex, interdependent, cross-market activities that generate an internal momentum that is difficult for any single actor to alter, however well placed. Howard Becker (1995) calls this momentum the "power of inertia." The details of the activity are means of integration and interdependency: the product standards, the requirements of importing and exporting, the rules for accounting, the sizes of containers for container ships, the barcodes on nearly every component, the modes of communication—all these and ten thousand other trivial and non-trivial details combine to interlink economic activities and make any attempt to change the direction of the whole a difficult, if not impossible, thing to do.

Insofar as politicians and state planners develop policies that complement the existing organization of the economy, such as industrial targeting in South Korea, then the role of the government will be to push the economy in the direction that it is already going. Such policies often have strong effects. In Korea's case, state policies undoubtedly favored some *chaebol* over others, which hastened the dominance of the top four or five *chaebol* over other business groups. In Taiwan's case, the development of government-sponsored initiatives in the computer industry to finance factories, such as Taiwan Semiconductor Manufacturing, to supply intermediate inputs for smaller firms downstream not only was tremendously successful in helping Taiwan build a viable high technology sector, but also purposefully built on existing patterns of allowing the exports manufactured by smaller firms to drive the demand for the intermediate inputs manufactured by larger upstream firms.

State policy often falls short of its objectives, in part because of the sheer complexity of all the activities involved in any large-scale institutional setting. For export-oriented economies like those of East Asia, and in an era when global intermediaries play a key role in the process of iterative matching of buyers and suppliers described in this chapter, we need to move beyond simplified models of market-driven or state-centered outcomes. Once the emergent global economic organization becomes a going concern, the viable options for the state's economic policies become progressively narrowed. For state officials and entrepreneurs alike, when economic organization develops its own internal momentum, it is like the proverbial tiger: once you begin riding it, you cannot get off.

PART III
WORKERS AND ACTIVISTS IN GLOBAL CHAINS

8 Mimicking "Lean" in Global Value Chains

It's the Workers Who Get Leaned On

Kate Raworth and Thalia Kidder

G LOBAL VALUE CHAIN ANALYSIS OFTEN TAKES THE FIRM AS its most micro unit of analysis.[1] For anyone interested in poverty reduction, this is a strange place to stop. Not only does it mean ignoring the role of workers in adding value, but it also misses a central dynamic in the analysis: the impact on labor standards and other outcomes affecting workers caused by the way that global value chains are managed. Good-practice "supply chain management," as it is known in the business literature, is increasingly taken to mean bringing the principles of "lean production" into global value chain relationships. Brands and retailers in the food and garment industries (among others) are demanding faster, more flexible, and cheaper production from internationally outsourced suppliers. These farms and factories, however, are not geared up to deliver because they lack the managerial and technical tools needed to cope with the demands of lean production, and they have little power to negotiate with buyers. As a result, suppliers transfer the pressure onto workers, who bear it in the form of precarious employment; workforces that are composed primarily of women and migrant workers endure insecure contracts, low wages, excessive hours, and few benefits. Because these workers are typically not organized or formally represented, they have little power to resist. Indeed, the success of retailers and brands in creating low-cost flexible supply chains appears to rely on the availability of a pool of workers who are socially and economically obliged to accept work on such terms.

What have been the responses to this problem? National governments, far from reinforcing respect for labor rights, have often weakened them in law or practice, implicitly accommodating the flexibility demanded in order to be a preferred competitive location for global sourcing. Meanwhile, as a defensive precaution against scandal, many leading food and clothing retailers and brands (also referred to here as lead firms) have adopted ethical codes of conduct specifying labor standards to be met by their suppliers. But the purchasing practices of buyers in those lead firms often undermine the very labor standards they claim to promote.

Trade unions and nongovernmental organizations have long been aware that the terms and conditions of employment for workers are at least in part determined by the dynamics of global value chains. In this chapter, we draw on research that was conducted by ourselves and colleagues at Oxfam International in collaboration with partner organizations to demonstrate how global value chain analysis can illuminate the situation of a too frequently forgotten constituency in these chains—the workers employed in the farms and factories on whose labor large retailers and brands depend.[2] We also note ways in which global value chain analysis is being used not just to document the dynamics of global industries but also to change industry- and firm-level practices in ways that can benefit workers and other stakeholders.

Research Methodology

The objective of the research that we report on here was twofold. Our primary aim was to understand and describe the impact of emerging commercial practices in global supply chain management on the terms and conditions of employment for workers at the labor-intensive stage of production in those supply chains, and the consequences of this work for women's unpaid domestic labor in the reproductive economy. Our secondary aim was to use this understanding of supply chain impacts on workers in order to support women workers' organizations, and to engage with multi-stakeholder initiatives in modifying supply chain purchasing practices so that they are consistent with respect for labor rights.

The research design consisted of a comparative analysis of the impact on workers of the pursuit of commercial efficiency in global value chains, with a specific focus on fresh produce (particularly fruit and flowers) and apparel.

The approach was to elicit multiactor viewpoints, using semistructured interviews, with five groups of actors across twelve countries. The research was conducted by a combination of academic researchers local to each country, national staff from Oxfam International country programs, and researcher staff in local nongovernmental organizations working with Oxfam, and it was carried out between June and December 2003.

First, interviews were conducted with 1,310 (predominantly female) workers employed on fruit farms and in apparel production. These interviews focused on the terms and conditions of employment as experienced by the workers, and on the subsequent implications of this paid labor for the unpaid work that they perform in the reproductive economy. Workers were initially contacted either through local worker organizations (although those interviewed were not limited to membership of these groups), or through permission from farm or factory management, and samples were obtained either through random sampling or through snowballing techniques, depending on what the context allowed. The interviews were conducted in the respondents' national languages and lasted on average sixty to ninety minutes.

Second, researchers conducted interviews with ninety-five managers and owners of apparel factories and thirty-three managers and owners of farms and plantations in which the workers concerned were employed. The interviews focused on understanding the attitude toward the workers of those managing, and especially their strategies for managing labor recruitment, productivity, and remuneration under the conditions generated in global value chains for fruit and apparel. Researchers sought to interview the manager who was responsible for operational decisions with respect to labor; where this person declined or was not available, then other management staff, or the owner, were interviewed instead.

Third, interviews were conducted with forty-eight government officials involved in labor law legislation or implementation, and with ninety-eight representatives of labor unions, workers' organizations, and other nongovernmental organizations. The aim in both cases was to elicit opinions about the reasons for the evident divergence between national labor legislation and its implementation, as documented by our and others' research.

Fourth, we conducted interviews with fifty-two agents, suppliers, and importers, who were largely selected on the basis of the contacts provided by farm and factory owners, or who were major agents or exporters in the country.

Last, we conducted interviews with seventeen staff of the brands and retailers who were the ultimate clients of the suppliers interviewed for this study. These brand and retail companies were identified by workers, or by farm and factory managers and mid-chain agents, and the staff interviewed included procurement managers and ethical purchasing managers.

Research on the fresh produce sector was conducted in Chile, Colombia, South Africa, and the United States, and research on the apparel sector was conducted in Bangladesh, China, Honduras, Kenya, Morocco, Sri Lanka, and Thailand. In addition to these two sectors, research was conducted in the United Kingdom, focusing on the context of female home workers engaged in light assembly, such as producing Christmas crackers.

The twelve countries and two sectors were selected on the basis of three criteria. We chose to focus on sectors in which women constitute a significant proportion of the labor force, so that we could investigate the impacts of employment terms and working conditions on the reproductive economy. In addition, we opted for countries that have become established sourcing locations in global value chains for those sectors. Finally, and of importance, we decided to conduct the research in countries in which Oxfam has established relations with local organizations supporting women workers, so that the interviews could be conducted in a context of social trust, and so that the results could be used to instigate or deepen national dialogue between workers' organizations, employers, governments, and international brands and retailers. The aim in covering two sectors across twelve diverse countries was to create a broad comparative analysis, which produced findings applicable to workers at the end of global value chains in a wide range of production locations.

On the basis primarily of the findings of this research (Oxfam International 2004), this chapter discusses the dynamics of these value chains, often as they were described or experienced by the individuals interviewed. We have changed the names of all the farm and factory workers interviewed to protect their identities, because many feared that they would lose their jobs for speaking out. We have also kept confidential the identities of the farm and factory managers and supply chain agents interviewed because many likewise feared losing their positions in the business networks of major retailers and brands. Some staff from the retail and brand companies were also only willing to be interviewed under conditions of anonymity.

The Rise and Spread of Lean Production

Lean production emerged from the assembly line manufacturing methodology developed between 1949 and 1975 by Toyota for producing cars, and was known originally as the Toyota Production System. It is a technique that aims at producing goods and services while eliminating "waste" from the process, in which waste is defined as "specifically any human activity which absorbs resources but creates no value . . . Lean thinking is lean because it provides a way to do more and more with less and less—less human effort, less equipment, less time and less space—while coming closer and closer to providing customers with exactly what they want" (Womack and Jones 1996).

There are common principles behind most approaches to eliminating waste the lean way. One core principle is just-in-time delivery, both of component parts required for assembly and of the finished product to the retail floor. This enables suppliers and retailers to maintain low inventories of goods, which reduces storage costs and enables rapid response to changing market demands. Product batches are made in smaller quantities, then repeated if there is demand, to enable flexible response to market conditions and to avoid the accumulation of stock. This places a high premium on manufacturing sites that can handle flexible production and can switch rapidly and at low cost between designs. There is of course strong emphasis on tight quality control in order to reduce errors and reworking.

Two additional principles in the original conception of lean production are particularly relevant. First, the philosophy of lean was developed in postwar Japan at a time when labor unions were strong. As a result, stability of the workforce and respect for the role of workers in the production process had to be built in as core principles of the approach. Hence, when practiced in its original form, lean production aims to create multiskilled workers who are able to reshape and improve the production process. They can, in this setting, play a critical role in increasing factory-floor efficiency, reducing human effort and costs at the same time. Second, the original philosophy of lean production places importance on seeking close technical and logistical cooperation with suppliers and customers in order to ensure a tight flow of communications within and between firms in the value chain.

By the 1980s, lean thinking was being introduced in U.S.-based manufacturing firms, and a consultancy industry spreading its principles sprang up (see for example Strategosinc.com). Today it is practiced in leading manufacturing firms in Japan, the United States, and the European Union, and its philosophy has been applied beyond industrial manufacturing to service organizations, logistics organizations, and a wide range of global value chains.

Mimicking Lean in Global Value Chains

Lean has proven profitable, and so it has been adopted by retail and branded firms as a means of managing their global value chains in the apparel and fresh produce industries, among many others. In the context of these GVCs, however, we argue that the lean production model is being mimicked in complex conditions with highly unequal power relations. As a result, it is most definitely the workers at the labor-intensive stage of production who are getting leaned on.

The reasons for the rise of outsourcing and offshoring in clothing and fresh produce retailing are diverse: falling transport costs, lower import tariffs, cheaper communication technology, and trade policy reforms, coupled with low costs of labor in developing countries, have provided lead firms with the incentive to source products from Asia, Eastern Europe, Latin America, and parts of Africa, while also maintaining advantageous supply sources in OECD countries (Hayter 2004; Gereffi 2005, 2006).

The process of outsourcing value-chain activities introduces new power relations between the actors in that chain, as is well documented by other contributors to this literature (Quan 2008; Appelbaum 2008). Offshoring production to farms and factories in developing countries makes the context additionally complex and different from that of manufacturing in postwar Japan. Some of the relevant characteristics may include

- Intense competition between mid-chain suppliers, and also between factory-level suppliers, for a place in the supply chain of major retailers and brands
- Insufficient communications both within lead firms (such as between the design and purchasing departments in apparel brand firms) and between lead firms and their suppliers
- Farm and factory managers with widely differing levels of training and capacity to manage people, manage production systems, and operate according to lean principles

- Sourcing from countries with widely differing labor laws, and differential implementation of those laws, including countries in which workers are not legally allowed to organize independently
- Global value chains spread across several countries, creating diverse perceptions among the governments, firms, and workers involved of what constitutes "the system" of concern, and hence what constitutes value or waste within it

These characteristics set a scene very different from that of domestic car manufacturing in postwar Japan, and it is largely due to these differences that lean is being mimicked, rather than practiced, in global value chains. The buying practices of lead firms, particularly, have strong influence over relations in the supply chain. Most buyers must respond to an incentive structure in which their week-on-week performance is assessed in terms of market share, total sales, and profit margins. In the fresh produce retail industry, many buyers are at early stages in their careers, and are under pressure to prove themselves within twelve to eighteen months before being moved on to a new product: a strategy of quick rotation preferred by lead firms wanting to prevent the relationship with suppliers from becoming too comfortable. According to one South African grape farmer who deals directly with supermarket buyers, "You can try to negotiate but you don't want to upset them. Every two years there's a new buyer, under pressure to perform; they must make margins and raise turnover, and they've got their ways and means of doing it."

Pressures on Suppliers, Passed on to Workers

The way that brand and retail firms in the garment and fresh produce industries are mimicking lean in their global value chains is experienced by suppliers as three kinds of pressure:

- *Time and speed,* such as pressures to deliver faster, reduce production lead times, and shorten design cycles
- *Flexibility and seasonality,* such as demands for quick changes in order size and the ability to switch rapidly between product designs
- *Costs and risks,* such as demands for higher quality at lower prices and contracts that shift price and profit uncertainty onto the producer (Acona and Insight Investment 2004)

The world's leading industrial farms and garment factories can meet the challenge of these pressures the smart way: through management training, rigorous production planning, and rewarding terms and conditions for workers. In Sri Lanka, for example, Oxfam found some leading factories that pay high wages and offer stable contracts, achieve high productivity, and so require zero overtime of their employees.

But such world-class production systems are the exception. Most farm and factory managers lack the production skills and management ethos needed. Although brand and retail firms invest significantly in the capacity of their own managers, very few are willing to invest in the tools and skills needed by their suppliers to deliver what they demand. "I have met a lot of factory managers who I feel extremely sorry for" said Rosey Hurst, a leading supply chain and labor standards consultant working in China. "I can't see how they can do their job with the tools they have and the pressures they are under, without exploiting the workers."

For workers at the labor-intensive stage of production, the result of the flexible supply chains set up by retailers and brands is precarious or "informal" employment.[3] These workers are typically women and often migrant workers. Why the predominance of women? First, some factory and farm managers adhere to gender-stereotyped ideas that female employees are more dexterous for this "hand work," more "flexible" about endless routine and unskilled tasks, or more "docile" and less likely to complain or assert their rights. Second, it is likely that more women than men apply for jobs on such terms: men are more able to travel in search of better opportunities, whereas women's family responsibilities may oblige them to accept seasonal, temporary, or home-based jobs. Third, the myth persists that women's jobs provide only "extra" household income, perpetuating the rationale among employers and governments that it is less important for their jobs to be stable, with employment benefits, training, or opportunities for promotion. In fact, Oxfam's research affirmed that these jobs are often the main income source for families, and that benefits, such as paid leave time, health and maternity coverage, and regular hours, are highly valued by women workers because it is these benefits that enable them to balance their paid work with their socially imposed role of unpaid caring work in the home.

For many individual women, their jobs on farms and in factories have facilitated personal empowerment, and in some cases economic independence or greater equality in the household. "May God bless the flowers, because they provide us with work," say the women in Colombia's flower greenhouses. But women workers may pay a high price due to the terms and conditions of these jobs: Oxfam's research found widespread experiences of insecurity, excessive stress, and subordination, particularly among women workers.

In response to the threat of scandal and reputation damage, brands and retailers in both the garment industry and the fresh produce industry are increasingly introducing ethical codes of conduct that specify the labor standards to be maintained by the supplying farms and factories producing their orders. Such codes are typically enforced through audits of labor conditions onsite. Codes have had some important positive impacts: they have reduced the use of child labor in factories and on farms, and they have generally improved visible, or "tickable" conditions, such as factory lighting and ventilation, lunchrooms and toilets, and health and safety measures. But the extent to which these codes can ensure farm and factory compliance with decent labor standards in part depends on the pressures created by the lead firm's own sourcing practices. Ethical teams responsible in lead firms for promoting supplier compliance with these codes often feel they are working at odds with the buyers—to the extent that in one lead firm, the buyers referred to their in-house ethical team as "the sales prevention team" (Acona and Insight Investment 2004). Suppliers are well aware of these contradictory pressures and, as Oxfam's research found, tend to prioritize meeting the buyers' demands over complying with labor standards.

The following sections show how these value chain pressures combine to create precarious terms and conditions for workers in the garment and fresh produce industries.

Mimicking Lean: Pressures in the Garment Industry

The changing nature of garment retailing and its rising performance bar is reflected in changing pressures in the supply chain, in terms of time and speed, flexibility and seasonality, and costs and risks. These pressures undermine other efforts to promote good labor standards, and reinforce bad practices of unscrupulous factory managers. As Auret van Heerden, executive director of a multi-stakeholder initiative called the Fair Labour Association, explained, "Most of the places I go all over the world, the contractor is not out of compliance because he wants to be or because he deliberately wants to cut corners. . . . The problems with overtime, the problems with minimum wages or piece rate, the problems with harassment and abuse are because these factories are run on an incredibly crude basis. The retailers and the big brands are expecting very, very high levels of performance, and they keep raising the bar in terms of speed, cost and quality. And what these contractors do when faced with that type of challenge is work harder rather than smarter" (cited in Drickhamer 2002: 2).

Time and Speed

Two to four fashion "seasons" each year was once an industry standard for garment retailing; now the norm is six to eight, and the Spanish retailer Zara has led the move toward a model that puts out twelve seasons a year. Quick response means shorter production lead times—that is, the period from when the order is received to when the garments must be shipped off to market. Research in diverse countries, from Thailand and China to Honduras and Morocco, found that these lead times are falling significantly, in step with the shorter seasonal cycles. According to one Sri Lankan factory owner we interviewed in 2003, "Last year the deadlines were about ninety days. . . . [this year] the deadlines for delivery are about sixty days. Sometimes even forty-five . . . They have drastically come down."

Compounding this trend is the lack of efficiency of critical path management within some lead firms. Several staff in lead firms admitted that internal communication, such as between the design, sampling, and purchasing teams, is not always as coordinated as it should be. This can mean that decisions that get forgotten internally turn into urgent orders for manufacturers, with no additional time built in for production.

Flexibility and Seasonality

Fashion is fickle, and so it is understandable that brands and retailers want to handle their product lines in ways that can respond to consumers' changing preferences. But rather than investing in better forecasting, which could help reduce market uncertainty, buyers typically demand increasingly rapid response flexibility from suppliers (Acona and Insight Investment 2004). Lead firms are placing orders for smaller initial batches of garments and then following up with rapid reorders for styles that sell well.

Costs and Risks

The combination of flat retail price points (such as $9.99), rising costs, and rising shareholder expectation of returns puts retailers and brands under pressure to cut their production costs, and so demand lower prices from suppliers. The effect is passed down the supply chain as price cuts year after year for many manufacturers in many countries.

According to a manager of a Sri Lankan factory that has maintained good labor standards, "Our wage and electricity costs have increased around 20 percent over the past five years yet the prices we receive have gone down by 35 percent in the past eighteen months alone. I feel that prices are reaching rock bottom in Sri Lanka, and I am not sure how we will survive." In Morocco, factory managers report rising expectations coupled with prices falling by nearly 30 percent in recent years. Said one, "[The buyers] always want higher-quality garments, the price goes down due to competition, and moreover, you're in no position to argue. Sometimes the orders are extremely short notice and we accept them."

The Coping Strategies of Managers: Impacts on Workers
As Rosey Hurst, director of an ethical supply chain consultancy called Impactt, explained, "The pressures to produce faster, more flexibly and at lower cost are clearly passed on by most garment factory managers to their workers through the terms and conditions on which they are hired. . . . Buyers pressure factories to deliver quality products with ever-shorter lead times. Most factories just don't have the tools and expertise to manage this effectively, so they put the squeeze on the workers. It's the only margin they have to play with."

Hiring Women and Migrants   Given factory managers' lack of power in the supply chain, it is not surprising that they tend to hire workers who have little power to negotiate their terms and conditions. Women, usually young and often migrants, dominate in the cut-make-trim stage of garment production. Women make up 65 percent of the factory workforce in Honduras, 70 percent in Morocco and Thailand, and 85 percent in Bangladesh. Many are migrants from rural areas: Guangdong province, China's economic powerhouse, is a temporary home to twenty-six million migrant workers. Four out of five of those in the garment sector are women under twenty-five. Under Chinese law, migrants lose their right of residence to live outside their home province if they lose their job. In any case, they lose their bargaining power: 60 percent of those interviewed by Oxfam had no written contract and 90 percent no social insurance.

Giving Short-Term Contracts and Fewer Employment Benefits   The lean philosophy of unionized postwar Japan has been distorted in terms of many contemporary factory managers' attitudes to workers' contracts and employment benefits. With the focus on eliminating waste, and when waste is defined as any activity not directly adding to value as perceived by the customer, then maternity leave, sick leave, paid holidays, and health benefits can quickly be recast as wasteful costs. This attitude was summed up by one Kenyan garment factory manager, who claimed, "We are here for production, not reproduction" in explaining why his factory did not provide maternity leave or child care facilities.

Subcontracting Pressures Away Brand and retail buyers keen to guard their reputation will typically place their orders with large factories that meet their quality requirements. But in order to meet those same buyers' requirements on delivery times and costs, many factories subcontract out. "The TNCs don't allow us to do this," admitted one Sri Lankan manager. "However, sometimes we are forced to in order to meet their deadlines. If a shipment of ten thousand pieces is due, we do about six thousand in the factory and give the rest to other factories who are willing to take them on." Time is saved and money too: workers in Sri Lankan subcontracted units earn around 60 percent of what those in formal factories earn, home workers often far less. These production units are not audited by ethical code inspectors.

In Kenya, large orders that a major American mass discount retailer placed with one factory in the export processing zone were then subcontracted out to many others. "We are never sure of whether the next order will be coming," said one manager receiving the subcontracts. "You cannot therefore engage people on a regular basis when you are not sure that there will be work." As a result, he hired workers on a daily basis for months on end. Out of sight of buyers and inspectors, workers in subcontracted units and home workers receive lower pay in cramped conditions and rarely have written contracts, and few are ever enrolled in social security systems.

Setting High Production Targets for Low Piece-Rate Pay Daily or hourly production targets are used to raise worker productivity, but they are often set so high that workers run themselves down simply trying to keep up. "Every hour the boss would count how many t-shirts my team had made," said Sonia, a thirty-four-year-old former garment worker in Honduras. "If we hadn't reached our quota it was added to the quota for the next hour. They used to tell us that we had to stay until we had reached our quota, but they wouldn't pay us overtime." One Thai former factory owner recalled, "I offered a bonus for those who could stitch at least 150 pieces in one day. . . . I remember one young woman phoned her supervisor at 3 A.M. to say 'I need just one more zip—I have almost done 150 pieces.' . . . Sometimes I pass my former employees in the street; I dare not ask them about their health."

Demanding Excessive Overtime Factories that miss their shipping deadlines can face hefty air-freight charges and lose their reputations. Instead, they will go to extreme lengths and long hours to deliver on time, as explained by one Morrocan factory manager: "We have a very young workforce of women between twenty-five and thirty-two years old. We prefer hiring women because they are more disciplined. At times, the women have to stay up working all night, and they understand perfectly the need for that flexibility."

Overtime and even night work are standard practice in many garment factories around the world. In China, overtime is limited in law to thirty-six hours per month but in Guangdong province, the vast majority of workers surveyed by Oxfam did over one hundred and twenty hours each month. It is often not optional: one factory rule book stipulated that "When workers cannot do overtime they have to apply to the supervisors for a written exemption from overtime." In another factory surveyed, the factory clinic recorded two or three sewing section workers suffering head injuries every week due to collapsing from exhaustion at their machines.

Some factories resort to extremely crude methods of raising production, such as restricting access to the toilets. One young woman in a large Sri Lankan export processing zone factory explained, "We have a token system. For the entire line there are about forty women and only two tokens. Workers have to compete among themselves to get the token. If we get caught using a toilet without the token, then we are given a warning and the bonus is reduced." In an attempt to cope with these restrictions, many workers skip meal breaks and drink as little water as possible, commonly resulting in cases of urinary tract and kidney infections.

Fiddling the Books: Bridging Purchasing Pressures and Ethical Demands Manufacturers are caught in the contradiction between the buyer's demands and the ethical auditor's requirements, but are well aware of the disjointed approach within lead firms. "I know how to deal with the ethical code people from my many years' experience," said one factory manager in Shenzhen, China. "I can judge the balance of power between buying departments and those responsible for codes of conduct to see where the real power lies." Like other factory managers, he admitted to prioritizing the buyers' demands while fooling the ethical inspectors. And if inspection visits are announced in advance, quick, and conducted by foreigners, it is relatively easy to do.

Double bookkeeping hides the long hours. Gita, working in a leading Sri Lankan garment factory, each month receives a paper bag that has her pay slip printed on it—but with no mention of her overtime hours. Inside the bag, with her earnings, is another piece of paper. She explained, "This is the overtime pay. The company does not include overtime payment in the pay-slip itself because then the people coming to the factory would know that we have been working more than the overtime hours allowed. We have been instructed by the company not to show this piece of paper when they come to question us."

Coaching and bribing workers is common. One pregnant Thai worker described the instructions she received from the personnel manager before an inspection. "He said the customer will ask, 'Do you work overtime?' and we have to say, 'No!' But in reality pregnant workers work overtime and on Sunday as well. We sometimes work until two in the morning or till dawn but we have to say that we work overtime only until eight in the evening. . . . If we lie we will get paid four hundred baht [two days wages]."

Governments, too, make it easy for factories to get away with poor labor standards. Labor ministries are usually underfunded and have little power in government and, with inspectors typically underpaid, bribery is common among factory managers seeking a clean report. In Kenya, labor inspectors did not have the right to enter export-processing zones until mid-2003. Fierce competition in China for foreign investment between provinces can make enforcing the law a low priority. "The labor regulations simply are not working here—nobody cares to enforce them, not even the trade union or the labor bureau," said one factory director in Shenzhen, China. In Morocco in 2003, inspectors were paid just above the minimum wage, leaving them open to corruption. "The labor inspection means nothing," said Fatima, a women workers' organizer. "When the inspector visits the company, he meets with management. He has a coffee with the personnel boss, goes into the control room, chooses a suit, tries it on, and off he goes." And in Bangalore, India's fashion-garment hub, one labor inspector admitted, "We have received instructions from above to be lenient in inspections, as these factories are contributing to the economic growth of the state."

Mimicking Lean: Pressures in the Fresh Produce Industry

The structure and operations of fresh produce supply chains differ from those in the garment industry largely due to the characteristics of the products and the markets they serve, but there are clear patterns in the pressures that suppliers face.

Time and Speed

Fresh produce that can be grown year round in hothouses is increasingly sent as air freight, such as cut flowers, mangetout (snow peas), and baby sweet corn grown in Kenya and Zambia and flown daily into the United Kingdom. Retailers can order these products for just-in-time delivery the next day and so send last-minute orders of fluctuating volumes direct to their suppliers, requiring significant flexibility in the size of the workforce needed to complete orders from one day to the next.

Flexibility and Seasonality

Major food retailers—also known as multiples and supermarkets—typically offer their suppliers an assured sale through "programs," which are commitments to buy a specified volume of produce at a specified time, but for a price to be confirmed on delivery. Many such agreements are verbal, so there is no written contract to break. "Only a very small portion of the fruit is traded under a signed, legally binding contract," explained one Chilean supplier of U.S. and EU markets, "It can sound incredible, but it is that informal."

Such informality enables buyers to break agreed programs if they find a more favorable last-minute supply, leaving the suppliers' agents to find alternative markets. "They shop and change their minds constantly," said one apple-packhouse manager in South Africa. "It takes one month for us to get the fruit there, but it takes two minutes for them to change their minds. They tell us there is no market for Gala [apples] and that we need to change our supply. . . . then the only thing we can do is dump it somewhere else." Wine producers selling to multiples can, likewise, face one-way uncertainty in their contracts. "We are penalized if the product is not delivered on time," explained one. "We are given three-month forecasts for what is required, but if the retailers decide they don't want it, it's up to the producer to sell it elsewhere."

Costs and Risks

Quality requirements for fresh produce have become increasingly exacting, because multiples typically use the appeal of their fresh produce displays to draw customers over from their competitors. "Now they are telling us that the size of a Fuji apple is ideally 65 millimeters not 63 millimeters," explained a South African apple farm manager, "So when you are thinning [the trees] you have to tell the workers to cut more deeply. . . . There is more skill involved, but it also takes longer and there is more labor."

These pressures show up in the packhouse, too, because the different multiples, especially in the United Kingdom, where retailing competition is particularly acute, now require the fruit to be packed using their own brand's bags, crates, and sizes. For packhouses, this greatly increases the complexity and hence length of work. "Tesco wanted us to change their grape packaging from open to sealed bags," according to a grape farmer in South Africa. "The new bags were three times as expensive, from 2.8 rand to 8 rand per carton. And the productivity in the packhouse went through the floor because it took workers 20 to 30 percent longer to seal those bags. But the price stayed exactly the same; it wasn't even discussed. And then the other supermarkets all demanded it too. That's the way it goes."

It can often be the farm-level suppliers who carry the financial risk when prices are low or volatile. The volume of fruit to be shipped may be agreed on in the "program," but usually not the price: some multiples specify a ceiling but no floor on what they will pay. And if the buyer decides to run a promotion, the farm-level supplier may bear the price cut. "They also change the prices: £1.49 is the price then suddenly they put it on sale and make it 99 pence. Then they sell it in bulk. The [technical] codes of conduct do not cost us half as much as these things do," explained a South African apple grower.

Some multiples fix their margins and let suppliers carry any price fluctuations that arise during the season. One South African grape supplier gave an illustrative example: "The supermarkets are looking for a 30 percent margin and say they want to sell grapes at 99 pence. So they tell the importer that he must underwrite the deal: if he can't supply them with grapes at 66 pence for the season, he must write them a check for the difference."

Hence farm-level suppliers may find they are footing the bill if their fruit is rejected on arrival, if buyers find a cheaper source, or if buyers run low-price promotions to capture market share from other retailers. "I talked to my financial manager the other day," commented one South African apple grower, "and he said 'When you deliver your fruit, who do you invoice?' I said no one, and that I wait for the price to be told to me. He said 'You're not farming, you're gambling.'"

The Coping Strategies of Managers: Impacts on Workers

"The only ham left in the sandwich is our labor costs. If they [the supermarkets] squeeze us, it's the only place where we can squeeze," said one South African apple farm owner. And the methods for squeezing workers are familiar.

Hiring Women and Migrants In Colombia, Ecuador, Guatemala, Kenya, Mexico, and Zimbabwe, women account for at least half of the employees in the fresh produce industries and tend to be employed in more insecure ways than men (Dolan and Sorby 2003). In Chile and South Africa, women get the temporary jobs in the fruit sector and are hired on rolling contracts for up to eleven months, year after year. Half of all deciduous fruit workers in South Africa are women, but they only have one quarter of the long-term jobs. In Chile, women's employment in the fruit sector quadrupled between 1982 and 1992, but in 2001 they held just 5 percent of the long-term jobs and over 50 percent of the temporary ones.

In high-income countries, too, women and migrant workers fill the most precarious jobs at the labor-intensive end of fresh produce value chains. Fraser Valley, in Canada's province of British Columbia, is famous for its fruit farms but not for protecting its farmworkers: in that province, they are excluded from important labor laws. Eighty percent of the valley's fruit pickers are Punjabi, three quarters of them women, mostly recent immigrants. Hired by contractors—usually higher-caste Punjabi men—they work long hours on low piece-rates and often do not receive the overtime pay due to them.

Likewise in the United Kingdom, a government investigation in 2003 found that contractors were charging Chinese, Ukrainian, and Portuguese immigrants high recruitment fees to work for excessive hours picking fruit and flowers on piece-rates far below the legally mandated minimum wage. The government's report concluded that "the dominant position of the supermarkets in relation to their suppliers is a significant contributory factor in creating an environment where illegal activity by gangmasters can take root. Intense price competition and the short time-scales between orders from the supermarkets . . . put pressure on suppliers who have little opportunity or incentive to check the legality of labor which helps meet these orders" (United Kingdom House of Commons Environment Food and Rural Affairs Committee 2002–2003: paragraph 25).

Making Workers "Permanently Temporary" "We employ people as we need them," explained one South African apple farm manager. "But you need to break their expectation of having a permanent position, so you hire for two to three weeks and then you let them off for a few weeks, and then you hire them again." Hiring farm workers through contractors, or gangmasters, is increasingly common in the countries of Oxfam's research. According to one South African apple grower who has halved his long-term workforce in the past five years and replaced them with contract workers, "Bad market conditions resulted in layoffs, [and] restructuring of the labor force . . . towards contract labor. What has happened with labor is that you can cut them out at short notice if the business profitability decreases." The impact of these practices on fruit-farm workers is stark. In one 2003 study in Ceres, a major fruit-producing area, over one in three households interviewed reported the loss of a long-term job in the past five years, and one in four households were entirely dependent on earnings from seasonal or temporary labor (du Toit 2003: 17).

The cost savings for farm managers from using contract labor were explained by one Chilean contractor in language that clearly reflects lean thinking: "Outsourcing helps firms to optimize the use of human resources, given that it 'eliminates deadweight' such as redundant payments during work delays or suspension of work due to weather conditions, and payments other than straight compensation." Temporary, seasonal, and casual farm workers get far fewer benefits and protections under law in most countries. In Colombia, Oxfam's research found some women flower workers who were paying out of their salaries for health coverage that they never received. "The employers deduct social security contributions," said one, "but when we go to the doctor, they say that the employer is not up to date or that we don't even appear in the system."

Paying Low Piece-Rates for Long Hours In Chile, our research found that one in three fruit pickers and packers paid by piece-rate earned the minimum wage or less. And they put in extraordinary hours to make it, facing an average working week of sixty-three hours, sometimes up to eighteen hours a day. Some workers reported their employers adjusted piece-rates earned to meet only minimum wage levels. As one worker, Ana, explained, "You're told you will earn so much per box, so you head off to work on that farm very satisfied, but once you are there, they don't pay you what you ought to get." In Colombia, flower workers' production targets have been significantly increased, from covering forty flower beds in 1996 to at least sixty beds in 2003, for the same pay. In the United States, at the height of the tomato-picking season in Florida, farm laborers work for seven days a week, eleven hours a day on piece-rates. For these hours, they would qualify for 148 hours of overtime pay per month, but U.S. federal and state laws exclude farm workers from that right.

Overtime is often far from voluntary: the requirements to meet shipping deadlines or same-day orders for just-in-time delivery frequently lead to compulsory late nights at short notice. Colombian flower workers can face up to seventy hours of compulsory overtime in a week, despite a legal limit of twelve, especially in the peak seasons of Valentine's Day and Mother's Day. And with the complex packing and labeling requirements of different supermarkets, fruit packhouse workers can also face up to eight hours of overtime in a day. "We are often told on the same day that we have to work overtime that evening," explained one South African woman packing fruit. "It is then our responsibility to make arrangements with the [transport] services we use. We have to pay for the phone call to change arrangements. . . . This is not fair—management should pay for these calls. . . . Women who have children have to make special arrangements. . . . We are not given adequate warning to come to work prepared" (Smith and others 2003: 10).

The industry-led drive for ethical practices in fresh produce supply chains is not yet as well-established or widespread as that in the garment industry, but the tensions with commercial practices are already clear. "We have met all the technical and social standards in Tesco's code [Nature's Choice]," said one table-grape grower in South Africa, "but instead of buying more of our fruit, they still go to other farms around here that have not. And then they ask why we are supplying their competitors. What do they expect us to do?" The contradiction between ethical and commercial performance is also felt by staff in the lead firms. According to a former fresh-produce buyer at a leading U.K. supermarket, "Buyers are caught in a high-pressure culture of weekly reporting on their sales and profit margin targets. Ethical trade just doesn't fit neatly into numbers, and so it gets left out of the picture."

Using Global Value Chain Analysis to Advocate for Change

Oxfam and many other NGOs and trade unions are increasingly using global value chain analysis as part of their strategies to improve labor conditions. Global value chain analysis is useful in three broad ways: leveraging greater impact through multi-stakeholder initiatives; informing strategies for innovative worker organizing; and helping to change the terms of public debate on flexible employment and national competitiveness. These are each described in this section.

Leveraging Greater Impact Through Multi-Stakeholder Initiatives

Improving labor rights often requires coordinated interventions addressing employer practices, government labor regulation, and efforts to strengthen worker organizations. Multi-stakeholder initiatives help to achieve this coordination by bringing together brand and retail firms with unions and nongovernmental organizations that are operating in both the country of production and the country of retail. Such initiatives, in early phases, typically focused their efforts around creating, implementing, and monitoring codes of conduct. Global value chain analysis has helped to change the terms of debate within these initiatives by redescribing the problem and so bringing far more evidence and attention to the role that brands' and retailers' own purchasing practices play in undermining the very labor standards their codes are intended to promote. Of course changing purchasing practices alone is no guarantee of farm and factory compliance with labor standards, because managers could appropriate for themselves the benefits provided by improved terms, instead of passing them on as better terms and conditions for workers. Codes of conduct are, hence, still critical as part of an integrated approach to change, along with worker organizing. Several initiatives are now under way to examine what can be done to change purchasing practices and to make them consistent with and complementary to existing efforts to implement codes of conduct.

The London-based Ethical Trading Initiative (ETI), whose members include leading retailers, NGOs, and trade unions, set up a multi-stakeholder pilot project in 2005, which includes six leading garment retailers, to examine the extent to which their purchasing practices are compatible with labor standard compliance in their supply chains.[4] The retailers are analyzing their critical paths from design to delivery, working with suppliers to understand the impact of key purchasing decisions, raising buyers' awareness of working conditions, and collaborating with other retailers to explore the impact of multiple buyers sourcing from one supplier. One company within this project, the clothing retailer Gap Inc., found that some of its practices were not only affecting working conditions but also causing problems for its own business regarding quality, on-time delivery, and cost. Steps that the company has considered to address the problems include improving their own adherence to a production calendar, redesigning their internal production processes, involving suppliers earlier, and encouraging feedback from them through a third party (Traidcraft 2006).

In a separate initiative, Impactt Limited, a supply chain management consultancy, worked with eleven purchasing companies (mostly U.K.-based brands and retailers) and a group of Chinese factories in a three-year project aiming to reduce the extreme overtime required of workers in those factories. The project showed that it is possible, through gradual change, to reduce workers' overtime while maintaining or even increasing their wages, by improving factory productivity, human resource management, and internal communications. These are, of course, areas of performance for which lead firms would provide training to any division of their own firm that they expected to operate as part of a lean production system. The project results show that if lead firms take steps to operationalize (rather than mimic) lean by investing in raising the management and production capacity of their suppliers, it can make a significant difference. Impactt's project also found, however, that these in-factory improvements were only sustainable so long as lead firms' buying practices were compatible with them, such as setting realistic lead times and sticking to agreed timetables (Impactt 2005).

On the basis of results obtained so far, global value chain analysis is very likely to grow in its usefulness for, and influence upon, multi-stakeholder initiatives. This will be particularly true if researchers producing sectoral studies more regularly integrate an analysis of value chain dynamics through to the level of workers in the production unit, rather than identifying the firm itself as the last level of analysis.

Women and Migrant Workers Creating Innovative Forms of Organizing

Women and migrant workers need to be able to organize effectively in order to redress power imbalances between themselves and both governments and firms, but traditional models of organizing—unionizing a permanent labor force working for a single employer—are unworkable in many of the contexts described here. Where stable jobs have been replaced by temporary, part-time, piece-rate, subcontracted, or home work, workers may even have difficulty identifying who is legally responsible for ensuring labor standards, or such workers may not be identified as stakeholders by ethical auditors. Global value chain analysis helps workers' organizations have a more accurate understanding of power relations in the industry and to identify the actors and practices that have the most negative impact. As a result, unions, women's organizations, and migrants' organizations have often built alliances, and combining their complementary skills, started organizing workers as a sector or within a community and negotiating with all employers in a certain supply chain in the area. These organizations have also collaborated with ethical code auditors to give voice to workers in flexible jobs.

The Nicaraguan organization of unemployed and working women "Maria Elena Cuadra" (MEC), for example, has a membership consisting of currently employed as well as laid-off garment workers and has negotiated with factory employers about ending violence and harassment and improving health and safety standards. Likewise, the Self-Employed Women's Association (SEWA) in India has developed a membership organization including industrial home workers capable of negotiating with employers in their sector or region. SEWA has supported the ETI Homeworkers Project, in which U.K.-based clothing retailers, supply chain agents, NGOs, and unions have worked together to modify practices that have a negative impact on the home workers' labor conditions. In the United Kingdom, the Trades Union Congress (TUC) has collaborated with organizations of home workers and migrants to do outreach to these groups of workers and to create a new category of membership status for workers in nonstandard jobs. In South Africa, the Women on Farms project has helped form a new union, Sikhula Sonke, of daily agricultural workers. Women on Farms and Sikhula Sonke have had meetings with leading U.K. supermarkets about evidence collected through global value chain analyses of the fresh produce industry. According to the project's director, Fatima Shabodien, the two organizations have successfully negotiated with employers for improvements in health and safety conditions on fruit farms.[5]

Changing the Perceptions of Governments Regarding Flexible Labor Laws
Part of the reason why governments are introducing more flexible labor laws and allowing excessive workplace practices is because these are perceived as enhancing the competitiveness of the industry, and hence the national economy. An extremely flexible workforce is sometimes seen as an inevitable dimension of foreign investment, rather than a consequence of certain ways of managing global supply chains. What is not counted in this assessment are the longer-term, hidden costs of precarious employment borne by women

workers, their families, and wider society. Global supply chain analysis can usefully contribute to public debates about the benefits and costs of flexible employment to various stakeholders, and thus about which labor legislation is optimum for the country.

Documenting the hidden costs of precarious employment will help generate alternative perspectives on what constitutes an efficient "value-creating" supply chain because it widens the range of stakeholders whose perception of value is taken into account. The assessment of value should not just be in terms of the value that accrues to the retailer that ordered the product, nor in terms of the immediate export value to the country that is now a popular sourcing location. It should also be made in terms of the value created by the industry with respect to the longer-term interests of the individuals employed and the society in which it is operating.

During Oxfam International's launch of *Trading Away Our Rights* (2004a), some discussions began between government officials and alliances of labor organizations about the "hidden costs" of these supply chain practices for women workers and their families. Many worker alliances, however, met with standard objections that labor flexibility was essential for the competitiveness of an industry and hence of the country, and therefore that the (small) costs to individuals were "worth it." The alliances saw that they needed additional documentation to support their claim that this is not always the case, both because global supply chain actors could operate differently and because of hidden costs for society and industry. Oxfam and partners began to identify and gather evidence about potential costs for society—for example, rising health care costs due to the chronic conditions suffered by garment workers required to work long hours at breakneck speeds, untreated illnesses of workers on temporary status who are denied social insurance benefits, or poor educational outcomes of children who have little parental supervision or attention. Likewise, we began to document the potential costs for industry itself—for example, the cost of rejects from low-quality production that is more likely from a transient, demoralized, and exhausted workforce.

There is a lack of evidence about the personal and social costs of "flexible labor." For example, we have not found longitudinal studies documenting the impact on labor force productivity and health caused by the intensive, long hours of work currently found in the garment industry. Only by documenting and understanding the long-term costs to workers' health and their

children's education, and the wider costs of family instability and social fragmentation, can we have a real debate about the benefits and costs of labor
force "flexibility."

Some government and industry officials are recognizing the negative impacts and so are slightly modifying their stance. Although changes in their
public statements are incremental steps toward significant change in workers'
lives, we believe that accepted ideas and beliefs, as expressed through public
statements, are an important element of creating that change. A significant
initial step in changing the situation is for governments simply to acknowledge that "flexible" employment can be problematic. Likewise, retail industry
representatives need to acknowledge the role played by their own purchasing
practices in perpetuating poor labor standards in their suppliers' farms and
factories.

Following the launch of *Trading Away Our Rights*, some officials publicly
affirmed that precarious employment was a development concern. The coor-
dinator of the United Nations Development Program's National Human Development Report in El Salvador acknowledged that labor market flexibility
did not bring automatic benefits, and that these policies should be assessed
in regard to human development.[6] In Indonesia, the director of the National
Board for Development Planning (BAPPENAS) revised downward his assessment of the benefits provided by labor flexibility reforms implemented in
2003. Although reforms were expected to stimulate employment and protect
subcontracted workers, he stated in November 2004 that provisions of the
Act needed to be improved, especially those dealing with subcontracting.[7] In
the United Kingdom, the secretary of state for trade and industry acknowledged the link between unprotected employment and gender and race inequality when announcing reforms to minimum wage regulations to benefit piece-rate workers: "The change to the home working rules will protect
people who work in an industry that has a history of exploitative rates of pay,
especially [to] minority ethnic and women workers" (Department of Trade
and Industry 2004).

Conclusion

We return to the definition of lean production with which we began: lin-
ing up all the value-creating activities for a specific product with the goal of

eliminating waste, defined as "any human activity which absorbs resources but creates no value" (Womack and Jones 1996). The problem with this conception of an efficient production system lies in the question of who defines what constitutes value. Victors traditionally write the history books, and in global value chains, it seems, lead firms define "value." But such a conception of value creates supply chains that offload costs and risks onto suppliers who, in turn, offload them onto workers. These translate into significant "disvalues" for workers in the way that they are employed and the impact it has on themselves, their families, and their communities. At the national level, the wider and longer-term social costs of this precarious employment typically go uncounted because they are not recognized to be significant, and are not documented along with data on jobs created and export revenues generated.

Global value chain analysis can provide a very effective framework for leveraging change and improving labor standards, as discussed in this chapter. Trade unions and NGOs such as Oxfam that are supporting women workers to secure their labor rights place high importance on getting workers' voices heard in debates on global industries (and seeing these voices reflected in the literature on global value chains) because they reveal a great deal about the development impacts of "mimicking lean." This potential can only be realized, however, if global value chain analysis does not take the firm to be the smallest unit of analysis but goes one step further to integrate the impacts on workers of chain pressures and dynamics. We hope that the research and initiatives cited in this chapter give an indication of the significant difference that this can make.

9 Unveiling the Unveiling

Commodity Chains, Commodity Fetishism, and the "Value" of Voluntary, Ethical Food Labels

Julie Guthman

LABELS AND STANDARDS FOR COMMODITIES THAT ARE PRODUCED with more attention to ecological or social values have become a key form of political action to mitigate neoliberalism's race to the bottom. These labels are especially common in the realm of food, as the well-known examples of "organic," "fair trade," and even "*terroir*" attest. As a form of politics, their purpose is twofold. One is to make transparent how the commodities are produced, under the assumption that if people know where their food comes from they will make more ethical consumption choices. The other is to protect land, other natural resources, and labor from the ravages of the market by shifting the loci of value production and retention. To this latter end, these protective labels are necessarily voluntary, in the sense of not being mandated by state regulation, and thus are designed to capture value for certain producers. To have a meaningful effect for either purpose, however, these labeling claims must demonstrate that the ascribed commodities are different from other commodities, and the claims must be substantiated. There is no credible label, that is, without standards and verification.

A crucial, if obvious question, is whether these voluntary labels are effective in meeting these twin purposes. What do they reveal (and hide)? What or who do they protect (and hurt)? One way, albeit a partial one, to adjudicate these questions is to put different labeling systems through a commodity or value chain lens. As discussed throughout this volume (as well as in this chapter), commodity chain methodologies are both descriptive and normative. In other words they can be employed to describe (to explain), to create transparency (to reveal), and to capture value (to redistribute). Yet, as I will demonstrate, even in the ideal, different sorts of labels significantly vary as to what they reveal and what they protect; as they are operationalized their differences (and weaknesses) are made even clearer. For one, they fundamentally depend on forms of exclusion to be effective. Yet despite my abiding skepticism of labels as a vehicle of social and environmental improvement, they may be all that there is. In other words, it may be that at this political juncture, to use Margaret Thatcher's unfortunate phrase, "there is no alternative." So then the question becomes, What sort of broader politics do they provoke (and constrain)? That is, is it possible that although their apparent effects are anemic, they put processes into motion with far larger potential to effect progressive change?

This chapter thus has three aims. Its primary purpose is to theorize the relationship between the commodity chain approach and these voluntary ethical food labels as a form of politics;[1] a secondary one is to subject the labels themselves to the scrutiny of a commodity chain approach to see (1) what they reveal or hide and (2) what or who they protect through value capture. A tertiary purpose is to suggest, albeit briefly, how these labels might provoke a broader politics beyond their immediate effects. Throughout the chapter I will be touching on the notions of commodity fetishism and value, because both are so central to the overall questions. Empirically, I will draw my examples mainly from organics, my particular area of research, although I will also make more cursory comments on other labeling schemes. I begin, then, with a discussion of the commodity chain approach and its politics.

Politicizing Commodity Chains

As should be clear from reading this volume, the commodity chain approach can be typologized in several different ways (for example, disciplinarily, schools of thought, even ontologically).[2] Some scholars, including some in this volume, focus on chain governance as the key differentiating variable. In light of many of the things I will be discussing, namely the proliferation of ethical products and the increasing power of private systems of regulation to construct and ensure quality in certain spheres of commodity production, they are now positing the existence of regulation- or consumer-driven commodity chains (Gereffi, Humphrey, and Sturgeon 2005; Gibbon 2001a). This surely demonstrates the blurring of descriptive and normative uses of the commodity chain approach, which I will differentiate. Nevertheless, for the purposes of this chapter I want to suggest a taxonomy that draws out just those programmatic distinctions and puts them on a short continuum.

The vast majority of work using commodity chain methodologies is fundamentally descriptive, albeit in various ways. For example commodity chains have been used to examine industrial organization, a usage that seems to have origins in French industrial economics. Montfort and Dutailly (1983) first used the term *filière* to refer to a set of firms linked vertically in the creation of a single product. The organizational structure of an economy could then best be understood and described as a collection of constituent *filières,* or commodity chains. Geographers and heterodox economists have borrowed from this usage to discuss technological and economic interdependencies between spatially proximate buyers and suppliers, as well as firms linked horizontally in relations of cooperation (Storper 1997). Implicit to this usage is the recognition that the specificity of the nature of and market for different commodities bears on, if not determines, the social relations that bring them to fruition (Barham, Bunker, and O'Hearn 1994).

Commodity chains have also been used to describe globalization. To be sure, in charting the geographical path commodities take from conceptualization to use, the approach has created a methodological window onto all sorts of questions relevant to economic geography. So, for example, although the global commodity chain approach highlights the vertical "slice" of a given product's trip from design and inputs to consumption (Gereffi and Korzeniewicz 1994), its inherent spatiality, along with commodity specificity, has afforded a new lens onto theorizations of uneven development. For that reason, among others, geographers Leslie and Reimer (1999) have recently argued that commodities and their components should be analyzed not only by how they travel *through* space, but also by how their production, consumption, and regulation are shaped by and produce space and place.

These insights as to how commodity chains shape social relations over space easily lead to more politically explicit uses of the commodity chain approach. For some scholars, the very justification for scrutinizing a commodity borrows from Marx's notion of commodity fetishism: the necessary masking of the social relations under which commodities are produced. Such masking allows capitalist commodity production to retain much of its legitimacy. Commodity chain analysis then becomes an unveiling of sorts—a way to show and have seen how commodities are really produced as a first step in transforming social relations (Hartwick 1998; Hudson and Hudson 2003). The idea that society-*nature* relations are equally concealed in commodity production but can also be opened up to scrutiny is in keeping with this perspective (Allen and Kovach 2000). There is a geographic dimension to this approach as well, for the distanciation putatively inherent to globalization makes the commodity all the more inscrutable as to how it is made and distributed (Harvey 1990; Hartwick 1998; Hudson and Hudson 2003). It should be noted that this particular emphasis has somewhat oblique origins in the world-systems approach that spawned early work in commodity chains analysis (Hopkins and Wallerstein 1986). As the chapters by Bair and Wallerstein in this volume remind us, in calling this linked set of processes a commodity chain, world-systems theorists sought to reaffirm the existence of an international division of labor and to recognize social reproduction (the production of workers as commodities) as part of this division of labor. Although this was originally a programmatic move to shift the unit of analysis in international political economy away from the nation-state, concerns with the transparency of commodity movements in relations of "unequal exchange" also raised the question as to where *value* is added, appropriated, and distributed, leading us to the third usage.

The third programmatic usage is explicitly redistributional, then, with the point being (borrowing from a familiar phrase) not to describe the chain but to change it. The idea here is that commodity chains can be regulated in such a way as to shift where value is appropriated, to favor some actors in the chain over others. The origins of this particular emphasis can also be found within the global commodity chain approach, most associated with Gereffi (1994). In bringing focus to *inter-firm behavior,* and specifically the power dynamics among different firms in a chain, researchers hoped to gain insight into nodes of value capture and retention. The conceit of the global value chain literature is precisely that national development prospects can be improved by industrial "upgrading" to processes that produce or capture more value (Gereffi, Humphrey, and Sturgeon 2005; Gibbon 2001a), although the overall approach remains elusive about where value actually comes from. Recently Kaplinsky (2004) has argued that surplus distribution along a given chain is a function of rent-generating barriers to entry that are in turn a function of chain governance. Rents thus become the source of value; rents make possible redistribution.

It is striking that similar ideas have been developed by agro-food scholars prior to or outside of the emergence of the commodity or value chain approaches. It is even arguable that value capture is more *possible* with food commodities because of certain characteristics of those commodities. This, then, is the topic of the next section.

Commodity Chains and Agro-Food Exceptionalism

Despite the recent surge in popularity for commodity and value chain analysis (as evidenced in this and other recent volumes), such analysis has long been a workhorse of scholars in the anthropology, sociology, and geography of food and agriculture. Yet it seems to have evolved somewhat independently from those approaches that focused on manufactured goods, in part because commodity chain methodologies in agro-food research developed precisely to address a number of methodological issues unique to food as an object of study. In this section I want to feature some of the major developments in this area, both to demonstrate how the uses of commodity chains in agro-food studies have differed and to suggest how it is that voluntary food labeling has become such a prevalent site of action. In doing so I hope to point to how such labeling schemes differ from, say, sweat-free apparel.

The seedling was Friedland's (1984; Friedland, Barton, and Thomas 1981) path-breaking work in "commodity systems analysis," which focused on the mutual interaction of production practices, grower organization, labor, science and extension, and marketing and distribution systems on the production of agricultural commodities. The purpose of this exercise was in part to show that food production is rarely internalized into one firm and, as a result, is highly influenced by the network of actors that are tangential to the fields. It also illustrated the importance of commodity specificity. Not only are tomatoes not like widgets, unable to conform perfectly to the exigencies of factory production, but tomatoes are also not like lettuce. In this regard, Friedland was building on—if sometimes reluctantly if one is familiar with his life's work—a large literature on agricultural exceptionalism, particularly that which highlighted how crop specificity, perishability, and seasonality, and the nonidentity of labor time and production time, affected the organization of production and distribution (Bunker 1989; Kautsky [1899] 1988; Mann 1989).

In a similar vein, early work by David Goodman and his colleagues (Goodman, Sorj, and Wilkinson 1987; Goodman and Redclift 1991) noted that food systems are fundamentally dependent on biophysical production, to the extent that much of the value received in the market is created by biological processes. Yet the riskiness of biological production has made agriculture relatively unattractive for industrial capitals. Capital has been more likely to enter into sectors in which technologies exist to overcome or regularize nature, and, they posited, these opportunities for more predictable profitmaking could be found in discrete activities that could be removed from the rural setting and put into factories. In that way they explained the rise of the agricultural input and food-processing industries more generally and certainly contributed to understandings of the salience of genetic engineering technologies today. Although they did not engage the language of commodity chains, at least initially (compare Goodman and Watts 1994), in effect their argument was that available technology would shape the length and complexity of a given commodity chain.

Ben Fine combined aspects of both approaches in his systems-of-provision framework. Seeking to explain food consumption, Fine gave centrality to the uniqueness of any given commodity in shaping its provision and, hence, its consumption (Fine and Leopold 1993; Fine 1994, 1998; Fine, Heasman, and Wright 1996). Besides his insistence on the verticality of any given system of provision as a way of understanding causality, he brought two further insights to the commodity system approach. One is that food systems are thoroughly dependent on agriculture and particularly land as a major factor of production. Consequently, the historically contingent ways in which landed property intervenes into the accumulation process and the various ways that rents are appropriated influences both the scale and intensity of accumulation (Fine 1994). The other is that food systems are shaped by the organic (that is, biological) content of the food in question at *all instances* along the commodity chain. Therefore, all systems of provision are necessarily affected by the metabolic processes of eating and digestion. Here, Fine went to great lengths to contrast this insight with that of Goodman and Redclift (1991) who, he claims, only considered the organic content at each end of the chain (in other words, the beginning as a growing plant or animal, the end as metabolized through the human body).

Since this early work, many agro-food scholars have attempted to lengthen and deepen commodity chain methodology, especially in reference to accusations that it is too economistic in light of the deep cultural content of eating and food. Friedland (2001) appended the idea of "commodity culture" to the commodity systems framework, suggesting that beliefs about certain commodities may also play a determinative role in their production (more so with certain commodities than others, he claims). Dixon's (1997) cultural economy approach proved to be a more integrative corrective to the problem of "culture" and consumption.[3] Recognizing how production has largely been relegated to the purview of economics with its privileging of material explanation, and consumption the purview of anthropology with its current favoring of the symbolic, Dixon aptly pointed to how production (the creation of value) has been too often understood as that which happens at the factory (or field) while consumption (the sharing of meanings) as that which happens within the household. Accordingly, there is a methodological and conceptual break when the consumer arrives home to cook the food; value added thereafter is not counted as work, adding a clear gender dimension to the problematic, as well. Alternatively, she said, we need to acknowledge production within the household and nonmarket exchanges in the whole chain of provision, including "the trade in representations and the processes of transferring symbolic value" (152). FitzSimmons and Goodman's (1998) discussion of the co-metabolism of symbolic and corporeal nourishment (also Goodman 1999) enriched and extended Dixon's schema even further, with its insight that the *ingestion* of food sustains both laboring bodies and thinking subjects.

Other correctives to commodity analysis have reflected new developments in social theory as well as disciplinary concerns. Following Fine's concerns with ground rent and pre-dating the recent flush of value chain analysis, Guthman (2002, 2004) explored how commodity meanings can produce economic rents, even to be imputed into land values. DuPuis (1998) suggested that commodity chain analysis (and political ecology) must take more seriously what happens at the "other end" of the chain, calling for what she calls a political ecology of the body. In recognition of the social embeddedness of actors (and their "agency"), others looked at how relations of trust are forged between buyers and sellers along what are otherwise quite tenuous chains, particularly when perishable crops are at stake (Arce and Marsden 1993; Freidberg 2004). Finally (but not exhaustively), the idea of a chain has been superseded with that of the network, in recognition that there are multiple and multidirectional influences on, in this case, commodity production (Whatmore and Thorne 1997).

Thus far I have made little mention of the labor process in agriculture other than noting the nonidentity of production and labor time (meaning that crops grow and animals graze with little human work going on). Yet this is significant too. Building on Chayanov ([1924] 1986), Mann (1989) argued that this nonidentity creates an obstacle to capitalist production, which seeks smoothness and regularity. She then went on to use this to explain the persistence of the family farm. Although she has been proven wrong empirically, the point that agricultural labor is irregularly applied is important, and, as many have argued, contributes to the more general social vulnerability of peasants and farm laborers. In addition, Benton (1989) has noted that agricultural labor tends to be what he calls "eco-regulatory" rather than productive. By this he means that labor processes in agriculture tend to create and improve the conditions of agricultural production but do not produce the product. The same could possibly be said of food production and processing—certainly labor processes must work around, enhance, or take care of the biological content. That labor itself is not always productive in the classic sense perhaps contributes to the social devaluation of food and agricultural labor. At the same time, that certain types of food labor are treated as crafts (for example, cheese and wine-making, restaurant cooking)—the exceptions that prove the rule—may provide some hints regarding the efficacy of voluntary food labels. For their point is in part to revalorize food and agricultural labor so the people who do this labor can be adequately compensated.

Finally, notwithstanding earlier accounts of a "world steer" (Sanderson 1986) nor the many studies of global food supply chains, most scholars of agrofood systems would agree that food supply chains are not equivalent to those of manufactured goods (Goodman and Watts 1994). They are usually simpler in terms of the number of contributing supply chains—even comparing, say, a frozen TV dinner to a car, and not forgetting the crop protection inputs, food processing aids, and genetic technologies that likely went into that dinner. They are often considerably shorter in terms of the number of intermediaries, particularly with perishable foods.

In short, much has been said about the uniqueness of agricultural commodities, and many of these ideas bear on the commodity chain methodology. But the primary reason I have rehearsed these arguments is to shed light on how it is that food has become such a locus for ethical commodity production. Taken together (and the points I make here are hardly exhaustive), this literature points to the need to take nature as biology seriously, as a source of value, as an "obstacle" to capitalist or at least factory production for certain segments of production, as a source of anxiety in the trade of agricultural products (here I discussed perishability but certainly food-borne disease looms large), and as a metabolic or digestive function in food (Olestra and such notwithstanding). All of these aspects in some sense uniquely shape the production, distribution, and consumption of agricultural commodities and provide some explanation for shorter supply chains.

I have also nodded to the intense cultural meanings associated with food and agriculture, which exist quite literally along the entire commodity chain, from soil to digestive waste. Although much more could be said—and has been said—many scholars rest this intensity of feeling on the fact that food is "the intimate commodity," one of the few that enters in and passes through our bodies. It seems, then, that it is some combination of the "ick factor" of food, the immediacy of its moral content, and the centrality of agriculture in both developmental and environmental imaginaries that makes food more subject to ethicalization. Yet one of the key reasons, I would argue, that food has become subject to these labeling schemes is that it can be. It seems relatively easy to make a food supply chain transparent; it is certainly thinkable that such chains can be regulated in a way that alters where value is appropriated. And it is precisely with these relatively attenuated supply chains that we see these labels flourishing: coffee, produce, cheese. For that matter, it is relatively easy to make a food label work as a regulatory space, particularly in so far as consumers are used to reading food labels for information. Nevertheless, to do so still requires the commodification of nontangibles. This leads us back to the two central problematics that weave through this entire discussion: commodity fetishism and the meaning of value.

Commodity Fetishism and the Indeterminacy of Value

As I have stated, the purpose of voluntary, ethical food labels is twofold. One is to make transparent how the transformation of nature and use of labor are different in the commodities they describe from that of common commodities; the other is to redistribute value along the supply chain to favor certain producers and land uses. These objectives are not straightforward analytically. The former assumes some version of commodity fetishism; the latter assumes the determinacy and stability of value.

If commodity chain analysis purports an unveiling of how commodities are produced in a global economy (Hartwick 2000; Harvey 1990), it should stand to logic that those commodities which are claimed to be produced in more ecologically sustainable or socially just ways are intended to *reveal* the social and natural conditions under which they are produced and circulated (see Hudson and Hudson [2003], who use the language of peeling away the veil quite liberally). This purposeful defetishization is seen by many as a sort of positive politics, and, again, it is particularly common with food. As Bell and Valentine (1997) suggest, food labeling in particular is a way to provide heretofore concealed information about the materials and processes that agricultural producers incorporate or avoid. I have observed that many producers of alternative food commodities trade on the presumption that if only people really knew what they were eating, they would act differently in their purchasing choices, and many consumers purchase their products precisely because they feel that commodities are "unveiled." This conviction surely has to do with the intimacy of food as well; the "ick" factor figures prominently (although then one also has to explain why it is that people eat McDonald's hamburgers despite what they know).

Nevertheless, the idea of commodity fetishism (along with false consciousness) has come under considerable intellectual attack of late. These criticisms, though related, employ three somewhat separate arguments. Some question macro-notions of social power in constituting food networks in the first place and therefore reject attempts to locate the sources of such power (Lockie and Kitto 2000). Some question whether unveiling the truth is even possible (Reimer and Leslie 2004). Instead, we are exhorted to "get with the fetish" by finding the ruptures and reworking them into other meanings (Cook, Crang, and Thorpe 2004). The most damning criticism of the commodity fetishism idea, however, is that it assumes the consumer to be a dupe, a final player in a top-down chain of provision, and not a conscious, reflexive actor in the semiotic-material world in which he or she takes part (Goodman and DuPuis 2002; Lockie 2002). It may well be that, in the case of fast food, consumers do know where their food comes from and are making a Faustian bargain for, say, cheaper, more convenient food (DuPuis 2001). This line of thinking, however, does not dispense with the commodity chain methodology and its implied relations of power and value, but rather takes the consumer quite seriously as an actor within the commodity chain.

Yet if the notion of commodity fetishism is made untenable, the idea that commodities, and in this case ethical commodities, "speak for themselves" so that consumers are wholly enlightened must be put to the same scrutiny. For it seems that the idea of ethical labeling puts a good deal of weight on the ability of the label to produce knowledge and the desire of the consumer to consume knowledge, thereby reinforcing neoclassical assumptions of consumer sovereignty. Commodity fetishism may not be tantamount to false consciousness, the latter of which implies a willful ignorance, but neither can defetishization produce perfect knowledge, or, for that matter, a willingness to pay for that knowledge.

The question of value is thus related. Assuming "normal" conditions of competition under capitalism, for a commodity to be protective of the environment, classes of people, or both, it must realize value for the targeted actors above and beyond what they would receive otherwise. This extra value is what provides the necessary cushion to preclude a competitive "race to the bottom." Optimally, this cushion would allow for all "needs" of social reproduction and the replacement or renewal of used natural resources; minimally it would create conditions less exploitive than existing arrangements. Even if the goal is not explicitly monetary, but rather, say, better working conditions, it seems a necessary if not sufficient condition that the unit of production retains more value to allow for lower productivity. In that way, ethical commodities by definition are redistributive. Although they may appropriate value from other nodes of the supply chain, they are more likely to target a redistribution of income from consumers to primary commodity producers and their productive assets. Of importance, attempts at ethicality that are not redistributive can worsen social conditions. This is best exemplified in the new European ethical trade initiatives, such as Eurepgap, which are designed to have all producers conform to what are presumably higher standards (Campbell 2005). The problem is that meeting these standards is so onerous and costly that, much like ethical initiatives in Britain, they force certain producers out of the market (Freidberg 2003a) or into informal or illicit markets (Dunn 2003).[4]

But what is the source of this value? Value is far too complicated to be critically examined in a chapter of this scope, so a few propositions will have to suffice. Classical political economy assumes that the origin of value is in the labor applied in producing a commodity—the labor theory of value. Roughly speaking, the source of profit (surplus value) is the difference between the remuneration of labor and the value of commodities as realized in the market in the form of prices. It also assumes that markets are clearing; in other words, that prices equilibrate supply and demand and, moreover, that perfect competition ensures that prices do not generally rise above costs plus a normalized profit margin. It follows that value received in the market beyond the "normal" rate of return is based on some sort of scarcity, whether naturally or socially created. These over-profits are what economists call rent—an unusually high return to a factor of production. And though generally these rents are founded on supposedly rare inputs, or temporary technological efficiencies in the case of so-called Schumpeterian rents, they can also result from consumers' culturally constructed wants and needs and regulations that create industry-specific monopoly conditions, including the establishment of intellectual property rights. As Kaplinsky (2004) notes, it is precisely these nontangible pieces of value chains that are increasingly sources of rent in today's political economy. Yet it is also these two sources of rent that figure into ethical commodities. As I will suggest, consumers' constructed desires to be ethical can be met in producers' intellectual property rights in the form of labels.

As with notions of commodity fetishism, this idea of the source of value is contentious. Besides arguments from neoclassical economics that see the origin of profit in exchange, even among scholars sympathetic to classical political economy, value is seen as more elusive than as implied in the labor theory of value and theories of rent. First of all, as Sayer (2003) argues, the use values of commodities can be inclusive of moral concerns, irrespective of how exchange values circulate. In other words, moral concerns do not necessarily enter into the commodified value of things. Second, as Graeber (1996) discusses, any system of value entails struggle over definition, in part because what is being exchanged is noncommensurable between two actors (although the exchange makes them so); that being obtained is an object of desire, that being let go is by definition expendable. But if value, as he says, is "something that mobilizes the desires of those who recognize it" (12), what does that suggest in a supply chain that involves many nodes between primary producers and consumers, especially when the object of desire is not just a thing but a desire to be just and ethical? Surely, value in such a case becomes pretty slippery. Henderson throws an additional wrench into the problematic when he states that "values that inhere in commodities become relative to each other," and that value is always in the process of being mediated by a nonvalued or devalued force, to the extent that "value itself can be a destabilizing force" (2004: 491). Such would seem to hold for ethical commodities; the devaluation of labor and natural resource renewal of primary producers under current conditions of neoliberalism are exactly what have to figure in their moral valuation for consumers. In such a situation, these two poles of value seem strikingly incommensurable and would certainly call into question whether the price paid by the ethical consumer can really make up the "true cost" of that devaluation, or if, instead, it constitutes a sort of moral rent.

The inherent relativity of value in ethical commodity chains (and likely elsewhere) returns us to the fetish. To defetishize a commodity is to make clear the value of the commodity by unveiling the many steps of value-added it has been through along the supply chain. This is no easy task, particularly when value is based on devaluation. For to really understand value, Graeber says, is to understand an object's history. Mistaking the history of the object for the object itself is the fetish. In that way, mirroring one's own desires to "do good" onto a commodity that has been tagged as ethical could arguably constitute a double fetish.

These are difficult issues, which are not easily resolved. Rather than attempt to adjudicate the debates on commodity fetishism and value once and for all, I want to look at what goes into making these voluntary commodities ethical qua commodities by focusing on the institutions and mechanisms that operationalize these labels. This attempt to unveil the unveiling will no doubt be construed as a suggestion that ethical consumers are indeed dupes. Although I would argue that it is the mechanism and not consumer knowledge and intention that is at the crux of the problem, I do ask the reader to countenance the idea that the ethical commodity is to some degree a fetish, and that its value is produced by regulatory mechanisms that capture moral concern and turn it into something akin to rent.[5] To these issues, I now turn.

Operationalizing Protective Labels

How then do these labels produce transparency or offer redistribution? In three key steps: standard setting, verification, and establishment of barriers to entry, all designed to produce an economic incentive (price premium) to reward (or compensate for) those who do things differently. Crucially, all involve boundary setting that is at once protective and exclusionary (DuPuis and Goodman 2005). Indeed, exclusion is what allows this sort of politics of consumption to transpire at all—a critical point to consider in terms of its political efficacy.

Standards are the first step to protection. Standards, as Busch says, are a way of defining what is socially desirable and what is not, of disciplining people and things (2000: 274). Standards thus delineate the production processes, material uses, employment practices, and so forth that are the basis of any sort of labeling claim and thus set boundaries around what is good and bad. Voluntary, proactive standards—the topic of this inquiry—must be based on demonstrable difference from conventional commodities. Accordingly, they must give the impression that only some can meet those standards—the first moment of exclusion. So in the case of organics, the standards are a product of a long and variegated political history, but in the United States boil down to the disallowance of certain materials that have been deemed "synthetic" (although that definition is much more complicated than I am portraying it here). Those without the technical know-how to avoid these inputs or who grow crops where adequate substitutes for such inputs have yet to be developed are effectively excluded from organic production, whether or not they incorporate other practices that may be associated with organic agriculture.

For standards to be a meaningful form of regulation, they also have to be verified. Verification is what makes supply chains legible, traceable, and believable. Verification is also central to what Power (1997) calls the new "audit society." Therefore, we must take seriously the effects of audit as well as the substance of the standards themselves. In the case of organics, verification is accomplished through third-party certification, a process that determines whether organic foods are produced in accordance with established standards. To be certified, growers must fill out elaborate paperwork, including a farm plan; agree to initial, annual, and perhaps spot inspections; fulfill whatever requirements there are for crop or soil sampling; pay various dues, fees, and assessments (which become part of a value chain); and, of course, agree to abide by the practices and input restrictions designated by that agency and the law itself. Once certified, growers have a right to sell that product as organic. The cost and hassle of going through certification, as well as the increased surveillance that verification entails, obviously exclude some people from participation. In fact, insofar as certification processes themselves are produced and consumed, they partially constitute the value chain (Mutersbaugh 2005).[6]

Finally, to realize the benefits of such standards—to ensure the protective price premium—depends on the construction and maintenance of quasi-monopoly conditions. Although all elements of organic regulation can be onerous, and the challenge of growing certain crops in compliance with organic standards is a barrier in its own right, the key barrier to entry is a required three-year transition to organic production. During the transition period, for instance, many growers operate on a lower margin or even a loss; yields generally decline at the initial withdrawal of conventional inputs, at the same time that crops must be sold at conventional prices. In return for meeting these regulatory burdens, organic growers expect to receive a price premium for the crops they sell. Here it is important to note that California (which was the basis of the now existing federal rule) once had a one-year transition period to organic production, and it was at the behest of already certified growers that it was extended to three years.

Although such rules are attempts to avoid the erosion of rents that the organic designation is designed to protect, rent-seeking competition is nevertheless unleashed. The erosion of the price premium in organics is a consequence of these rent-seeking dynamics. As it turns out, the entry barriers to organic production proved to be fairly surmountable. Many growers have skirted the three-year transition period by bringing fallow or marginal land into production. Rent-seeking has also taken the form of political interventions in the standards or verification to allow easier entry. The most recent and significant example of this is Tyson's intervention in organic livestock regulations to remove the organic feed requirement. Starbucks's recent attempts to eliminate the price guarantee from fair trade (which would basically eviscerate any meaning for fair trade) tell a similar tale. The paradox, of course, is that those who are already protected by such labels are often hurt by the proliferation of the very thing they want to advocate for. The tension between spreading the practices of sustainable agriculture and upholding a "strong" organic standard that few can meet has been the central fight of organic regulation.

The construction of barriers, then, is the key moment, and the form they take determines who can participate and on what terms. And though all give rise to monopoly rents of sorts (an argument I pursue at length in Guthman 2004), they may offer protection from the ravages of the market. But then, it behooves us to examine what or who is being protected by these labels (what redistributive potential they hold) and, of course, who is being excluded. For example, those labels that aim to protect other than a set of environmental production practices have different sorts of enforcement and different sorts of barriers. Craft labels, such as Parmigiana Reggiano, arguably are designed to protect an unalienated labor process and thus retain value for the cheese maker. The gatekeepers of these labels are usually those already trained in the craft who apprentice a select group of newcomers. In contrast, *terroir* purports to safeguard particular qualities of land that are supposed to produce a certain taste. Access to designated land provides a formidable barrier to entry, protecting those who already have that access and giving rise to monopoly ground rent. The commonality of these two designations is that they are protective of existing producers with access to land and craft; they are not redistributive per se, but they can protect against erosion of those producers' livelihoods. Fair trade labels, then, are the only existing food labels that are clearly redistributive in their intent, and perhaps in their practice, although emerging research is calling fair trade into question for other reasons (Shreck 2005).

The point, though, is that even fair trade is necessarily exclusionary, as it requires standards and verification processes that at the very least impose certain startup costs on producers. It seems impossible to have a protective label without some sort of created scarcity, and it appears that the most effective of these labels are highly exclusionary, protecting those with existing access to land or a craft. Meanwhile, those voluntary labels in which protection is implied but no evidence is given that they are operationalized at all are the worse sort of "green-washing," and thus fetishization of ethicality itself.

Conclusion

I have attempted to demonstrate that to transform productive relations to those that are less exploitive takes redistribution and a mechanism to prevent further redistributions of values—in other words, barriers to entry. That these barriers to entry are necessarily political and regulatory points to the *indeterminacy* of value distribution (although it still presumes that value itself is determinable). Even still, protective labels are not a panacea; they can only protect certain people no matter how they are construed, and unfortunately, people with something of value for consumers. Among other things, this puts a tremendous amount of moral onus on wealthy consumers to choose wisely. Consider all the producers in the world of commodities that are not of interest to latte lovers or, for that matter, producers of nonfood commodities. They are looked over entirely in what Michael Goodman (2004) calls "developmental consumption." So even in the best of circumstances, protection is highly uneven.

So what about the unveiling part—the defetishization that commodity chain analysis promises? On the one hand, these analyses unveil the distribution of value, but they never unveil the meaning of value itself—for ultimately value itself is relative, not just its distribution. Furthermore, the idea that transparency and accountability can induce change without spelling out the normative foundations of "ethical" behavior, or, for that matter, justice, seems to fetishize ethicality. On the other hand, if labels are one of the few tools available to mitigate the injustices and destruction of neoliberalization, it may be worth saving the bathwater over the baby in this case. Because although the labels themselves may be limited in their positive effect and even produce perverse outcomes, their saving grace may be in their unintended consequences. That is, in a world where activist politics have been highly constrained by larger political economic forces, voluntary labeling may be one of the few tools available to provoke a broader politics. They may help embarrass (or encourage) major suppliers into changing their practices, as Unilever did in nearly abandoning the use of genetically engineered supplies of grain for its European market. They may make transparent corporate vulnerabilities that activists can exploit (see Chapter 10, by Munro and Schurman, in this volume). They might even produce new political subjects, who will create still unimagined forms of collective action and resistance in a rapidly changing world.

10 Chain (Re)actions

Comparing Activist Mobilization Against Biotechnology in Britain and the United States

William A. Munro and Rachel A. Schurman

D URING THE LAST HALF OF THE 1990S, EUROPEAN PUBLICS were barraged with media stories about genetically modified organisms (GMOs). Articles on "Frankenfoods" splashed across the pages of daily newspapers; television news stations reported on GMO trade disputes and public safety questions; and one of the longest-running radio shows in Britain—*The Archers*—even featured a fictional series about the issue. Government officials, public figures, and a wide array of organizations took stands on agricultural biotechnology, declaring themselves either very supportive of, or deeply opposed to, the use of these new technologies. Animating this public debate was a small group of activists based in several dozen nongovernmental organizations (NGOs). Indeed, as a result of these activists' actions and the public and consumer support they generated, European publics turned firmly away from genetically modified (GM) foods at the turn of the century, and catalyzed important new regulatory restraints on the technology (Schurman 2004). These included a six-year de facto moratorium on new GM crop approvals, followed by the application of stringent labeling and "traceability" laws for foods containing GMOs.[1] In Britain, major supermarkets committed themselves to ridding their "own brand" products of GM ingredients, as did a host of the continent's food-processing giants, including Nestlé, Unilever, and Cadbury Schweppes. As a result, the mainly U.S.-based agricultural biotechnology industry was sent reeling.[2]

Although social activism around genetically modified foods is most commonly associated with the "anti-biotech" movement in Europe, there has also been a long-standing social movement opposed to the use of GMOs in agriculture in the United States (Schurman and Munro 2006; Tokar 2001).[3] In fact, concerns about genetic engineering were raised by activists in the United States as early as 1977 and have remained a focus of organizing for the past thirty years. Indeed, the development of anti-biotech movements followed a similar course on both continents. Both movements initially relied on a politics of counterexpertise and pressed for legal and regulatory changes when they discovered how hard it was to arouse public concern about a not-yet-commercialized technology. Both movements also broadened their strategies when GM foodstuffs and crops were approved and introduced into the marketplace and it became politically feasible to attack GM food products directly. Where these movements diverged was in their success in mobilizing public opposition to GMOs and influencing the state. Unlike in Europe, the U.S. anti-biotech movement has gained relatively little traction. Although it has raised public awareness of the use of these technologies in the U.S. food supply and stimulated a few changes in government regulatory policy, it has not been able to catalyze anything like the response that occurred in Europe. This is true despite the fact that U.S. activists tried many of the same tactics that their European counterparts used so successfully, including direct actions, public education, and supermarket campaigns.

So why was the European anti-biotech movement so efficacious, while the U.S. movement was not? We address this question through a comparative analysis of anti- biotechnology activism in the United States and in the United Kingdom. We focus on the United Kingdom because the movement there was so successful in turning public opinion around and forcing change at the government level, and because focusing on one European country allows us to avoid the problems posed by cross-national variation in European cultures and institutional contexts. As other studies of the biotechnology controversy have shown, although there are certain unifying features of the European context (such as the presence of the European Union institutions), there are important national differences in the way European publics have interpreted and responded to activism around GMOs, and the technologies themselves (Gaskell and others 2000, Heller 2002).

Most people who have attempted to explain why the United Kingdom turned against GMOs in the late 1990s emphasize one or more of several factors: an intense fear of innovation in the food supply precipitated by Britain's experience with bovine spongiform encephalopathy, or "Mad Cow" disease, in the 1990s; a culturally rooted suspicion among the British public of the putative benefits of science and technology, particularly compared with Americans, who tend to be highly accepting of both (Priest 2001); and a protectionist sensibility among European farmers and governments, who fear that these technologies threaten their own domestic agricultural industries (author interviews; see also Bernauer 2003). Certainly, all of these explanations hold part of the truth. But none takes proper account of the critical role played by activists in galvanizing public responses to the technology. Nor do they appreciate the ways in which the structural and organizational characteristics of the commodity chain opened or constrained opportunities for mobilization that allowed activists to exploit conjunctural political conditions and cultural traditions in building public opposition to the technology. As such, they do not illuminate the political dynamics of the struggle over agricultural biotechnology.

In this chapter, we suggest that a more fruitful approach is to explore these politically usable openings through an analysis of the intersection between the structural characteristics of the global commodity chain for food, on the one hand, and conjunctural events, cultural factors, and political interests, on the other.[4] The commodity chain literature has stressed the ways in which the organization of particular commodity chains is characterized by specific patterns of competition between firms, as well as specific relationships of power and dependency at various points in the chain. These patterns establish points of vulnerability, or "weak links," in the chain in specific places and times.

Yet these weak links are not *only* structural. They are also determined by the kinds of relationships and alliances that are established among the networks of social actors along the commodity chain, and these are informed by cultures of consumption, production, and competition, as well as traditions of political engagement and participation. Our explanation takes both structure and culture into account by focusing on the relationship between the socioeconomic organization of the global commodity chain for food, on the one hand, and the cultural and political construction of networks among actors involved in the chain, on the other.

In thinking about the political construction of these networks, we draw on aspects of actor-network theory (ANT). ANT holds that actors engaged in a defined activity produce particular outcomes by "enrolling" in "networks" that mobilize around the specific knowledge claims, physical processes, conventions for action, established wisdoms, and actor-interests that make that activity possible. All the actors necessary for the success of the activity (and the achievement of the outcomes) are components of the network.[5] We adapt this notion of actor enrollment by focusing on the ways in which particular actors involved in the biotechnology commodity chain contribute to the expansion and consolidation of pro- or anti-GM networks through their chain-oriented activities and interactions. For instance, farmers buy and cultivate seed (GM, non-GM, or both) through farming practices that entail a range of interactions with other actors, including seed suppliers and distributors, bank and loan officers, farm equipment, biotic resources, insurance adjustors, and so on. All of these interactions are essential not only for them to be successful farmers, but also for GM seeds to have a successful "career."

Similarly, food consumers affect not only the operation of the food commodity chain but also the trajectory of the biotechnology industry if they decide to eschew GM food, either by changing the basket of products they shop for or by shopping elsewhere. Thus these actors' production or consumption decisions profoundly affect the fortunes of agricultural biotechnology. In this light, an analytical focus on the enrollment of actors in pro- or anti-GM networks along the commodity chain is useful because it helps us understand not only the factors that worked together to create a resistance to these new technologies in Europe, but also why GMOs were *not* rejected in the United States.

Anti-Biotechnology Activism in the United Kingdom

Anti-biotechnology activism in the United Kingdom began in the 1980s when a handful of people became concerned about the health, safety, and meaning of the new techniques of genetic engineering, and began organizing around the issue.[6] In the early phase of the movement, before the science had successfully produced much in the way of genetically modified organisms, anti-biotech activism centered on what social movement scholars call a "politics of counter-expertise" (Purdue 2000). Most of the movement's energy was devoted to "fighting science with science," pressuring government agencies to take a precautionary approach to these new technologies, and using political and legal means to challenge the extension of intellectual property rights law to life forms (Emmott 2001; Purdue 2000).

When the first GM cereal crops were introduced into Britain from the United States in 1996, the movement's strategy and tactics changed substantially, beginning with a Greenpeace blockade of ships unloading unsegregated GM and non-GM grain in Southampton. This shift partly reflected the new organizing possibilities that accompanied the commercial introduction of GM foods, but it also reflected the changing composition of the movement, which had grown to include many more organizations, including some that were mass-membership groups (such as Friends of the Earth, the British Soil Association, Greenpeace UK).[7] Reflecting the new blood and energy flowing into the movement, activists expanded their "repertoire of contention" (Tilly 1978) to include more symbolic acts of protest, mass demonstrations and civil disobedience (for example, the destruction of field trials of GM crops), and grassroots education campaigns. The movement also mobilized an alternative discourse around the technology (using metaphors such as "genetic pollution" and "Frankenfoods") and targeted the industry leader, Monsanto, in an aggressive anticorporate campaign, denouncing it for valuing profit over people and for seeking to gain control over the world's food supply through its growing portfolio of crop patents.

Perhaps most important of all, activists initiated a major campaign aimed at urging food processors and retailers to stop using and selling GM foods. Anti-biotech activists specifically targeted the leading British supermarket chains and played one off against another in an attempt to force them to reject GM food. This tactic yielded a major victory in March 1998, when Iceland Foods, a large frozen-food producer and supermarket chain, agreed to eliminate all GM foods from its shelves and to ensure that its own-label products would not contain GM ingredients (BBC News 1998).

Largely as a result of these new tactics and the movement's skill in getting its message out to the mass media (see further on), U.K. citizens' awareness of GM food increased markedly after 1996, and public opinion began to turn against it. Whereas the majority of Europeans were agnostic about agricultural biotechnology in the early part of the decade, "widespread public ambivalence about GM foods . . . [gave] way to widespread public hostility" by the decade's end (Gaskell 2000: 938). By the summer of 1998, only one out of six British people was found to be "happy" with the introduction of GM foods, and virtually 96 percent wanted them labeled (*The Economist* 1998). Over the ensuing year, many food processors and supermarket chains followed the lead set by Iceland Foods and moved to clear their shelves or brands of GM ingredients and products. Among them were Sainsbury's and Tesco, the two largest U.K. food retailers (Henson and Northern 1998, Table 1), and Unilever, the world's largest food manufacturer (Waugh 1999).

Activists in the United Kingdom and in a number of other European countries were also instrumental in pushing their governments, and ultimately the EU as a whole, to alter their regulatory positions on agricultural biotechnology. Although the British government had looked favorably upon GM crop approval requests during the early 1990s, it was forced to reverse its support after 1997. In June 1999, the European Union amended its regulatory framework for GM crop approval, Directive 90/220, such that it became impossible to get any new crops approved (Carr 2000: 15; Charles 2001). This de facto moratorium had a powerful influence on keeping new GM crops out of Europe and served as an important political complement to the closure in the retail market described earlier. Even after this directive was officially lifted in May 2004, the EU created a new set of challenges for firms seeking to introduce GMOs into the food supply by establishing a stringent set of labeling and "traceability" requirements that require documentation of a food's ingredients from farm to fork.

The shift in public opinion toward GM foods together with the aforementioned market and policy changes had major reverberations on the geography and length of the commodity chain for processed foods. Supermarkets in the United Kingdom began searching for countries that could provide them with GMO-free corn, soy, and canola, leading to a new geography of production and the creation of new supply relationships (for example, with "officially" GMO-free Brazil). Moreover, as Europe's trade partners, particularly its former colonies in Africa, observed what was happening on the continent, they became highly reticent to plant GM crops. Europe's rejection of GMOs also helped stimulate an industry dedicated to producing "identity preserved" crops for export to Europe.

Explaining Activist Efficacy in the United Kingdom

There were three mutually reinforcing factors that facilitated the ability of the British anti-biotech movement to smother the commercialization of agricultural biotechnology in the United Kingdom. One was the *structure of the com-*

modity chain for processed foods, which established the processing and retail sectors as particularly vulnerable links for attacking the technology. A second was the *strong culture of popular distrust* regarding the ability of government regulatory agencies to protect the public's health and safety. This culture both established agricultural biotechnology as a hot political issue that kept it in the jaundiced eye of the media and enabled activists to paint the government as more closely allied with the industry than with its citizenry. The third was the *transnational character of the commodity chain,* which exacerbated political and cultural, as well as structural, tensions in the chain. Through strategic action, activists were able to exploit all of these tensions.

The Structure of the Processed Foods Commodity Chain

Agricultural biotechnology firms do not sell their products, that is, GM seeds, directly to food consumers, but to farmers, who plant and grow them. Farmers sell their crops to grain elevators or handlers, who then sell the milled grain to food processors. Food processors' products are then sold to supermarkets, the fast food industry, and restaurants, which sell them to final consumers (Figure 10.1). Furthermore, unlike the rubber or plastics industries, which produce products for a wide variety of uses and markets, the main output of the agricultural biotechnology industry (GM seeds) is used to produce food for human consumption. Consequently, even though final food consumers are not the *direct* customers of ag-biotech companies, activists could exert consumer pressure at the downstream end of this "closed loop" commodity chain to harm the firms at the upstream end, that is, the biotechnology industry. By

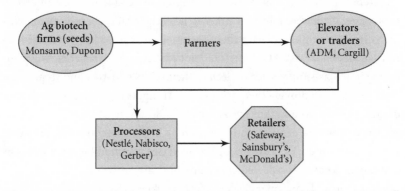

FIGURE 10.1. Supply chain for the ag-biotech industry

giving GMO foods a tremendous amount of negative press and mobilizing consumers to put pressure on retailers and processors, this is precisely what they did.

The structure of the British food retail sector significantly augmented the impact of the movement's retail-sector activism. Following the abolition of the Retail Price Maintenance mechanism in 1964, which had allowed manufacturers and suppliers to dictate their prices to retailers, pricemaking power shifted toward supermarkets. At the same time, the supermarket sector became highly concentrated, dominated by five companies that held some 60 to 75 percent of market share (*The Guardian* 2003, Michaels 2003).[8] Competition within this sector was extremely fierce, and rested on competitive pricing, as well as on these firms' abilities to establish themselves as purveyors of quality, which was captured in their house brands. In this highly competitive environment, any significant customer defection posed a serious threat. This made supermarkets an excellent target for activist attacks, particularly when those attacks were aimed at questioning the quality of a firm's store brand.[9]

Consequently, when GM foodstuffs appeared on the retail horizon in the mid-1990s, supermarkets faced two challenges. One was how to respond to the consumer campaigns that organizations such as Greenpeace and Friends of the Earth began to mobilize. The other was how to respond to the GM labeling laws introduced by the EU in 1997. These laws, which were based on the idea that consumers had a right to know what they were eating, mandated the labeling of GM foodstuffs. This placed retailers in a quandary. Faced with intense competition for market share, activist campaigns, and consumer research that showed that consumers wanted to be able to make informed choices, retailers were reluctant either to label their house brands as containing GM ingredients or to have their operations disrupted by activists if they resisted labeling. Even if GM foods did not particularly alarm company management, it was simply safer to declare themselves GM-free and to pressure their suppliers to provide them with non-GM inputs than to take the chance of losing customers and thus market share.

The desirability of "preemptive" action by British processors and retailers was bolstered by the fact that among the main GM commodities were soybeans and canola (known as rapeseed in Britain). Both are processed into a very wide range of food and consumer products, from cookies to frozen chicken pot pies. This meant that once consumers became suspicious of GMOs, a wide range of supermarket items became vulnerable to rejection. EU labeling and trace-ability laws enabled consumers to turn their suspicions into decision-making criteria, and raised the cost and retail risk of selling GM products. This gave retailers an added incentive to reject GM products *tout court.*

The interests of U.K. farmers further militated against the acceptance of GMOs in Britain, though the situation played out somewhat differently in soy and rapeseed markets. On the one hand, Britain is not a soy-farming country; almost all soy is imported. Consequently, there was no local audience for industry arguments about the benefits to *producers* of using GM seed. In addition, because soy was not widely grown in the United Kingdom, British retailers could switch their sources of soy supply without hurting local farmers. Rapeseed, on the other hand, *is* a major British crop. But given the tremendous power of retailers and EU labeling and traceability requirements, the possibility of "contamination" of their crops and fields by GM seeds carried multiple financial risks for farmers. One was that they might lose their immediate market for their crops if they were found to be GM. Another was that they might lose their markets in the long-term for crops raised on land once known to be "contaminated." A third was that they might lose access to EU subsidies (Lean, Angres, and Jury 2000; Ministry of Agriculture, Fisheries and Food 2000). British farmers thus found it more sensible to try to protect their own crops and fields from "contamination" than to coalesce in support of genetic engineering.

Public Distrust of Government Authorities

Behind the risk-aversion of retailers was the fact that retail risk only existed if public consciousness was particularly elevated or inflamed. Survey data show a rapid increase in public opposition to GMOs in the late 1990s associated with the expansion of public knowledge about the technology (Tiberghien and Starrs 2004). This opposition was not rooted in any strong *cultural* tradition of healthy eating manifested in a desire for unadulterated food. Indeed, the British eating public is not particularly health conscious. In a Food Standards Agency survey in September 2001, for example, 46 percent of respondents said that price was the key determinant for choosing their food, and only 12 percent put health first (Michaels 2003).[10] Rather, the root of opposition was political, associated with a rash of food scares that swept Europe in the 1990s (Friedberg 2004). The most important of these, of course, was Mad Cow disease and its human variant, Creutzfeldt-Jakob disease. Creutzfeldt-Jakob disease had a particularly terrifying impact in the United Kingdom, where it caused almost seven hundred human deaths in the 1990s.[11] In this context, it is not surprising that consumers would be frightened by any large-scale tinkering with their food supply. At the same time, public attention focused less on *inherent* concerns about health than on the government's readiness to protect public health and safety.

This focus on the government's regulatory capacity and will had two mutually reinforcing implications for anti-GMO politics. First, activists were able to invoke this concern strategically to exploit any glitches in the technology's deployment that might indicate inadequate government regulation or uncontrollability of the technology. One key strategy was to publicize contamination of non-GM seed shipments by GM seeds. In one noteworthy case, a political firestorm erupted in 2000 when Advanta Seeds UK admitted that GM rapeseed had inadvertently been mixed with conventional seed imported from Canada and sold in the United Kingdom and Europe over the previous two years.[12] Activist organizations immediately called for the destruction of the entire contaminated crop, berating the Food Standards Agency for failing in its public watchdog role. The issue also ignited a rancorous debate in Parliament during which the government was assailed not only by opposition parties but by its own backbenchers for its "frightening complacency" (Hickman and Roberts 2000, Waugh 2000).

Growing fears of the environmental impact of a poorly regulated or uncontrollable technology also brought a wider range of organizations and public interest groups into the fray. For instance, mainstream and venerable organizations such as the Royal Society for the Protection of Birds became engaged because they feared the loss of vital bird habitats if GM traits should make plants unpalatable or should stray across species. Organizations such as the Soil Association, which represented organic farming interests (farmers, suppliers, consumers), took up the issue because they worried that GM crops would spread across fields and destroy the possibility of growing uncontaminated organic crops. In effect, suspicions about ineffective regulation and control galvanized a broad range of public interest groups to form a coalition against the technology.

The second implication of the broad skepticism about the efficacy of government regulation is that it placed public debates over GMOs in the context of party and government politics, an area of great interest to the media. Here activists were aided by Prime Minister Tony Blair's resolute enthusiasm for GM technology, which created a context in which both the popular press and the establishment press found an ongoing theme on which to scrutinize government actions. As one British activist noted,

> I think that . . . newspapers like the *Daily Mail* [were] looking for a way to attack Tony Blair. He was the new prime minister, he was squeaky-clean, there was nothing wrong with him, and they were looking for a weak spot, and it was very clear that GM foods was a very big weak spot. . . . And . . . his science minister had . . . a lot of money invested in GM companies (author interview 2005).

In 2001, the *Guardian* newspaper argued that "One of the biggest failures of Tony Blair's first term was missing the public mood on genetically modified food and crops. . . . The fact that during his first term every supermarket chain has withdrawn genetically modified foods from its shelves and gone to extensive lengths to insist suppliers are GM free seems to have passed the prime minister by." As a result, the paper noted, "The perception that the prime minister is a pushover for big business interests is partly tied up with his perceived lack of interest in genuine public concerns about the consequences of embracing this technology" (Brown 2001). In part, then, the strong association of Tony Blair with GMOs, and the controversy this created even within his own party, gave the issue media "legs." Both print and television media persistently covered GM debates and controversies, thereby sustaining the air of unease around the technology and helping to keep the movement bubbling.

The Transnational Commodity Chain

The fact that the core of the biotech industry lay in the United States had both structural and cultural implications for the organizing opportunities confronting the British anti-biotech movement. In the first place, when Monsanto rolled its GM products into European markets, it thoroughly, and disastrously, ignored the cultural sensibilities of European consumers (see Shapiro 1999). Second, Monsanto failed to pursue buy-in among British retailers and processors, who were not expecting a change in their products' ingredients (authors' interviews). In 2000, Monsanto CEO Hendrik Verfaillie acknowledged that "Monsanto focused so much attention on getting the technology right for our customer—the grower—that we didn't fully take into account the issues and concerns it raised for other people" (Van Yoder 2001). This strategic error had important ramifications at both ends of the commodity chain. At the consumer end in Britain, it created what the *Guardian* called "the central problem that there is no gain in the technology for the consumer and only perceived threats" (Brown 2001). This threw the industry back on a public relations strategy that could only stress the safety of the product rather than its benefits to consumers. In an environment made hostile by activists and kept under scrutiny by the media, the industry was left very much on the defensive. Further, the industry could not look to the British government for strong public support, because the government was being pushed into tighter and tighter testing through activist pressure and EU regulations. This created the cumulative effect of a weak industry appeal and a government that, while wanting to be supportive, was not able to say with any great credibility that it would protect the public from risks associated with the technology.

At the producer end of the GCC, the U.S.-based industry had given no serious consideration to strategies for maintaining strict segregation of GM and non-GM products, and this made it vulnerable to charges of "contamination" when these products reached Britain. By the time that U.S. processors and farmers became fully attuned to the need to segregate GM and non-GM products, the horse was out of the stable and the expense of segregation was prohibitive. In effect, in a kind of ironic twist, the consolidated strength of pro-GM networks in the United States (see next section) helped to consolidate the strength of anti-GM networks in the United Kingdom.

This transnational disconnect had further political ramifications. As the EU elaborated its labeling and traceability requirements in the early 2000s, the only feasible response for the U.S. biotech industry was to seek government assistance in opening European markets using the World Trade Organization (Ford 2001; Woolf 2001). This fueled growing anti-American sentiments in Europe. When the anti-GM movement portrayed Monsanto as the leader in American food imperialism—trying to shove a dangerous technology down people's throats—they were acting strategically (Schweiger 2001; Specter 2000).[13] In 2001, a leaked memo concerning negotiations between British ministers and high-level U.S. officials on the GMO issue enabled Friends of the Earth activists to stress "how much pressure the U.S. is now putting on the British Government to back its move to force GM products into the European market. . . . President Bush obviously hopes that Britain will play its usual role as a Trojan horse for U.S. interests inside the EU" (Woolf 2001).

In sum, the anti-biotech movement's success in Britain was defined not only by conjunctural political conditions or by local food cultures but also by specific characteristics of the transnational commodity chain, which enabled activists to exploit key weak links to mobilize public opposition to agricultural biotechnology. The features of the commodity chain that contributed to Britain's market closure included a highly concentrated and competitive retail sector, and a supermarket chain (Iceland Foods) that was willing to be a first mover on the issue in order to gain a competitive advantage. In addition, the transnational structure of the commodity chain enabled British activists to engage a cultural politics that presented the industry not only as corporate and uncaring but as imperialist. Under these conditions, the anti-GM movement was able to bring off the crucial victory of scaring the major food processors and retailers into renouncing the use and sale of GM foods. The primary means by which it did so was by shaping public opinion and mobilizing the public to express its concerns to supermarket managers, thereby threatening retailers and processors with a loss of market share. Conditions in the United States were very different.

Anti-Biotechnology Activism in the United States

As was the case in Europe, much of the U.S. anti-biotechnology movement's energies up until the late 1980s were devoted to raising public awareness of the potential risks and hazards of genetic engineering, stemming the tide toward "life patenting," and forcing the U.S. government to take biotechnology regulation more seriously.[14] Toward these goals, activists in the movement adopted a multipronged strategy. First, they set out to raise public consciousness through public speeches, writings, and teach-ins. Second, groups such as the Center for Food Safety and the Foundation for Economic Trends, both in Washington, D.C., spearheaded a string of lawsuits against the industry that attempted to prevent product field-testing and, later, the introduction of the first applications of GM technologies. Third, U.S. activists used science-based arguments and data to challenge decisions made by the three government agencies that represented the gateway to the marketplace (the Department of Agriculture, the Environmental Protection Agency, and the Food and Drug Administration).

Although the movement did enjoy some victories, such as slowing down the introduction of certain applications of the technology by a few years[15] and turning a small class of consumers into organic food buyers, most of their tactics met with limited success. For example, despite the fact that the movement

promulgated numerous lawsuits against state regulatory agencies, none suc-
ceeded in changing these agencies' fundamentally pro-biotechnology bias in
decision making. Nor were they able to push the government to strengthen its
oversight of the industry by replacing its "coordinated framework" of regulation with a system that centralized decision-making power over biotechnology.[16] More significant, perhaps, they could not ignite the public's imagination. Frequently, the information on which law cases turned was esoteric, and
industry or government spokespeople were able to cast them as attacks on
U.S. farmers who, as we show in the next section, were enthusiastic users (and
boosters) of the technology and are invariably an object of sympathetic coverage in the U.S. media. What the activists did seemingly achieve with their
lawsuits was to augment the amount of scientific data that firms submitted to
government regulatory agencies about the safety of their technologies. Even
now, however, these data are considered proprietary (and are not required to
be made public), and are not routinely used by the agencies as a basis for rejecting GM products.[17]

In the latter part of the 1980s, the anti-biotech movement expanded its
strategies and began to target the products that were starting to enter the
market. The movement's first attack took the form of a consumer campaign
against bovine somatotropin, a growth hormone developed for use in milk
production. Groups in three small-dairy states (Wisconsin, Minnesota, and
Vermont) worked with Jeremy Rifkin and his organization, the Foundation
on Economic Trends, to try to stop the marketing of bovine growth hormone (BGH) by the biotechnology industry. But they struggled to gain traction in the public's consciousness, partly because BGH is a natural hormone
already present in milk and partly because the industry responded with its
own vigorous campaign stressing the safety of the technology. In addition,
the technology benefited large farmers over small farmers, and the industry
was able to exploit the bimodal distribution of the dairy industry to weaken
farmers' reservations. As a result, the impact of anti-BGH activism remained
geographically limited, reaching little further than the few small dairy states
where there was an organized movement. No doubt the failure of this campaign boosted the confidence of pro-GM interests, allowing the biotechnology industry to conclude that American consumers did not really care much
about GM technologies and were unlikely to revolt against the technology. In
short, if they did not react negatively to a product such as milk, which parents

routinely give to their kids, they certainly were not going to lose any sleep over GM corn or soy. Given this industry view, it was virtually impossible for the movement to scare the industry with a credible consumer threat, as we argue further on.

In the wake of European movements' success in the late 1990s, organizations such as Greenpeace and the Organic Consumers' Union launched a series of consumer campaigns, modeled on European strategies, to push food processors and retailers away from GM products. Some campaigns were successful. In 1999, McDonald's, fearing a threatened boycott, decided not to use genetically engineered potatoes in its French fries. When Wendy's and Burger King followed suit, Monsanto pulled its genetically engineered NewLeaf potato from the market. Frito-Lay, a major food processor, also declared its products GM-free in some markets. In 2001, the California-based supermarket chain Trader Joe's responded to a consumer campaign by agreeing to stock its stores only with GM-free products. But other campaigns failed. An effort to pressure Kellogg's to reject GM corn was simply shrugged off by the company. And despite the intense pressure it placed on the Shaw's supermarket chain in New England as part of its True Food Now campaign, Greenpeace was never able to get the company to capitulate. By 2003, with financing dwindling, these consumer campaigns largely fizzled out.

Explaining (the Lack of) U.S. Movement Efficacy

If the structural and cultural features of the food commodity chain in the United Kingdom established several key points of vulnerability that anti-GM activists could exploit, the opposite was true in the United States: there the mutually reinforcing structure and culture of the food commodity chain helped to marginalize anti-GM networks and to strengthen those who were supportive of GMOs. Two features, almost mirror-imaging conditions in the United Kingdom, played key roles. One was the consolidation of power at the producer end of the commodity chain, which enabled the GM industry, led by Monsanto, to establish a resilient pro-GM network comprising seed companies, distributors, and farmers. The other was the structure and culture of the food retail sector, which inhibited the ability of activists to enroll expanding networks of anti-GM actors. Two crucial elements of this environment were the size of the retail market, which made supermarkets resilient against

consumer campaigns, and a trusting consumer culture, which made it difficult for activists to capture the public's imagination and to turn them against
GMOs. The cumulative effect of these features was that U.S. activists were never
able to effectively "cut" the chain in the way their British counterparts were.

Consolidating Power Upstream

Following the failure of its biotech rollout in European markets, Monsanto
leaders acknowledged that they had ignored the sensibilities of consumers because they assumed that most people would share their belief in the social and
environmental benefits of the technology, and because they had focused their
efforts on producing products that would offer advantages to their direct customers, namely, farmers (Shapiro 1999; Van Yoder 2001). In the context of the
U.S. market, however, their decision to focus on farmers made absolute sense.
If U.S. farmers did not respond favorably to the commercialization of GM
seeds (for instance, by rejecting the technology fee and sticking with tried-
and-true hybrids), or even if they responded sluggishly enough to push down
the biotech companies' stock value, the enterprise would have been doomed.
It was therefore crucial for agricultural biotechnology companies to enroll
seed companies, seed distributors, and farmers in a pro-GM network, and to
keep critics out.

As it turned out, American farmers took up agricultural biotechnology
with remarkable speed and confidence. (As many observers have noted, GM
technologies have had the steepest adoption curve of any technology in U.S.
agricultural history.) To fully understand why this happened, it is necessary
to consider the upstream end of the U.S. commodity chain. For historical and
structural reasons, the seed industry is the "driver" in this chain. In the 1970s,
the seed industry began undergoing a process of dramatic consolidation, as
small seed firms were bought up by large conglomerates whose primary investments lay in cognate sectors, such as pharmaceuticals, petrochemicals,
and food (Fernandez-Cornejo 2004). This pattern of consolidation intensified
over the 1980s and 1990s while crop biotechnology was developed and tested.
Some companies interested in biotechnology—such as Monsanto, Novartis,
and AgrEvo—developed "life sciences" complexes based on agricultural chem-
icals, seeds, foods and food ingredients, and pharmaceuticals. The ensuing
frenzy of mergers and acquisitions helped these large agrochemical conglomerates to strengthen their market shares in the seed and agrochemical businesses while expanding their distribution infrastructures and capacities.[18]

By buying seed companies outright or entering into other legal and financial arrangements with them, these firms also ensured that they would have a vehicle for getting their genes out of the laboratory and into the fields.[19]

The consolidation of power in the hands of vertically integrated multinational agrochemical companies was enhanced by the regime of strong plant breeders' rights that characterized the seed industry, especially following the 1970 Plant Variety Protection Act (Boyd 2003; Kloppenburg Jr. 1988). As Fernandez-Cornejo points out, "where each breeder holds the exclusive rights to produce and distribute his or her variety, competition tends to be based more on product performance—yield, disease resistance, quality—than price. Given the size of their R&D investments, these plant breeders play a central role in managing the entire production, distribution, and marketing processes in the seed industry, resulting in extensive vertical integration in the industry" (2004: 28). The large seed-producing companies maintained direct access to farmers through dense networks of seed distributors as well as middle-order seed producers that used their licensed technology. In this context, the companies built strong relationships with farmers who believed in the quality of their product and were prepared to pay a premium price for it.

The vertically integrated structure of the seed sector created an environment that facilitated an extensive enrollment of farmers and seed suppliers in pro-GM networks at the upstream end of the commodity chain. Given the high stakes of ensuring the successful uptake of the technology, biotechnology companies—notably Monsanto, the most aggressive developer—worked to protect and expand these networks. Before rolling out its GM seeds commercially, Monsanto decided strategically to cut seed dealers and distributors in on the financial benefits of its new, genetically modified RoundUp® Ready corn and soy products (author interview with former Monsanto official 2004). The company also carried out extensive field trials with farmers, showing them firsthand how these technologies worked to address problems such as the corn borer. In doing so, the company appealed to and fostered farmers' deeply held belief in scientific agriculture and their long tradition of respect for seed technology.

Thus, in seeking to bring U.S. farmers on board, Monsanto and other firms benefited from U.S. farmers' growing enthusiasm for the technology. Farmers in the U.S. Midwest were attracted to GM seed because it eased farm management and reduced their herbicide applications. Furthermore, farmers were used to playing by the seed companies' rules. For all of these reasons, farmers were culturally predisposed against distinguishing between biotech and conventional hybrid seeds. Grumble though they did about the licensing fee and about the need for "refuges" of non-biotech crops required by government regulation, they psychologically and financially bought in and paid up.

In effect, then, if Monsanto failed to properly prepare the ground for its product rollout among European end-consumers, it prepared the ground among American producers impeccably. As a result, the top end of the commodity chain was tightly sealed against activist influence. Indeed, in many cases, the resentment that European consumers felt toward imperialist American agriculture found its mirror image in U.S. farmers' contempt for European consumers and resentment over market bottlenecks created by European consumers' squeamishness. Anyone echoing European sentiments locally was guaranteed a hostile audience.

Retail Sector and Consumer Culture

The public campaigns against agricultural biotechnology that activists developed in the United States during the late 1990s and early 2000s were strongly influenced by the success of the British campaigns. Modeling their strategies on these campaigns, U.S. activists set out to "push back on the commodity chains," as one activist put it, by trying to scare supermarkets into rejecting GM products (author interview with Greenpeace activist 2005). Supermarkets were an obvious target. As in the United Kingdom, national supermarket chains in the United States have a great deal of power to determine the conditions for the supply, procurement, and marketing of agricultural and food products. Thus if activists could turn a national supermarket chain such as Kroger or Albertsons away from GM products, the market ripples would be tsunamic. But supermarket campaigns were much harder to pull off in the United States, in part because these chains were so large and sprawling that it was difficult for a chronically underfunded and understaffed movement to target them comprehensively. Indeed, this was a lesson that the movement learned from the failure of the campaign against Kellogg's (author interview with U.S. activist 2005). In addition, the structure of the U.S. food retail sector made it possible for retailers to accommodate the concerns of a wide range of consumers: supermarkets could easily diversify into organic produce in order to hold onto customers, and local chains and health food groceries could cater to customers who were prepared to spend a bit more on organic food.[20]

Farmers markets (which doubled in number between 1994 and 2004, from around 1,500 to around 3,000) also provided an increasingly viable outlet for consumers seeking non-GM food. In short, while mainstream consumers could indulge their overriding concern with price, those concerned about or opposed to GMOs (who are generally more affluent) had a relatively easy exit strategy.

In a situation in which a national-level campaign was beyond the mobilizing capacity of the anti-GM movement, activists had to design their consumer campaigns around smaller regional supermarkets whose corporate cultures biased them toward "healthy" foods, in the hope of starting a snowball effect. They selected Trader Joe's in California and Shaw's in New England; the latter was chosen because it was owned by the British firm Sainsbury's, which activists hoped might make it sensitive to GM food issues. But even though the Trader Joe's campaign worked, the snowball effect never occurred. Trader Joe's was not a significant enough player in the supermarket sector to pose a competitive threat to other chains. Shaw's, the second largest supermarket chain in the northeast, had its own subsidiary group of natural food stores, and was resilient enough to hold off the Greenpeace campaign before being bought by Albertsons in 2004.

The limited success of anti-GM activism points to a broader constraint on the movement: anti-GM activists were never able to capture the imagination of U.S. consumers on a significant scale in the way that they had in Britain. Some analysts have noted that Americans are culturally predisposed to trust regulatory authorities, technology, and corporations far more readily than are European citizens (see Bernauer 2003). Furthermore, in interviews, several activists lamented that Americans could not be galvanized without a significant health-threatening regulatory failure or catastrophe such as Love Canal or Three Mile Island (author interviews 2001). But other environmental factors were no doubt also instrumental in shaping U.S. food consumer culture. For one thing, there was no "foreign enemy" of imperialist corporations that the activists could point to in the way that European activists could. Activists also had a very different relationship with the media in the United States than they had in the United Kingdom. In the latter case, as we have seen, the media treated agricultural biotechnology as a political issue, and activist organizations were regarded as speaking with some authority on the issue. In the United States, even though there was a burst of increased media interest in GMOs in the early 2000s, mainstream media coverage was generally the preserve of business, science, or agriculture reporters who tended to report from within the hegemonic framework of the establishment, thereby muting critical voices (Priest 2001).[21]

Activists were also hurt by their inability to win the battle to label GM food. The U.S.-based industry and food and grain processors had lobbied hard for a regulatory approach that emphasized the similarities (or "substantial equivalence") between GM- and non-GM products, rather than the distinctions between them which EU regulation stressed.[22] Such an approach, they argued, made labeling unnecessary and prohibitively expensive. This argument prevailed with U.S. regulatory agencies. When activists tried to push for a labeling regime, as they did in an Oregon ballot measure in 2002, they faced both an industry with deep pockets and a hostile state. In Oregon, a corporate coalition that included Monsanto, DuPont, General Mills, and H.J. Heinz spent some $5.5 million to defeat the measure, while the FDA warned that labeling was illegal because it would violate interstate commerce rules. The measure failed by a large margin (Cohen and Gillam 2002). It stands, perhaps, as a marker of the inability of anti-GM activists in the United States to "push back on the commodity chain" effectively.

Conclusion

It seems clear that the dynamics and the outcomes of the struggles over agricultural biotechnology, in both Britain and the United States, were overdetermined—albeit in opposite directions. This makes it difficult to assign overwhelming causal weight to any one factor. Nonetheless, we have argued that fruitful analysis of anti-GM movement efficacy might well focus on the ability of activists to exploit "weak links" in the global commodity chain. Thus, although the commodity chain cannot *explain* the dynamics or outcome of anti-GM activism, our comparative analysis shows that the nature and structure of the commodity chain does shape the terrain of struggle in important ways. In both Britain and the United States, the structure of competition between companies and the patterns of power and dependency up and down the commodity chain opened up spaces for opposition in some locations and narrowed those spaces in others.

In Britain, where supermarkets were focused intensely on the threat of losing market share and the biotechnology companies could make no compelling argument about the technology's benefit to consumers or to retailers, activists were able to break the chain by enrolling a widening anti-GM network, among both retail decision makers and the general public. Here the transnational character of the commodity chain helped by adding a cultural disjuncture at the consumer end. Pro-GM networks, in contrast, remained weak, partly because the central position of GM traits and seed supply was dominated by American companies, and partly because of the stringency of EU regulation. British farmers also had a smaller stake in the technology, both because they were worried about a potentially disappearing market and because they were concerned about the potential long-term effect on the value of their land.

In the United States, the opposite was true. Here the organizational structure and the cultural construction of the commodity chain converged to make pro-GM networks at the upstream end robust and resilient, while anti-GM networks at the downstream (consumer) end remained weak. Consolidation in the seed industry, strong plant breeders' rights, and U.S. farmer culture had established strong relationships of dependency and trust between seed companies, farmers, and distributors. Firms involved in agricultural biotechnology had secured a labeling regime that was cost-effective for distributors and processors and therefore defended vigorously by them. Farmers' cultural adherence to a notion of progressive, scientific farming made defections from the pro-GM network very rare. At the consumer end of the commodity chain, activists were stymied by a vast and sprawling retail sector, by a consumer culture of trust in industry and government fostered by a quiescent media, and by the exit strategies available to concerned consumers offered by niche organic stores and farmers' markets. Under these conditions, activists were unable to build anti-GM networks extensive and dense enough at the national level to successfully exploit the weak links in the commodity chain.

REFERENCE MATTER

Notes

Chapter 1

1. See also Chapter 9, by Julie Guthman, in this volume.

2. Other contributions to the GPN literature include Coe et al. 2004, Coe and Hess 2005, Hess and Coe 2006, and Hess and Yeung 2006.

3. I am grateful to Raphie Kaplinsky for bringing this article to my attention.

4. These references to the origins of commodity chain analysis often accompany critical or dismissive discussions of the GCC framework; see, for example, Thompson (2003: 210) and Fine (2002: 120).

5. Examples of this literature that give some indication of the range of industries studied include Bair and Gereffi 2001; Clancy 1998; Dolan and Humphrey 2000; Fitter and Kaplinsky 2001a; Fold 2002; O'Riain 2004; Phyne and Mansilla 2003; Ponte 2002; Rabach and Kim 1994; and Rammohan and Sundaresan 2003.

6. Of course, Marx's understanding of the term *commodity* is quite different, and it may well have been this meaning that Hopkins and Wallerstein meant to evoke with their choice of the "commodity chain" terminology.

7. This likely reflects the influence of Sturgeon's turnkey model on the development of this theory, given that Sturgeon's argument regarding modular manufacturing was based on the changing relationship between brand-name electronics companies and their key component manufacturers.

Chapter 2

1. Other coffee scholars such as Thurber (1886), Samper K. (2003), Talbot (2004), and Topik and Samper K. (2006) have not been so audacious; they did not attempt to examine the coffee chain over such a wide sweep of history.

2. Calculated from Greenhill 1993: 307; Ocampo 1984: 303; and Brazil, IBGE. 1986: 84.

3. Calculated from Greenhill 1993: 330–331; and Wakeman 1911: 193.

Chapter 3

1. Various analysts of the political economy of food and agriculture have long argued that this is a critical, but understudied, part of the global economy and worldwide trade (Dickinson and Mann 1978; Friedmann 1982). More recently, John Talbot (2004) clearly grounds the political economy of international coffee production in terms of global commodity chain analysis.

2. The UN commodity categories we analyze here represent the "commodity bundles" derived in a factor analysis of all bilateral international exchange originally described in Smith and Nemeth 1988. The five empirically defined clusters of commodity trade used in Smith and White 1992, Mahutga 2006, and this chapter are interpretable along a rough two-dimensional scale that contrasts production versus extraction and capital-intensive versus labor-intensive.

3. Both semi-peripheries close the gap between themselves and the core in the 1965–1980 period, though the strong semi-periphery reverses this trend in the 1980–2000 period. The net effect is still a smaller gap. The strong-semi-periphery is a rather interesting group. It is composed of downwardly mobile countries from Eastern and Western Europe, and upwardly mobile countries from East Asia, along with Brazil.

Chapter 4

1. The original discussion is to be found within the framework of a research program of the Fernand Braudel Center (Hopkins and Wallerstein 1977). For subsequent statements, see Hopkins and Wallerstein 1986 and 1994, and the special issue of *Review* (2000).

Chapter 5

1. The tropical commodities are agricultural commodities that, because of their ecology, can be grown profitably only in tropical climates. The most important ones, in order of their value in world trade, are coffee, sugar, tropical timber, natural rubber, tropical oils and oilseeds, cocoa, tea, bananas, jute, and hard fibers.

2. In this chapter, I use the phrase "the structure of a chain" as shorthand to refer collectively to the characteristics that Gereffi identifies as the "dimensions" of commodity chains—that is, their input-output structures, the geography of different activities or links in the chain, and governance structures. See Gereffi 1994: 96–97.

3. One exception is the analysis of the aluminum commodity chain in Barham, Bunker, and O'Hearn 1994. There are very few studies of mineral commodity chains, which is unfortunate, given that they are the forgotten extractive beginnings of many manufacturing chains.

4. The apparel chains analyzed by Gereffi have probably been more highly regulated than many other manufacturing chains, given the important influence of the Multi-Fibre Arrangement until very recently. Nevertheless, states and other actors have more directly governed segments of agricultural and other primary commodity chains than has been the case for most manufacturing chains.

5. The existence of this data is due to a combination of factors. Coffee's importance as a consumption item in developed-country shopping baskets meant that good data on retail prices were available (used in calculating consumer price indexes). Coffee's importance as a commodity in world trade meant that good records of export and import prices were kept. Coffee's importance in the economies of producing countries meant that data on prices paid to growers were also kept. Finally, the collective action of producers that led to the establishment of the International Coffee Organization enabled the standardization and centralization of all of this data in a form that could be easily used.

Chapter 6

1. This chapter was supported by Doshisha University's ITEC 21st Century COE (Centre of Excellence) Program's Synthetic Studies on Technology, Enterprise and Competitiveness Project. Participants in the Global Value Chains Initiative contributed to the development of the concepts advanced, especially Hubert Schmitz, Peter Gibbon, Florence Palpacur, Raphie Kaplinsky, Mike Morris, Meenu Tewari, and Katherine McFate. John Talbot, Richard Appelbaum, Rachel Schurman, Sanjaya Lall, William Millberg, and Andrew Schrank provided useful feedback during a workshop held at Yale University on May 13 and 14, 2005. Jennifer Bair, Gary Gereffi, John Humphrey, and two anonymous reviewers provided helpful editorial suggestions on an earlier draft. All responsibility for the final text, of course, lies with the author.

2. This group met under the auspices of the "Global Value Chains Initiative," sponsored largely by the Rockefeller Foundation (a meeting held in Rockport, Massachusetts, in April 2004 was sponsored by the Alfred P. Sloan Foundation). The participants in the first workshop, a seven-day event held at the Rockefeller conference center in Bellagio, Italy, were Catherine Dolan (U.K.), Peter Gibbon (Denmark), Gary Gereffi (United States), Afonso Fleury (Brazil), John Humphrey (United Kingdom), Raphie Kaplinsky (United Kingdom), Ji-Ren Lee (Taiwan), Dorothy McCormick (Kenya), Katherine McFate (United States), Mike Morris (South Africa), Florence Palpacuer (France), Hubert Schmitz (United Kingdom), and Meenu Tewari (United States). Subsequent workshops included many of these core participants, additional academics researchers, and policymakers and NGO activists from the United Nations

Industrial Development Organization, the United Nations Conference on Trade and Development, the World Trade Organization's International Trade Centre, the World Bank's Development Economics Research Group, the International Labour Organization's World Commission on the Social Dimension of Globalization, the International Centre for Trade and Sustainable Development, the AFL-CIO, Oxfam, India's National Council of Applied Economic Research, the Merrimack Valley (Massachusetts) Workforce Investment Board, and the Maquila Solidarity Network/Ethical Trading Action Group.

3. A list of more than three hundred GVC-related publications can be found at www.globalvaluechains.org.

4. Feenstra and Hamilton (2006) describe, in detail, the ways in which retailers gained power relative to manufacturers, beginning in the United States in the 1960s, a trend that continues to the present day. On one hand this "retail revolution" has been a major factor in deindustrialization within the United States, as retailers increased overseas sourcing of apparel, electronics, and consumer goods, in turn forcing manufacturers to move their own facilities offshore and increase sourcing in low-cost locations in East Asia. The other side of this coin was the spurring of "late" industrialization and industrial upgrading, first in Japan, and later in Korea and Taiwan (Amsden 1989; Wade 1990; Evans 1995).

5. Of course, a second variable in the transactions cost framework, frequency of transactions, acknowledges that asset-specific activities tend to remain outsourced when minimum-scale economies cannot be reached through internal consumption, a notion that was developed separately in a classic article by Richardson (1972).

6. Nevertheless, this distinction failed to penetrate the field of economics very far beyond the immediate debates just mentioned, and economistic accounts of the globalization process still emphasize only two options: market or hierarchy (see, for example, Arndt and Kierzkowski 2001). Firms either invest offshore directly (hierarchy) or buy goods and services from firms located offshore (markets).

7. I owe this observation to conversations with Jennifer Bair, Stefano Ponte, Peter Gibbon, and Florence Palpacuer.

8. In fact, an accurate mapping of the chain can be all that is needed for activists and policymakers to identify leverage points for effecting change. For example, in this volume Schurman and Munro (Chapter 10) show how "anti-biotech" activists were able to usher in a multiyear moratorium on new genetically modified food crop approvals in Europe by focusing pressure on the region's tenth-largest food retailer. When this firm increased its market share by labeling its stores "GMO free," its larger competitors soon followed suit.

9. To the well-known cases of the structuring role that Intel microprocessors and Microsoft's operating system play in the personal computer industry (Borrus and Zysman 1997) and that Shimano's component systems play in the bicycle industry (Galvin and Morkel 2001), I can add several others, including Applied Materials' manufacturing equipment in the semiconductor and flat panel display industries (Murtha, Lenway, and Hart 2001), Qualcomm's chip sets for mobile phone technologies based

on Code-Division Multiple Access (CDMA) technologies, ARM's chip technology for mobile phone systems based on the Global System for Mobile Communications (GSM) standard, and grinders in the coffee industry (Fold 2002).

10. Of course, all forms of firm-level power are related in some way to simple market power, and the notion that industry concentration is, to some degree, compatible with competition is quite venerable (Chamberlin 1933: 205).

11. These remarks were made at the conference "Organisational Configurations and Locational Choices of Firms: Responses to Globalisation in Different Industry and Institutional Environments," held at the Centre for Research in the Arts, Social Sciences and Humanities, Cambridge University, Cambridge, United Kingdom, on April 14, 2005.

12. These remarks were made at the MIT Working Group on Services Offshoring Workshop, held in Cambridge, Massachusetts, on October 28, 2005.

Chapter 7

1. The authors would like to thank Jennifer Bair and Mark Mizruchi for their comments on this paper. We also want to thank the Rockefeller Foundation for supporting portions of the research reported here.

2. In this chapter, we will not discuss the ties between global commodity chains and the closely related global value chains approach. This is handled very ably by other contributors to this volume, particularly in the chapters by Jennifer Bair (Chapter 1) and Timothy Sturgeon (Chapter 6).

3. Also, having found positions in business schools, most of these researchers worked more or less exclusively on intra-firm and inter-firm data and ignored most other levels of analysis, including national and global levels.

4. Collected by the U.S. Custom Service, the data report the country of origin for U.S. imports at a seven-digit level known as the Tariff Schedule of the U.S. Annotated (TSUSA) for 1972–1988, and at the ten-digit Harmonized System (HS) level from 1989 on. Both the TSUSA and HS series consist of data fine enough to distinguish between hundreds of different types of shoes and apparel and between any final product and the components that go into it. These data are available from the Website of the Center for International Data, UC Davis, at www.internationaldata.org.

5. For additional examples and dates related to the emergence of U.S. big buyers, see Gereffi 2001b: 32–34.

6. The following section is a summary of an argument made in considerably more detail in Feenstra and Hamilton 2006.

Chapter 8

1. Many thanks to Mary Sue Smiaroski for help with this chapter, and to the many individuals who conducted research for Oxfam International and whose findings are cited here.

2. Unless otherwise cited, all data and quotes in this chapter are from Oxfam International 2004.

3. In 2002 the ILO revised its definition of informal employment away from a focus on the characteristics of the enterprise. Informal employment is now defined as work lacking secure contracts, worker benefits, or social protection. See ILO 2002.

4. For more information on the Ethical Trading Initiative's purchasing practice project, see www.ethicaltrade.org/Z/actvts/exproj/purchprac/index.shtml.

5. Fatima Shabodien, director, Women on Farms, personal communication, March 14, 2006.

6. Comment made by William Plietez in an Oxfam International forum on women workers in export industries, San Salvador, El Salvador, February 10, 2004.

7. See *Kompas* newspaper, Nov. 30, 2004; available online at www.kompas.com/kompas-cetak/0411/30/ekonomi/1405306.htm.

Chapter 9

1. The shorthand of *ethical commodities* is borrowed from Bell and Valentine (1997), although I have reservations about using this term. As Freidberg (2003a) argues in regard to British retailing practices, *ethical* is an ascription that supermarkets have chosen as a sort of greenwashing that is not tantamount to "fair" much less "just." Indeed, any labeling system that does not significantly enroll those on whose behalf it appears to act is necessarily problematic (Esbenshade 2004).

2. See Leslie and Reimer 1999, as well as Bair (this volume, Chapter 1) for useful taxonomies and reviews of the commodity chains literature much more comprehensive than what I provide here.

3. Dixon also appended state regulation to the commodity systems approach.

4. Paradoxically, though, these sorts of standards aim for a much larger swath of producers and their practices than do the voluntary protective labels.

5. I have forwarded different elements of this argument elsewhere in much more extensive form than I can do here (Guthman 2002; 2003; 2004).

6. In that way, certification services should also be put to the test of transparency and value capture in commodity chain analysis, although that would be outside the scope of this chapter.

Chapter 10

1. The de facto moratorium ended in 2004 with the EU's passage of the new traceability and labeling requirements.

2. See Schurman 2004 for details.

3. Although we use the term *anti-GMO movement* for expediency, it is important for readers to recognize that not all of the individuals and groups involved in this

movement are firmly opposed to the use of any genetic engineering in agriculture. Although there are some that take an extreme position ("not on Planet Earth"), others are not philosophically or morally opposed, but want to see the technology better studied, regulated, and subjected to more democratic debate.

4. These openings are broadly analogous to the "political opportunity structures" discussed by some social movement theorists. See especially McAdam 1982; McAdam, McCarthy, and Zald 1996. They differ, however, in being defined by the organizational structure of industry rather than by political institutions (see Schurman 2004).

5. Thus actor-networks comprise both structural and agential properties. They are structural inasmuch as they constitute strands of relationships between actors. They are agents inasmuch as they embody a set of actor-interests that congeal into the conditions that produce a particular outcome. Yet it is not necessary for particular actors' actions and interactions to be strategically geared toward advancing that outcome; they can do so simply by being part of the network. In this sense, actor-networks differ from the strategic notion of networking that characterizes conventional social network theory or advocacy networks (cf. Keck and Sikkink 1998).

6. For more detail on the history of this movement, see Purdue 2000.

7. This in turn reflected an increase in financial support for anti-GM groups by some private foundations, including Edward Goldsmith's foundation. Goldsmith is editor of *The Ecologist*.

8. The "big five" include Tesco, ASDA, Sainsbury's, Morrisons, and Somerfield.

9. There are clear similarities here to strategies employed by the anti-sweatshop campaigns; see, for instance, O'Rourke 2005 and Gereffi, Garcia-Johnson, and Sasser 2001.

10. The first genetically engineered food marketed in Britain, a tomato paste introduced by Zeneca in 1996 and proudly labeled "genetically altered," became a bestseller (Charles 2001: 168); for a skeptical view of British cultural opposition to GMOs, see Millstone 2000.

11. These figures come from www.cjd.ed.ac.uk/figures.htm, downloaded on April 28, 2003.

12. This case illustrates how closely integrated European markets are for agricultural imports from America. The seed had been sold in Sweden, France, Germany, and the United Kingdom. The contamination was in fact discovered in a field test in Germany.

13. These resentments had been severely heightened by the prolonged trade war over European resistance to the importation of hormone-treated beef from the United States in the mid-1990s. The United States ultimately won that battle.

14. In the interest of space, we do not detail the movement's actions here. For more detail, see Schurman and Munro 2006.

15. One of the technologies whose introduction the United States anti-biotech movement was able to forestall was the "ice minus bacterium." (See Krimsky 1982 for a detailed case study.) The movement also slowed down Monsanto's introduction of bovine somatotropin for several years.

16. The coordinated framework was established in 1986 by the Reagan government and relies upon a decentralized system of decision making involving the USDA, the EPA, and the FDA. None of these agencies has taken up the mantle of risk assessment in a serious way. The EPA comes the closest, but throughout the 1980s and 1990s, government spending on biotech risk assessment was only 1 to 2 percent of the revenue devoted to biotechnology research.

17. Some firms have shown a willingness to share these data in recent years, although this decision remains a discretionary one for the firm.

18. In the 1990s, Monsanto was particularly aggressive in seeking to expand its market share (author interviews; also see Charles 2001).

19. During the 1990s, it became increasingly obvious to firms that gaining access to seed companies was crucial for getting their genes into the marketplace (author interviews with various industry representatives 2006; Mergermarket Limited 2005).

20. According to U.S. organic regulations, organically certified products may not include genetically modified ingredients.

21. Survey data indicate that public knowledge of genetic engineering has remained at a relatively low level (Pew Charitable Trusts 2005).

22. Bernauer (2003) draws the distinction between the EU's process-oriented approach to regulation and the United States's product-oriented approach. The former resulted in a stringent labeling regime; the latter did not.

References

Abernathy, Frederick, John Dunlop, Janice Hammond, and David Weil. 1999. *A stitch in time: Lean retailing and the transformation of manufacturing—Lessons from the apparel and textile industries.* New York: Oxford University Press.

Abreu, Marcelo de P., and Afonso S. Bevilaqua. 2000. Brazil as an export economy, 1880–1930. In *The export age: The Latin American economies in the late nineteenth and early twentieth centuries.* Vol. 1 of *An economic history of twentieth-century Latin America,* ed. Enrique Cardenas, José Antonio Ocampo, and Rosemary Throp, 32–54. New York: Palgrave.

Acona and Insight Investment. 2004. Buying your way into trouble? The challenge of responsible supply chain management. *Insight Investment;* available at www .insightinvestment.com/Documents/responsibility/responsible_supply_chain_ management.pdf.

Adler, Paul. 2001. Market, hierarchy, and trust: The knowledge economy and the future of capitalism. *Organization Science* 12(2):215–234.

Alderson, Arthur, and Jason Beckfield. 2004. Power and position in the world city system. *American Journal of Sociology* 109(4):811–851.

Allen, Patricia, and Martin Kovach. 2000. The capitalist composition of organic: The potential of markets in fulfilling the promise of organic agriculture. *Agriculture and Human Values* 17(3):221–232.

Amin, Samir. 1980. The class structure of the contemporary imperialist system. *Monthly Review* 31(8):9–26.

Amsden, Alice. 1989. Asia's next giant: South Korea and late industrialization. New York: Oxford University Press.

———. 2001. *The rise of "the rest": Challenges to the West from late-industrializing economies.* New York: Oxford University Press.

Anderson, Oscar E. 1958. *The health of a nation: Harvey W. Wiley and the fight for pure food*. Chicago: University of Chicago Press.

Appadurai, Arjun. 1986. Introduction: Commodities and the politics of value. In *The social life of things*, ed. Arjun Appadurai, 3–63. Cambridge, UK: Cambridge University Press.

Appelbaum, Richard P. 2008. Giant transnational contractors in East Asia: Emergent trends in global supply chains. *Competition and Change* 12(1):69–87.

Appelbaum, Richard P., and Gary Gereffi. 1994. Power and profits in the apparel commodity chain. In *Global production: The apparel industry in the Pacific rim,* ed. Edna Bonachich, Lucie Cheng, Norma Chinchilla, Nora Hamilton, and Paul Ong, 42–62. Philadelphia: Temple University Press.

Appelbaum, Richard P., and David A. Smith. 2001. Governance and flexibility: The East Asian garment industry. In *Economic governance and the challenge of flexibility in East Asia,* ed. Frederic C. Deyo, Richard F. Doner, and Eric Herschberg, 79–105. Boulder, CO: Rowman and Littlefield.

Arce, A., and Marsden, T. K. 1993. The social construction of international food: A new research agenda. *Economic Geography* 69(3):293–311.

Arndt, Sven, and Henryk Kierzkowski, eds. 2001. *Fragmentation: New production patterns in the world economy*. Oxford: Oxford University Press.

Arrighi, Giovanni. 1990. The developmentalist illusion: A reconceptualization of the semiperiphery. In *Semiperipheral states in the world-economy,* ed. William Martin, 11–42. New York: Greenwood Press.

Arrighi, Giovanni, and Jessica Drangel. 1986. The stratification of the world-economy. *Review* 10(1):9–74.

Bacha, Edmar. 1992. "Política brasileira de café." In *150 anos de café,* ed. Marcellino Martins and E. Johnston, 20. Rio de Janeiro: Marcellino Martins and E. Johnston.

Bair, Jennifer. 2002. Beyond the maquila model? NAFTA and the Mexican apparel industry. *Industry and Innovation* 9(3):203–225.

———. 2005. Global capitalism and commodity chains: Looking back, going forward. *Competition and Change* 9(2):153–180.

———. 2008. Analysing economic organization: Embedded networks and global chains compared. *Economy and Society* 37(3):339–364.

Bair, Jennifer, and Gary Gereffi. 2001. Local clusters in global chains: The causes and consequences of export dynamism in Torreon's blue jeans industry. *World Development* 29(11):1885–1903.

Bairoch, Paul. 1974. Geographical structure and trade balance of European foreign trade from 1800 to 1970. *Journal of European Economic History* 3(3):606.

Balconi, Margherita. 2002. Tacitness, codification of technological knowledge and the organisation of industry. *Research Policy* 31(3):357–379.

Baldwin, Carliss, and Kimberly Clark. 2000. *Design rules: Unleashing the power of modularity*. Cambridge, MA: MIT Press.

Barham, Bradford, Stephen Bunker, and Denis O'Hearn. 1994. *States, firms, and raw materials: The world economy and ecology of aluminum*. Madison: University of Wisconsin Press.

Barney, Jay. 1991. Firm resources and sustained competitive advantage. *Journal of Management* 17(1):99–120.

Barrientos, Stephanie, Catherine Dolan, and Anne Tallontire. 2003. A gendered value chain approach to codes of conduct in African horticulture. *World Development* 31(9):1511–1526.

Barrientos, Stephanie, and Andrienetta Kritzinger. 2004. Squaring the circle: Global production and the informalization of work. *Journal of International Development* 16(1):81–92.

Bartels, Lambert. 1983. Oromo religion: Myths and rites of the western Oromo of Ethiopia—An attempt to understand. Berlin: Reimer.

Bates, Robert. 1997. Open-economy politics: The political economy of world coffee. Princeton, NJ: Princeton University Press.

BBC News. 1998. Iceland freezes out "genetic" foods. BBC Online Network, March 18.

Becker, Howard S. 1995. The Power of Inertia. *Qualitative Sociology* 18(3):301–309.

Bell, David, and Gill Valentine. 1997. *Consuming geographies: We are where we eat.* London: Routledge.

Benton, Ted. 1989. Marxism and natural limits: An ecological critique and reconstruction. *New Left Review* 178:51–86.

Berger, Suzanne, and Ronald Dore, eds. 1996. *National diversity and global capitalism.* Ithaca, NY: Cornell University Press.

Berger, Suzanne, and the MIT Industrial Performance Center. 2005. *How we compete.* New York: Doubleday.

Bernauer, Thomas. 2003. Genes, trade, and regulation: The seeds of conflict in food biotechnology. Princeton, NJ: Princeton University Press.

Bhatta, Saurav Dev. 2002. Has the increase in world-wide openness to trade worsened global income inequality? *Papers in Regional Science* 81:177–196.

Biggart, Nicole Woolsey. 1990. Institutionalized Patrimonialism in Korean Business. *Comparative Social Research* 12:113–133.

Biggart, Nicole Woolsey, and Mauro F. Guillén. 1999. Developing difference: Social organization and the rise of the auto industries of South Korea, Taiwan, Spain, and Argentina. *American Sociological Review* 64:722–747.

Block, Fred. 1987. *Revising state theory: Essay in politics and postindustrialism.* Philadelphia: Temple University Press.

Block, Fred, and Peter Evans. 2005. The state and the economy. In *Handbook of economic sociology,* 2nd edition, ed. Neil Smelser and Richard Swedberg, 505–526. Princeton, NJ: Princeton University Press.

Bluestone, Barry, Patricia Hanna, Sarah Kuhn, and Laura Moore. 1981. *The retail revolution: Market transformation, investment, and labor in the modern department store.* Boston: Auburn House.

Bluestone, Barry, and Bennett Harrison. 1982. *The deindustrialization of America.* New York: Basic Books.

Bonacich, Edna. 2005. Labor and the global logistics revolution. In *Critical globalization studies,* ed. Richard Appelbaum and William Robinson, 359–368. New York: Routledge.

Bonacich, Edna, and Jake B. Wilson. 2007. *Getting the goods: The logistics revolution and the ports of Southern California.* Ithaca, NY: Cornell University Press.

Borgatti, Stephen P. 1994. How to explain hierarchical clustering. *Connections* 17(2):78–80.

Borgatti, Stephen P., and Martin G. Everett. 1999. Models of core/periphery structures. *Social Networks* 21(4):375–395.

Bornschier, Volker, and Christopher Chase-Dunn. 1985. *Transnational corporations and underdevelopment.* New York: Praeger.

Borrus, Michael, Dieter Ernst, and Stephen Haggard, eds. 2000. *International production networks in Asia.* London and New York: Routledge.

Borrus, Michael, and John Zysman. 1997. *Wintelism and the changing terms of global competition: Prototype of the future?* Working paper 96B, Berkeley Roundtable on the International Economy, February.

Boyd, John, William Fitzgerald, Matthew C. Mahutga, and David A. Smith. 2006. *Computing continuous core/periphery structures for social relations data using MINRES SVD.* Paper presented at the 26th annual Sunbelt Social Network Conference of the International Network for Social Network Analysis, April 28th, in Vancouver, British Columbia, Canada.

Boyd, William. 2003. Wonderful potencies? Deep structure and the problem of monopoly in agricultural biotechnology. In *Engineering trouble: Biotechnology and its discontents,* ed. Rachel Schurman and Dennis D. Kelso, 24–62. Berkeley and Los Angeles: University of California Press.

Boyer, Robert. 1990. *The regulation school.* New York: Columbia University Press.

Brazil, IBGE. 1986. *Séries estatísticas retrospectivas,* vol. 1. Rio de Janeiro: IBGE.

Brinton, Mary, ed. 2001. *Women's working lives in East Asia.* Stanford, CA: Stanford University Press.

Brown, P. 2001. Frankenfoods debate in the UK rages on. *The Guardian* (UK), May 15.

Brusoni, Stefano, and Andrea Principe. 2001. Unpacking the black box of modularity: Technology, products, and organisations. *Industrial and Corporate Change* 10(1):179–205.

Bunker, Stephen. 1984. Modes of extraction, unequal exchange, and the progressive underdevelopment of an extreme periphery: The Brazilian Amazon, 1600–1980. *American Journal of Sociology* 89(5):1017–1064.

———. 1985. Underdeveloping the Amazon: Extraction, unequal exchange, and the failure of the modern state. Urbana: University of Illinois Press.

———. 1989. Staples, links and poles in the construction of regional development theory. *Sociological Forum* 4(4):589–610.

Bunker, Stephen, and Paul Ciccantell. 2005. *Globalization and the race for resources.* Baltimore: Johns Hopkins University Press.

Burt, Ronald S. 1992. *Structural holes: The social structure of competition.* Cambridge, MA: Harvard University Press.

———. 2004. Structural holes and good ideas. *American Journal of Sociology* 110(2): 349–399.

Busch, Lawrence. 2000. The moral economy of grades and standards. *Regional Studies* 16(3):273–283.

Buzby, Jean C., and Stephen Haley. 2007. Coffee consumption over the last century. *Amber Waves* (June):5.

Cain, P. J., and A. G. Hopkins. 1993. *British imperialism: Innovation and expansion 1688–1914*. London: Longman.

Campbell, Gwyn. 2003. The origins and development of coffee production in Réunion and Madagascar, 1711–1972. In *The global coffee economy in Africa, Asia and Latin America, 1500–1989*, ed. William Clarence-Smith and Steven Topik, 67–99. New York: Cambridge University Press.

Campbell, Hugh. 2005. The rise and rise of EurepGAP: European (re)invention of colonial food relations? *International Journal of Sociology of Agriculture and Food* 13(2):1–19.

Cardoso, Fernando H. 1973. Associated-dependent development: Theoretical and practical implications. In *Authoritarian Brazil*, ed. Alfred Stepan. New Haven, CT: Yale University Press.

Carr, Susan. 2000. *EU safety regulation of genetically-modified crops: Summary of a ten-year country study*. Milton Keynes, UK: The Open University.

Caves, Richard. 1996. *Multinational enterprise and economic analysis*. 2nd ed. Cambridge, UK: Cambridge University Press.

Chamberlin, Edward. 1933. *The theory of monopolistic competition*. Cambridge, MA: Harvard University Press.

Chandler, Alfred D., Jr. 1977. *The visible hand: The managerial revolution in American business*. Cambridge, MA: Harvard University Press.

———. 1990. *Scale and scope: The dynamics of industrial capitalism*. Cambridge, MA: Harvard University Press.

Charles, Daniel. 2001. *Lords of the harvest: Biotech, big money, and the future of food*. Cambridge, MA: Perseus Publishing.

Chase-Dunn, Christopher. 1989. *Global formation: Structures of the world-economy*. Cambridge, MA: Blackwell.

Chayanov, Aleksandr Vasil'evich. [1924] 1986. *The theory of peasant economy*. Madison: University of Wisconsin Press.

Cheng, Lu-lin. 1996. *Embedded competitiveness: Taiwan's shifting role in international footwear sourcing networks*. Ph.D. dissertation, Duke University.

Chirot, Daniel. 1977. *Social change in the twentieth century*. New York: Harcourt Brace Jovanovich.

Chow, Peter C. Y., and Mitchell H. Kellman. 1993. *Trade—The engine of growth in East Asia*. Oxford: Oxford University Press.

Clancy, Michael. 1998. Commodity chains, services and development: Theory and preliminary evidence from the tourism industry. *Review of International Political Economy* 5(1):122–148.

Clarence-Smith, William Gervase. 2003. The coffee crisis in Asia, Africa, and the Pacific, 1870–1914. In *The global coffee economy in Africa, Asia and Latin America,*

1500–1989, ed. William Clarence-Smith and Steven Topik, 100–119. New York: Cambridge University Press, 2003.

Coase, Ronald. 1937. The nature of the firm. *Economica* 4(16):386–405.

Coe, Neil, and Martin Hess. 2005. The internationalization of retailing: Implications for supply network restructuring in East Asia and Eastern Europe. *Journal of Economic Geography* 5:449–473.

Coe, Neil, Martin Hess, Henry Wai-chung Yeung, Peter Dicken, and Jeffrey Henderson. 2004. Globalizing regional development: A global production networks perspective. *Transactions of the Institute of British Geographers* 29(4):468–484.

Cohen, Deborah, and Carey Gillam. 2002. Oregon GMO label defeat spells uphill battle ahead. *Reuters News,* November 11.

Cohen, Robert B., Nadine Felton, Morley Nkosi, and Jaap van Liere, eds. 1979. *The multinational corporation: A radical approach—Papers by Stephen Hymer.* New York: Cambridge University Press.

Collins, J. 2005. New directions in commodity chain analysis of global development processes. *Research in Rural Sociology and Development* 11:1–15.

Cook, Ian, and Philip Crang. 1996: The world on a plate: culinary culture, displacement and geographical knowledges. *Journal of Material Culture* (1):131–153.

Cook, Ian, Philip Crang, and M. Thorpe. 2004. Tropics of consumption: "Getting with the fetish" of "exotic" fruit. In *Geographies of commodity chains,* ed. Alex Hughes and Suzanne Reimer, 173–192. London: Routledge.

Cowan, Brian. 2005. *The social life of coffee: The emergence of the British coffeehouse.* New Haven, CT: Yale University Press.

Cramer, Christopher. 1999. Can Africa industrialize by processing primary commodities? The case of Mozambican cashew nuts. *World Development* 27(7):1247–1266.

Cronon, William. 1991. *Nature's metropolis.* New York: W. W. Norton.

Crosby, Alfred. 1986. *Ecological imperialism.* New York: Cambridge University Press.

Cumings, Bruce. 1984. The origins and development of the Northeast Asian political economy: Industrial sectors, product cycles, and political consequences. *International Organization* 38:1–40.

Curtin, Philip D. 1984. *Cross-cultural trade in world history.* Cambridge, UK: Cambridge University Press.

Czaban, Laszlo, and Jeffrey Henderson. 1998. Globalisation, institutional legacies and industrial transformation in Eastern Europe. *Economy and Society* 27(4):585–613.

Daviron, Benoit, and Peter Gibbon. 2002. Global commodity chains and African export agriculture. *Journal of Agrarian Change* 2(2):137–161.

Daviron, Benoit, and Stefano Ponte. 2005. The coffee paradox: Global markets, commodity trade and the elusive promise of development. London: Zed Books.

Davis, A., P. R. Goeverts, D. M. Bridson, and P. Stoffelen. 2006. An annotated taxonomic conspectus of the genus *Coffea* (*Rubiaceae*). *Botanical Journal of the Linean Society* 152:465–512.

Davis, Kingsley, ed. 1945. *World population in transition.* Philadelphia: American Academy of Political and Social Science.

Department of Trade and Industry. 2004. Pay raise for low paid worker, press release, September 30; available at http://archive.nics.gov.uk/eti/040930d-eti.htm; accessed April 22, 2008.

Dicken, Peter. 1992. *Global shift: The internationalisation of economic activity.* London: Paul Chapman Publishing.

———. 2005. Tangled webs: Transnational production networks and regional integration. *SPACES Working Paper 2005-04.* Geography, Phillips-University of Marburg, Germany, 1–27.

———. 2007. *Global shift: Mapping the contours of the world economy,* 5th ed. London: Sage.

Dicken, Peter, P. Kelly, K. Olds, and Henry Wai-chung Yeung. 2001. Chains and networks, territories and scales: Towards a relational framework for analysing the global economy. *Global Networks* 1(2):89–112.

Dickinson, James M., and Susan A. Mann. 1978. Obstacles to the development of a capitalist agriculture. *Journal of Peasant Studies* 5(4):466–481.

Dicum, Gregory, and Nina Luttinger. 1999. *The coffee book: Anatomy of an industry from crop to last drop.* New York: New Press.

Dixon, Jane. 1997. A cultural economy model for studying food systems. *Agriculture and Human Values* 16(2):151–160.

Dobbins, Frank. 1994. *Forging industrial policy: The United States, Britain, and France in the Railway Age.* Cambridge, UK: Cambridge University Press.

Dolan, Catherine, and John Humphrey. 2000. Governance and trade in fresh vegetables: The impact of UK supermarkets on the African horticulture industry. *Journal of Development Studies* 37(2):147–176.

Dolan, Catherine S., and Kristina Sorby. 2003. *Gender and employment in high-value agricultural and rural industries.* Agriculture and Rural Development World Paper Series No. 7. Washington, DC: World Bank.

Domhoff, C. William. 1967. *Who rules America?* Englewood Cliffs, NJ: Prentice-Hall.

Dowrick, Steve, and Muhammad Akmal. 2005. Contradictory trends in global income inequality: A tale of two biases. *Review of Income and Wealth* 51(2):201–229.

Drickhamer, David. 2002. Under fire. *Industry Week,* June:30–36.

du Toit, Andries. 2003. *Hunger in the valley of fruitfulness: Globalisation, "social exclusion" and chronic poverty in Ceres, South Africa. Programme for Land and Agrarian Studies.* Draft paper to be presented at Staying Poor: Chronic Poverty and Development Poverty Conference, April 7–9, in Manchester, United Kingdom.

Dunn, Elizabeth. 2003. Trojan pig: Paradoxes of food safety regulation. *Environment and Planning A* 35(8):1493–1511.

DuPuis, E. Melanie. 1998. The body and the country: A political ecology of consumption. In *New forms of consumption: Consumers, culture and commodification,* ed. Mark Gottdiener, 131–152. Lanham, MD: Rowan & Littlefield.

———. 2001. *Nature's perfect food.* New York: New York University Press.

DuPuis, E. Melanie, and David Goodman. 2005. Should we go "home" to eat? Towards a reflexive politics of localism. *Regional Studies* 21(3):359–371.

The Economist. 1998. Food fights. June 13, 1998.

Emmanuel, Arghiri. 1972. *Unequal exchange: A study of the imperialism of trade.* New York: Monthly Review Press.

Emmott, Steve. 2001. No patents on life: The incredible ten-year campaign against the European patent directive. In *Redesigning life? The worldwide challenge to genetic engineering,* ed. Brian Tokar. London: Zed Books.

Ernst, Dieter. 1999. *Globalization and the changing geography of innovation systems.* Paper presented at the Workshop on the Political Economy of Technology in Developing Countries, October 8–9, in Brighton, United Kindgom.

Esbenshade, Jill. 2004. *Monitoring sweatshops: Workers, consumers, and the global apparel industry.* Philadelphia: Temple University Press.

Evans, Peter B. 1979a. Beyond core and periphery: A comment on the world system approach to the study of development. *Sociological Inquiry* 49(4):15–20.

———. 1979b. *Dependent development: The alliance of multinational, state, and local capital in Brazil.* Princeton, NJ: Princeton University Press.

———. 1987. Class, state, and dependence in East Asia: Lessons for Latin Americanists. In *The political economy of the new Asian industrialism,* ed. Frederic C. Deyo, 203–226. Ithaca, NY: Cornell University Press.

———. 1995. *Embedded autonomy: States and industrial tranformation.* Princeton, NJ: Princeton University Press.

Evans, Peter B., and James E. Rauch. 1999. Bureaucracy and growth: A cross-national analysis of the effects of "Weberian" state structures on economic growth. *American Sociological Review* 64:748–765.

Evans, Peter B., Dietrich Rueschemeyer, and Theda Skocpol, eds. 1985. *Bringing the state back in.* Cambridge, UK: Cambridge University Press.

Evans, Peter B., and John Stephens. 1988. Development and the world economy. In *Handbook of sociology,* ed. Neil Smelser. Newbury Park, CA: Sage.

Faroqhi, Suraiya. 1994. Trade: Regional, inter-regional, and international. In *An economic and social history of the Ottoman Empire,* vol. 2, ed. Suraiya Faroqui et al., 474–530. Cambridge, UK: Cambridge University Press.

Faust, Katherine. 1988. Comparison of methods for positional analysis: Structural and general equivalences. *Social Networks* 10:313–341.

Feenstra, Robert C. 1998. Integration of trade and disintegration of production in the global economy. *Journal of Economic Perspectives* 12(4):31–50.

Feenstra, Robert C., and Gary Hamilton. 2006. *Emergent economies, divergent paths: Economic organization and international trade in South Korea and Taiwan.* Cambridge: Cambridge University Press.

Fernandez-Cornejo, J. 2004. *The seed industry in U.S. agriculture: An exploration of data and information on crop seed markets, regulation, industry structure, and research and development.* Washington, DC: United States Dept. of Agriculture, Economic Research Service.

Fernando, M. R. 2003. Coffee cultivation in Java, 1830–1917. In *The global coffee economy in Africa, Asia and Latin America, 1500–1989,* ed. William Clarence-Smith and Steven Topik, 157–172. New York: Cambridge University Press.

Feuntes, Annette, and Barbara Ehrenreich. 1984. *Women in the global factory*. Boston: South End Press.

Fine, Ben. 1994. Towards a political economy of food. *Review of International Political Economy* 1(3):519–545.

———. 1998. *The political economy of diet, health and food policy*. London: Routledge.

———. 2002. *World of consumption: The material and the cultural revisited*. New York: Routledge.

Fine, Ben, and Ellen Leopold. 1993. *The world of consumption*. London: Routledge.

Fine, Ben, Michael Heasman, and Judith Wright. 1996. *Consumption in the age of affluence: The world of food*. New York: Routledge.

Firebaugh, Glenn. 1999. Empirics of world income inequality. *American Journal of Sociology* 104(6):1597–1630.

———. 2000a. Observed trends in between-nation income inequality, and two conjectures. *American Journal of Sociology* 106:215–221.

———. 2000b. The trend in between-nation income inequality. *Annual Review of Sociology* 26(1):323–339.

———. 2003. *The new geography of global income inequality*. Cambridge, MA: Harvard University Press.

Firebaugh, Glenn, and Brian Goesling. 2004. Accounting for the recent decline in global income inequality. *American Journal of Sociology* 110(2):283–312.

Fitter, Robert, and Raphael Kaplinsky. 2001a. Who gains from product rents as the coffee market becomes more differentiated? *IDS Bulletin* 32(3):69–82.

Fitter, Robert, and Raphael Kaplinsky. 2001b. *Can an agricultural "commodity" be decommodified, and if so, who is to gain?* IDS Discussion Paper 380, Institute of Development Studies, University of Sussex, December.

FitzSimmons, Margaret, and David Goodman. 1998. Incorporating nature: Environmental narratives and the reproduction of food. In *Remaking reality: Nature at the millennium*, ed. Bruce Braun and Noel Castree, 194–220. London: Routledge.

Fligstein, Neil. 1985. The spread of the multidivisional firm. *American Sociological Review* 50:377–391.

———. 1990. *The transformation of corporate control*. Cambridge, MA: Harvard University Press.

———. 1996. Markets as politics: A political-cultural approach to market institutions. *American Sociological Review* 61(4):656–673.

———. 2001. *The architecture of markets: An economic sociology of twenty-first-century capitalist societies*. Princeton, NJ: Princeton University Press.

———. 2005. States, markets, and economic growth. In *The economic sociology of capitalism*, ed. Victor Nee and Richard Swedberg, 119–143. Princeton, NJ: Princeton University Press.

Fold, Niels. 2001. Restructuring of the European chocolate industry and its impact on cocoa production in West Africa. *Journal of Economic Geography* 1(3):405–420.

———. 2002. Lead firms and competition in "bi-polar" commodity chains: Grinders and branders in the global cocoa-chocolate industry. *Journal of Agrarian Change* 2(2):228–247.

Ford, Peter. 2001. Europe invites biotech debate. *The Christian Science Monitor,* September 11.

Frank, Andre Gunder. 1969a. *Latin America: Underdevelopment or revolution?* New York: Monthly Review Press.

———. 1969b. The sociology of development and the underdevelopment of sociology. *Catalyst* 3:20–73.

———. 1978. *World accumulation, 1492–1789.* New York: Monthly Review Press.

———. 1979. *Dependent accumulation and underdevelopment.* New York: Monthly Review Press.

Freidberg, Suzanne. 2003a. Cleaning up down south: Supermarkets, ethical trade, and African horticulture. *Journal of Social and Cultural Geography* 4(1):27–42.

———. 2003b. Culture, conventions and colonial constructs of rurality in South-North horticultural trades. *Regional Studies* 19:97–109.

———. 2004. *French beans and food scares: Culture and commerce in an anxious age.* Oxford: Oxford University Press.

Fridell, Gavin. 2007. *Fair trade coffee: The prospects and pitfalls of market-driven social justice.* Toronto: University of Toronto Press.

Friedland, William H. 1984. Commodity systems analysis: An approach to the sociology of agriculture. In *Research in rural sociology and development,* ed. Harry K. Schwarzweller, 221–235. London: JAI Press.

———. 2001. Reprise on commodity systems methodology. *International Journal of Sociology of Agriculture and Food* 9(1):82–103.

Friedland, William H., Amy E. Barton, and Robert J. Thomas. 1981. *Manufacturing green gold.* Cambridge, UK: Cambridge University Press.

Friedman, Lawrence M. 1973. *A history of American law.* New York: Simon & Schuster.

Friedmann, Harriet. 1982. The political economy of food: The rise and fall of the post-war international food order. *American Journal of Sociology* 88(Supplement):248–286.

Fröbel, Folker, Jürgen Heinrichs, and Otto Kreye. 1980. *The new international division of labor.* London: Cambridge University Press.

Gallagher, John, and Ronald Robinson. 1953. The imperialism of free trade. *Economic History Review,* 2nd series 6(1):1–15.

Galtung, Johan. 1971. A structural theory of imperialism. *Journal of Peace Research* 8(2):81–117.

Galvin, Peter, and Andre Morkel. 2001. The effect of product modularity on industry structure: The case of the world bicycle industry. *Industry and Innovation* 8(1):31–47.

Gaskell, George, et al. 2000. Biotechnology and the European public. *Nature Biotechnology* 18(September):935–938.

Gellert, Paul. 2003. Renegotiating a timber commodity chain: Lessons from Indonesia on the political construction of global commodity chains. *Sociological Forum* 18(1):53–84.

Gereffi, Gary. 1983. *The pharmaceutical industry and dependency in the Third World.* Princeton, NJ: Princeton University Press.

———. 1990. Paths of industrialization: An overview. In *Manufacturing miracles: Paths of industrialization in Latin America and East Asia*, ed. Gary Gereffi and Donald L. Wyman. Princeton, NJ: Princeton University Press.

———. 1992. New realities of industrial development in East Asia and Latin America: Global, regional, and national trends. In *States and development in the Asian Pacific Rim*, ed. Richard Appelbaum and Jeffrey Henderson, 85–112. Beverly Hills, CA: Sage.

———. 1994. The organization of buyer-driven global commodity chains: How U.S. retailers shape overseas production networks. In *Commodity chains and global capitalism*, ed. Gary Gereffi and Miguel Korzeniewicz, 95–122. Westport, CT: Praeger.

———. 1995. Global production systems and Third World development. In *Global change, regional response: The new international context of development*, ed. Barbara Stallings, 100–142. Cambridge, UK: Cambridge University Press.

———. 1996. Global commodity chains: New forms of coordination and control among nations and firms in international industries. *Competition and Change* 1(4):427–439.

———. 1999. International trade and industrial upgrading in the apparel commodity chain. *Journal of International Economics* 48(1):37–70.

———. 2001a. Shifting governance structures in global commodity chains, with special reference to the Internet. *American Behavioral Scientist* 44(10):1617–1637.

———. 2001b. Beyond the producer-driven/buyer-driven dichotomy: The evolution of global value chains in the Internet era. *IDS Bulletin* 32(3):30–40.

———. 2005. The global economy: Organisation, governance and development. In *The handbook of economic sociology*, 2nd ed., ed. Neil J. Smelser and Richard Swedberg, 160–182. Princeton, NJ: Princeton University Press and Russell Sage Foundation.

———. 2006. *The new offshoring of jobs and global development.* Geneva: ILO.

Gereffi, Gary, Ronie Garcia-Johnson, and Erika Sasser. 2001. The NGO-industrial complex. *Foreign Policy* July/August(125):56–65.

———. 2007. American consumers to blame for huge trade deficit with China. *Baltimore Sun*, February 8.

Gereffi, Gary, John Humphrey, Raphael Kaplinsky, and Timothy Sturgeon. 2001. Introduction: Globalisation, value chains, and development. *IDS Bulletin* 32(3):1–8.

Gereffi, Gary, John Humphrey, and Timothy Sturgeon. 2005. The governance of global value chains. *Review of International Political Economy* 12(1):78–104.

Gereffi, Gary, and Miguel Korzeniewicz. 1990. Commodity chains and footwear exports in the semiperiphery. In *Semiperipheral states in the world-economy*, ed. William Martin, 45–68. New York: Greenwood Press.

———, eds. 1994. *Commodity chains and global capitalism.* Westport, CT: Praeger.

Gereffi, Gary, Miguel Korzeniewicz, and Roberto Korzeniewicz. 1994. Introduction: Global commodity chains. In *Commodity chains and global capitalism*, ed. Gary Gereffi and Miguel Korzeniewicz, 1–14. Westport, CT: Praeger.

Gereffi, Gary, and Olga Memdovic. 2003. *The global apparel value chain: What prospects for upgrading by developing countries?* Vienna: United Nations Industrial Development Organization.

Gereffi, Gary, and Mei-Lin Pan. 1994. The Globalization of Taiwan's Apparel Industry. In *Global production: The apparel industry in the Pacific Rim,* ed. Edna Bonacich et al., 126–146. Philadelphia: Temple University Press.

Gereffi, Gary, and Donald Wyman. 1990. Manufacturing miracles: Paths of industrialization in Latin America and East Asia. Princeton, NJ: Princeton University Press.

Gerlach, Michael. 1992. *Alliance capitalism: The strategic organization of Japanese business.* Berkeley: University of California Press.

Gibbon, Peter. 2001a. Upgrading primary production: A global commodity chain approach. *World Development* 29(2):345–363.

———. 2001b. Agro-commodity chains: An introduction. *IDS Bulletin* 32(3):60–68.

———. 2003a. *Commodities, donors, value-chain analysis and upgrading.* Paper prepared for UNCTAD, November.

Gibbon, Peter, Jennifer Bair, and Stefano Ponte. 2008. Governing global value chains: An introduction. *Economy and Society* 37(3):315–338.

Gibbon, Peter, and Stefano Ponte. 2005. *Trading down: Africa, value chains, and the global economy.* Philadelphia: Temple University Press.

Goesling, Brian. 2001. Changing income inequalities within and between nations: New evidence. *American Sociological Review.* 66:745–761.

Goetzinger, M. E. 1921. *History of the house of Arbuckle.* n.p.: The Percolator.

Gold, Thomas B. 1986. *State and society in the Taiwan Miracle.* Armonk, New York: M.E. Sharpe.

Goodman, David. 1999. Agro-food studies in the "age of ecology": Nature, corporeality, bio-politics. *Sociologia Ruralis* 39(1):17–38.

Goodman, David, and E. Melanie DuPuiss. 2002. Knowing food and growing food: Beyond the production-consumption debate in the sociology of agriculture. *Sociologia Ruralis* 42(1):5–22.

Goodman, David, and M. R. Redclift. 1991. *Refashioning nature.* London: Routledge.

Goodman, David, Bernardo Sorj, and John Wilkinson. 1987. *From farming to biotechnology.* Oxford: Basil Blackwell.

Goodman, David, and Michael Watts. 1994. Reconfiguring the rural or fording the divide. *Journal of Peasant Studies* 221(1): 1–49.

Goodman, Michael K. 2004. Reading fair trade: Political ecological imaginary and the moral economy of fair trade foods. *Political Geography* 23(7): 891–915.

Gower, Annabell, and Michael Cusumano. 2002. *Platform leadership: How Intel, Microsoft, and Cisco drive industry innovation.* Cambridge, MA: Harvard Business School Press.

Grabher, Gernot. 2006. Trading routes, bypasses, and risky intersections: Mapping the travels of "networks" between economic sociology and economic geography. *Progress in Human Geography* 30(2):163–189.

Graeber, David. 1996. Beads and money: Notes toward a theory of wealth and power. *American Ethnologist* 23(1):4–24.

Graham, Richard. 1968. *Britain and the onset of modernization in Brazil.* Cambridge, UK: Cambridge University Press.

Granovetter, Mark. 1973. The strength of weak ties. *American Journal of Sociology* 78:1360–1380.

———. 1974. *Getting a job: A study of contacts and career.* Cambridge, MA: Harvard University Press.

———. 1985. Economic action and social structure: The problem of embeddedness. *American Journal of Sociology* 91(3):481–510.

———. 1992. Economic institutions as social constructions: A framework for analysis. *Acta Sociologica* 35(1):3–11.

———. 1994. Business groups. In *Handbook of economic sociology,* ed. Neil Smelser and Richard Swedberg, 453–475. Princeton, NJ: Princeton University Press.

———. 2005. Business groups and social organization. In *Handbook of economic sociology,* ed. Neil Smelser and Richard Swedberg, 429–450. Princeton, NJ: Princeton University Press.

Greenhill, Robert. 1977. Shipping. In *Business imperialism, 1840–1930. An inquiry based on British experience in Latin America,* ed. D.C.M. Platt, 119–155. Oxford: Clarendon Press.

———. 1993. E. Johnston: 150 anos em café. In *150 anos de café,* ed. Marcellino Martins and E. Johnston. Rio de Janeiro: Marcellino Martins and E. Johnston.

———. 1995. Investment group, free-standing company or multinational? Brazilian warrant 1909–1952. *Business History* 37(1):86–111.

The Guardian (UK). 2003. Special report: Supermarkets. In Guardian Unlimited.

Guillén, Mauro F. 2001. *The limits of convergence: Globalization and organizational change in Argentina, South Korea, and Spain.* Princeton, NJ: Princeton University Press.

Guthman, Julie. 2002. Commodified meanings, meaningful commodities: Re-thinking production-consumption links through the organic system of provision. *Sociologia Ruralis* 42(4):295–311.

———. 2003. Eating risk: The politics of labeling transgenic foods. In *Remaking the world: Genetic engineering and its discontents,* ed. Rachel A. Schurman and Dennis Doyle Takahashi-Kelso, 130–151. Berkeley: University of California Press.

———. 2004. Back to the land: The paradox of organic food standards. *Environment and Planning A* 36(3):511–528.

Haji-Salleh, Abdul Latif. 1997. *Competition, coalitions, and coordination in the global personal computer industry.* Ph.D. dissertation, Duke University.

Hall, Peter, and David Soskice, eds. 2001. *Varieties of Capitalism.* Oxford: Oxford University Press.

Hamilton, Gary G., and Nicole Woolsey Biggart. 1988. Market, culture, and authority: A comparative analysis of management and organization in the Far East. *American Journal of Sociology* 94 (Supplement):S52–S94.

Hamilton, Gary G., and Cheng-shu Kao. 2007. Taiwan's industrialization: The rise of a demand-responsive economy. In *Social Transformation in Chinese Societies,* vol. 3, 91–128. Boston: Brill.

Hamilton, Gary G., Misha Petrovic, and Robert C. Feenstra. 2006. Remaking the global economy: U.S. retailers and Asian manufacturers. In *Commerce and capitalism in Chinese societies*, ed. Gary G. Hamilton, 146–184. London: Routledge.

Hamilton, Gary G., Benjamin Senauer, and Misha Petrovic. Forthcoming. *The market makers: How retailers are reshaping the global economy.*

Harley, C. Knick. 1996. Late nineteenth century transportation, trade and settlement. In *The integration of the world economy, 1850–1914*, vol. 1, ed. C. Knick Harley, 236. Cheltenham, UK: Edward Elgar.

Hartwick, Elaine. 1998. Geographies of consumption: A commodity-chain approach. *Environment and Planning D: Society and Space* 16(4):423–437.

———. 2000. Towards a geographical politics of consumption. *Environment and Planning A* 32(7):1177–1192.

Harvey, David. 1989. *The condition of postmodernity.* Cambridge, MA.: Blackwell.

———. 1990. Between space and time: Reflections on the geographical imagination. *Annals of the Association of American Geographers* 80(3):418–434.

Hattox, Ralph. 1985. *Coffee and coffeehouses: The origins of a social beverage in the medieval Near East.* Seattle: University of Washington Press.

Hayter, Susan. 2004. *The social dimension of global production systems: A review of the issues.* Working Paper 35, World Commission on the Social Dimension of Globalisation. Geneva: ILO.

Helleiner, Gerald K. 1973. Manufactured exports from less-developed countries and multinational firms. *The Economic Journal* 83(329):21–47.

Heller, Chaia. 2002. From scientific risk to paysan savoir-faire: Peasant expertise in the French and global debate over GM crops. *Science as Culture* 11(1):5–37.

Helper, Susan. 1991. Strategy and irreversibility in supplier relationships: The case of the U.S. automobile industry. *The Business History Review* 65(4):781–824.

Henderson, George. 2004. "Free food": The local production of worth, and the circuit of decommodification: Toward a value theory of the surplus. *Environment and Planning D: Society and Space* 22(4):485–512.

Henderson, Jeffrey, Peter Dicken, Martin Hess, Neil Coe, and Henry Wai-chung Yeung. 2002. Global production networks and the analysis of economic development. *Review of International Political Economy* 9(3):436–464.

Henson, Spencer, and James Northern. 1998. Economic determinants of food safety controls in supply of retailer own-branded products in United Kingdom. *Agribusiness* 14(2):113–126.

Hess, Martin, and Neil Coe. (2006) Making connections: Global production networks, standards, and embeddedness in the mobile-telecommunications industry. *Environment and Planning A* 38:1205–1227.

Hess, Martin, and Henry Wai-chung Yeung. (2006) Wither production networks in economic geography? *Environment and Planning A* 38:1193–1204.

Hickman, Mark, and Bob Roberts. 2000. Commons statement over GM seed row. *PA News* (wire service), May 18.

Hirschman, Albert. 1981. *Essays in trespassing: economics to politics and beyond.* New York: Cambridge University Press.

Hollingsworth, J. Rogers, and Robert Boyer, eds. 1997. *Contemporary capitalism: The embeddedness of institutions.* Cambridge, UK: Cambridge University Press.

Hollingsworth, J. Rogers, Philippe Schmitter, and Wolfgang Streeck, eds. 1994. *Governing capitalist economies.* New York: Oxford University Press.

Hopkins, Terence K., and Immanuel Wallerstein. 1977. Patterns of development of the modern world-system. *Review* 1(2):11–145.

———. 1986. Commodity chains in the world-economy prior to 1800. *Review* 10(1):157–170.

———. 1994. Commodity chains: Construct and research. In *Commodity chains and global capitalism,* ed. Gary Gereffi and Miguel Korzeniewicz, 17–20, 48–50. Westport, CT: Praeger.

Hudson, Ian, and Mark Hudson. 2003. Removing the veil? Commodity fetishism, fair trade, and the environment. *Organization and Environment* 16(4):413–430.

Hughes, Alex, and Suzanne Reimer, eds. 2004. *Geographies of commodity chains.* New York: Routledge.

Humphrey, John. 2003. Globalization and supply chain networks: The auto industry in Brazil and India. *Global Networks* 3(2):121–141.

Humphrey, John, and Olga Memdovic. 2003. *The global automotive industry value chain: What prospects for upgrading by developing countries?* Vienna: United Nations Industrial Development Organization.

Humphrey, John, and Hubert Schmitz. 2001. Governance in global value chains. *IDS Bulletin* 32(2):19–29.

———. 2002. How does insertion in global value chains affect upgrading in industrial clusters? *Regional Studies* 36(9):1017–1027.

ILO. 2002. *Decent work and the informal economy.* Report VI, Report to the International Labour Conference 90th session, ILO Geneva.

Impactt. 2005. *Changing over time: Tackling supply chain labour issues through business practice.* London: Impactt Limited.

International Coffee Organization. 2007. *Total production of exporting countries;* available at www.ico.org/prices/po.htm.

Ito, Takatoshi. 2001. Growth, crisis, and the future of economic recovery in East Asia. In *Rethinking the East Asian miracle,* ed. Joseph E. Stiglitz and Shahid Yusuf, 55–94. New York: Oxford University Press.

Jackson, Peter, Neil Ward, and Polly Russell. 2006. Mobilising the commodity chain concept in the politics of food and farming. *Regional Studies* 22(2):129–141.

Jacobides, Michael, Thorbjørn Knudsen, and Mie Augier. 2006. Benefiting from innovation: Value creation, value appropriation and the role of industry architectures. *Research Policy* 35(8):1200–1221.

Jacobidies, Michael, and Sidney Winter. 2005. The co-evolution of capabilities and transaction costs: Explaining the institutional structure of production. *Strategic Management Journal* 26(5):395–413.

Jarillo, Jose-Carlos. 1988. On strategic networks. *Strategic Management Journal* 9:31–41.

Jessop, Bob. 1982. *The capitalist state.* New York: New York University Press.

Johanson, Jan, and Lars-Gunner Matsson. 1987. Interorganizational relations in industrial systems: A network approach compared with the transaction-cost approach. *International Studies of Management and Organization* 27(1):34–48.

Johnson, Chalmers. 1982. *MITI and the Japanese miracle: The growth of industrial policy, 1925–1975.* Stanford, CA: Stanford University Press.

Kaplinsky, Raphael. 1998. *Globalisation, industrialisation and sustainable growth: The pursuit of the Nth rent.* IDS Discussion Paper 365. Brighton, UK: Institute of Development Studies, University of Sussex.

———. 2000a. *Spreading the gains from globalization: What can be learned from global value chain analysis?* IDS Working Paper 110. Brighton, UK: Institute of Development Studies, University of Sussex.

———. 2000b. Globalisation and unequalisation: What can be learned from value chain analysis? *Journal of Development Studies* 37(2):117–146.

———. 2004. Spreading the gains from globalization: What can be learned from value chain analysis? *Problems of Economic Transition* 47(2):74–115.

———. 2005. *Globalization, poverty and inequality: Between a rock and a hard place.* Cambridge, UK: Polity Press.

———. 2006. How can agricultural commodity producers appropriate a greater share of value chain incomes? In *Agricultural commodity markets and trade: New approaches to analyzing market structure and instability,* ed. Alexander Sarris and David Hallam, 356–379. Cheltenham, UK: Food and Agriculture Organization of the United Nations and Edward Elgar.

Kaplinsky, Raphael, Mike Morris, and Jeff Readman. 2001. *Globalisation and upgrading: Innovation and learning in the wood furniture value chain.* Vienna: United Nations Industrial Development Organization.

———. 2002. The globalization of product markets and immiserizing growth: Lessons from the South African furniture industry. *World Development* 30(7):1159–1177.

Kautsky, Karl. [1899] 1988. *The agrarian question.* London: Zwan Press.

Keck, Margaret E., and Kathryn Sikkink. 1998. *Activists beyond borders: Advocacy networks in international politics.* Ithaca, NY: Cornell University Press.

Kick, Edward L. and Byron L. Davis. 2001. World-system structure and change: An analysis of global networks and economic growth across two time periods. *American Behavioral Scientist* 44(10):1567–1578.

Kick, Edward L., Byron L. Davis, Marlene Lehtinen, and Thomas J. Burnes. 2000. World-system position, national political characteristics and economic development outcomes. *Journal of Political and Military Sociology* 28(1):131–155.

Kimura, Seishi. 2007. *The challenges of late industrialization: The global economy and the Japanese commercial aircraft industry.* London: Palgrave Macmillan.

Kloppenburg, J. Jr. 1988. *First the seed: The political economy of plant biotechnology,* 1st ed. Cambridge, UK: Cambridge University Press.

Kohli, Atul. 2004. *State-directed development: Political power and industrialization in the global periphery.* New York: Cambridge University Press.

Korzeniewicz, Roberto, and Timothy P. Moran. 1997. World-economic trends in the distribution of income, 1965–1992. *American Journal of Sociology* 102:1000–1039.

———. 2000. Measuring world income inequalities. *American Journal of Sociology* 106:209–214.

Krimsky, Sheldon. 1982. *Genetic alchemy: The social history of the recombinant DNA controversy.* Cambridge, MA: MIT Press.

Krueger, Anne. 1997. Trade policy and economic development: How we learn. *The American Economic Review* 87(1):1–22.

Krugman, Paul R. 1995. Growing world trade. *Brookings Papers on Economic Activity,* 1:327–377.

———. 1996. *The self-organizing economy.* Oxford: Blackwell.

Laerne, C. F. Van Delden. 1885. *Brazil and java: Report on coffee-culture in America, Asia, and Africa to H.E. the Minister of Colonies.* London: W.H. Allen & Co.

Langlois, Richard N. 2003. The vanishing hand: The changing dynamics of industrial capitalism. *Industrial and Corporate Change* 12: 351–385.

Lardy, Nicholas R. 2003. United States-China Ties: Reassessing the Economic Relationship. Testimony Before the House Committee on International Relations, U.S. House of Representatives, Washington DC, October 21.

Laseter, Tim, and Keith Oliver. 2003. When will supply chain management grow up? *Strategy + Business* 32:20–25.

Lean, Geoffrey, Volker Angres, and Louise Jury. 2000. GM genes can spread to people and animals. *Independent,* May 28.

Lee, Ji-Ren, and Jen-Shyang Chen. 2000. Dynamic synergy creation with multiple business activities: Toward a competence-based business model for contract manufacturers. In *Advances in applied business strategy, 6A (Theory development for competence-based management),* ed. Ron Sanchez and Aime Heene, 209–228. Stamford, CT: JAI Press.

Leff, Nathaniel H. 1982. *Underdevelopment and development in Brazil,* vol. 1. London: Allen and Unwin.

Leslie, Deborah, and Suzanne Reimer. 1999. Spatializing commodity chains. *Progress in Human Geography* 23(3):401–420.

Leung, H-C. 1997. *Local lives and global commodity chains: Timing, networking, and the Hong Kong-based garment industry 1957–1993.* Ph.D. dissertation, Duke University.

Levi, Margaret, and April Linton. 2003. Fair trade: A cup at a time? *Politics and Society* 31(3):407–432.

Levinson, Marc. 2006. *The box: How the shipping container made the world smaller and the world economy bigger.* Princeton, NJ: Princeton University Press.

Levy, Brian. 1991. Transactions costs, the size of firms, and industrial policy: Lessons from a comparative case study of the footwear industry in Korea and Taiwan. *Journal of Development Economics* 34:151–178.

Levy, Frank, and Richard Murnane. 2004. *The new division of labor: How computers are creating the next job market.* Princeton, NJ: Princeton University Press.

Lewis, W. Arthur. 1978. *Growth and fluctuations, 1870–1913.* London: Allen and Unwin.

Light, Ivan. 2005. The ethnic economy. In *The Handbook of Economic Sociology,* 2nd ed., ed. Neil J. Smelser and Richard Swedberg, 650–677. Princeton, NJ: Princeton University Press.

Light, Ivan, and Edna Bonacich. 1988. *Immigrant entrepreneurs: Koreans in Los Angeles, 1965–1982.* Berkeley: University of California Press.

Lockie, Stewart. 2002. "The invisible mouth": Mobilizing "the consumer" in food production-consumption networks. *Sociologia Ruralis* 42(4):278–294.

Lockie, Stewart, and Simon Kitto. 2000. Beyond the farm gate: Production-consumption networks and agri-food research. *Sociologia Ruralis* 40(1):3–19.

Lorenz, Edward. 1988. Neither friends nor strangers: Informal networks of subcontracting in French industry. In *Trust: Making and breaking cooperative relations,* ed. Diego Gambetta, 194–210. Oxford, New York: Basil Blackwell.

Lundvall, Bengt-Åke. 1992. *National systems of innovation: Towards a theory of innovation learning.* London: Pinter Publishers.

Lundvall, Bengt-Åke, Bjorn Johnson, Esben Sloth Andersen, and Bent Dalum. 2002. National systems innovation and competence building. *Research Policy* 31(2):213–231.

Mahutga, Matthew. 2005. *Measuring global and actor level change in core/periphery structures with correspondence analysis: An application to international trade.* Paper presented at the 25th annual Sunbelt Social Network Conference, February 19, in Redondo Beach, California.

———. 2006. The persistence of structural inequality?: A network analysis of international trade, 1965–2000. *Social Forces* 84(4):1863–1889.

Mann, Susan Archer. 1989. *Agrarian capitalism in theory and practice.* Chapel Hill: University of North Carolina Press.

Martínez-Torres, Maria Elena. 2006. *Organic coffee. Sustainable development by Mayan farmers.* Athens, Ohio: Ohio University Press.

Martins, Marcellino, and E. Johnston, 1992. *150 anos de café.* Rio de Janeiro: Marcellino Martins and E. Johnston.

Marx, Karl. [1867] 1992. *Capital,* Vol. I. New York: International Publishers.

McAdam, Doug. 1982. *Political process and the development of black insurgency, 1930–1970.* Chicago: University of Chicago Press.

McAdam, Doug, John D. McCarthy, and Mayer N. Zald, eds. 1996. *Comparative perspectives on social movements: Political opportunities, mobilizing structures, and cultural framings.* Cambridge, UK: Cambridge University Press.

McRobbie, Angela. 1997. Bridging the gap: Feminism, fashion and consumption. *Feminist Review* 55:73–89.

Melchior, Arne, and Kjetil Telle. 2001. Global income distribution, 1965–1998: Convergence and marginalization. *Forum for Development Studies* 1 (June):75–98.

Mergermarket Limited. 2005. *Genetic seed competition among giants to lower prices.* New York: SeedQuest.

Meyer, John W., and Brian Rowan. 1977. Institutionalized organizations: Formal structure as myth and ceremony. *American Journal of Sociology* 83(2):340–363.

Michaels, Lucy. 2003. *What's wrong with supermarkets?* Oxford, UK: The Agricultural Project at Corporate Watch UK.

Miller, Rory. 1993. Britain and Latin America in the nineteenth and twentieth centuries. Cambridge, UK: Cambridge University Press.

Mills, C. Wright. 1956. *The power elite.* New York: Oxford University Press.

Millstone, Erik. 2000. Analyzing biotechnology's traumas. *New Genetics and Society* 19(2):117–132.

Ministry of Agriculture, Fisheries and Food. 2000. Communication on GM presence in UK oilseed rape crop. London: Ministry of Agriculture.

Mintz, Beth, and Michael Schwartz. 1985. *The power structure of American business.* Chicago: Chicago University Press.

Mintz, Sidney. 1985. *Sweetness and power: The place of sugar in modern history.* New York: Viking.

Montfort, Jean, and Jean-Claude Dutailly. 1983. *Les filières de production.* Paris: INSEE.

Moran, Timothy P. 2003. On the theoretical and methodological context of cross-national inequality data. *International Sociology* 18(2):351–378.

Mortensen, Dale T. 1988. Matching: Finding a partner for life or otherwise. *American Journal of Sociology* 94 (Supplement):S215–S240.

Murray, Douglas, and Laura Raynolds. 2000. Alternative trade in bananas: Obstacles and opportunities for progressive social change in the global economy. *Agriculture and Human Values* 17(1):65–74.

Murtha, Thomas, Stefanie Lenway, and Jeffrey Hart. 2001. *Managing new industry creation: Global knowledge formation and entrepreneurship in high technology.* Stanford, CA: Stanford Business Books.

Mutersbaugh, Tad. 2005. Just-in-space: Certified rural products, labor of quality, and regulatory spaces. *Regional Studies.* 21(4): 389–402.

Nee, Victor. 2007. China in transition: An interview with Victor Nee. *Accounts* (ASA Economic Sociology Section Newsletter) 7(1):2–6.

Nelson, Richard. 1994. Evolutionary theorizing about economic change. In *The handbook of economic sociology,* ed. Neil Smelser and Richard Swedberg, 108–136. Princeton, NJ: Princeton University Press.

Nelson, Richard, and Sidney Winter. 1982. *An evolutionary theory of economic change.* Cambridge, MA: Harvard University Press.

Nemeth, Roger, and David Smith. 1985. International trade and world-system structure: A multiple network analysis. *Review* 8:517–560.

Newfarmer, Richard, ed. 1985. *Profits, progress and poverty: Case studies of international industries in Latin America.* Notre Dame, IN: University of Notre Dame Press.

North, Douglass. 1958. Ocean freight rates and economic development, 1750–1913. *Journal of Economic History* 18(4):537–555.

———. 1990. *Institutions, institutional change and economic performance.* New York: Cambridge University Press.

Nugent, Jeffrey, and James Robinson, 2000. *Are endowments fate?* Working paper, University of Southern California.

Ocampo, José Antonio. 1984. *Colombia y la economia mundial 1830–1910.* Bogotá: Siglo Ventiuno.

Okunade, Albert A. 1991. Functional former habit effects in the U.S. demand for coffee. *Applied Economics* 24(11):1203–1212.

O'Riain, Sean. 2004. The politics of mobility in technology-driven commodity chains: Developmental coalitions in the Irish software industry. *International Journal of Urban and Regional Research* 28(3):642–663.

O'Rourke, Dara. 2005. Market movements: Nongovernmental strategies to influence global production and consumption. *Journal of Industrial Ecology* 9(1–2):115–128.

Oxfam International. 2004. *Trading away our rights: Women workers in global supply chains.* Oxford: Oxfam GB.

Özveren, Ëyup. 1994. The shipbuilding commodity chain, 1590–1790. In *Commodity chains and global capitalism,* ed. Gary Gereffi and Miguel Korzeniewicz. Westport, CT: Praeger.

Paige, Jeffery. 1987. Coffee and politics in Central America. In *Crises in the Caribbean basin,* ed. Richard Tardanico, 141–187. Newbury Park, CA: Sage.

Palpacuer, Florence. 2000. Competence-based strategies and global production networks: A discussion of current changes and their implications for employment. *Competition and Change* 4(4):353–400.

———. 2008. Bringing the social context back in: Governance and wealth distribution in global commodity chains. *Economy and Society* 37(3):393–419.

Pan, Mei-Lin. 1998. *Organizations in global capitalism: The case of Taiwan-based production networks in the apparel and computer industries.* Ph.D. dissertation, Duke University.

Pan American Coffee Bureau. 1970. *Coffee drinking in the United States.* New York: Pan American Coffee Bureau.

Pelizzon, Sheila. 1994. The grain flour commodity chain, 1590–1790. In *Commodity chains and global capitalism,* ed. Gary Gereffi and Miguel Korzeniewicz. Westport, CT: Praeger.

Penrose, Edith. 1959. *The theory of the growth of the firm.* Oxford: Basil Blackwell.

Perrow, Charles. 1981. Markets, hierarchies, and hegemony: A critique of Chandler and Williamson. In *Perspectives on organizational design and behavior,* ed. Andrew H. Van de Ven and William F. Joyce, 371–386. New York: Wiley.

———. 1986. *Complex organizations: A critical essay,* 3rd ed. New York: Random House.

———. 2002. *Organizing America: Wealth, power, and the origins of corporate capitalism.* Princeton, NJ: Princeton University Press.

Petkova, Iva. 2006. Shifting regimes of governance in the coffee market: From secular crisis to a new equilibrium. *Review of International Political Economy* 13(2):313–339.

Petrovic, Misha. 2005. *Market makers and market making: The evolution of consumer goods markets in the United States, 1870–2000.* Ph.D. dissertation, University of Washington.

Petrovic, Misha, and Gary Hamilton. 2006. Making global markets: Wal-Mart and its suppliers. In *Wal-Mart: Template for 21st Century Capitalism,* ed. Nelson Lichtenstein. New York: New Press.

Pew Charitable Trusts. 2005. "Americans' knowledge of genetically modified foods remains low; Majority are skeptical about animal cloning," Initiative on Food and Biotechnology, press release, November 15.

Phyne, John, and Jorge Mansilla. 2003. Forging linkages in the commodity chain: The case of the Chilean salmon farming industry. *Sociologia Ruralis* 43(2):108–127.

Piore, Michael, and Charles Sabel. 1984. *The Second Industrial Divide.* New York: Basic Books.

Platt, D.C.M., ed. 1977. *Business imperialism, 1840–1930: An inquiry based on British experience in Latin America.* Oxford: Oxford University Press.

Podolny, Joel M. 1993. A status-based model of market competition. *American Journal of Sociology* 98(4):829–872.

———. 2005. *Status signals: A sociological study of market competition.* Princeton, NJ: Princeton University Press.

Podolny, Joel M., and Karen L. Page. 1998. Network forms of organization. *Annual Review of Sociology* 24:57–76.

Polanyi, Karl. 1957. *The great transformation.* Boston: Beacon.

Ponte, Stefano. 2002. The "latte revolution"? Regulation, markets and consumption in the global coffee chain. *World Development* 30(7):1099–1122.

Ponte, Stefano, and Peter Gibbon. 2005. Quality standards, conventions and the governance of global value chains. *Economy and Society* 34(1):1–31.

Porter, Michael. 1985. *Competitive advantage: Creating and sustaining superior performance.* New York: Free Press.

———. 1990. *The competitive advantages of nations.* New York: Free Press.

Posthumus, Nicolaas Wilhelmus. 1946. *Inquiry into the history of prices in Holland.* Leiden: E.J. Brill.

Poulantzas, Nicos. 1969. The problem of the state. *New Left Review* 58: 67–78.

Powell, Walter. 1987. Hybrid organizational arrangements: New form or transitional development? *California Management Review* 30(1):67–87.

———. 1990. Neither market nor hierarchy: Network forms of organization. *Research in Organizational Behavior* 12:295–336.

Powell, William, Kenneth Koput, and Laurel Smith-Doerr. 1996. Interorganizational collaboration and the locus of innovation: Networks of learning in biotechnology. *Administrative Science Quarterly* 41(1):116–145.

Power, Michael. 1997. *The audit society: Rituals of verification.* Oxford: Oxford University.

Prechel, Harland. 1990. Steel and the state. *American Sociological Review* 55: 648–668.

———. 2000. *Big business and the state: Historical transitions and corporate transformation, 1880–1990s.* Albany: State University of New York Press.

Priest, Susanna Hornig. 2001. *A grain of truth: The media, the public, and biotechnology.* Lanham, MD: Rowman and Littlefield.

Purdue, Derrick A. 2000. *Anti-genetiX: The emergence of the anti-GM movement.* Aldershot, UK: Ashgate.

Quack, Sigrid, Glen Morgan, and Richard Whitley, eds. 2000. *National capitalisms, global competition, and economic performance.* Amsterdam: John Benjamins.

Quan, Katie. 2008. Use of global value chains by labor organizers. *Competition and Change* 12(1):89–104.

Rabach, Eileen, and Eun Mee Kim. 1994. Where is the chain in commodity chains? The service sector nexus. In *Commodity chains and global capitalism,* ed. Gary Gereffi and Miguel Korzeniewicz. Westport, CT: Praeger.

Rafeq, Abdul-Karim. 2001. The socioeconomic and political implications of the introduction of coffee into Syria, 16th–18th centuries. In *Le commerce du café avant l'ère des plantations colonials espaces, réseaux, sociétés (xve–xixe siècle),* ed. Michel Tuchscherer, 126–141. Cairo: Institut Français d'Archéologie Orientale.

Raikes, Philip, and Peter Gibbon. 2000. "Globalisation" and African export crop agriculture. *Journal of Peasant Studies.* 27(2):50–93.

Raikes, Philip, Michael Friis Jensen, and Stefano Ponte. 2000. Global commodity chain analysis and the French filière approach: Comparison and critique. *Economy and Society* 29(3):390–417.

Rammohan, K. T., and R. Sundaresan. 2003. Socially embedding the commodity chain: An exercise in relation to coir yarn spinning in Southern India. *World Development* 31(5):903–923.

Raynolds, Laura. 2002. Consumer-producer links in fair trade coffee networks. *Sociologia Ruralis* 42(4):404–424.

———. 2004. The globalization of agro-food networks. *World Development* 32(5):725–743.

Reimer, Suzanne, and Deborah Leslie. 2004. Knowledge, ethics and power in the home furnishings commodity chain. In *Geographies of commodity chains,* ed. Alex Hughes and Suzanne Reimer, 250–269. London: Routledge.

Renard, Marie-Christine. 1999a. Los intersticios de la globalización. Un label (Max Havelaar) para los pequeños productores de café. Mexico, DF: Misceláneas.

———. 1999b. The interstices of globalization: The example of fair coffee. *Sociologia Ruralis* 39(4):484–500.

Review. 2000. Special issue on commodity chains in the world-economy, 1590–1790. 23(1).

Richardson, George. 1972. The organisation of industry. *The Economic Journal* 82: 883–896.

Rischbieter, Julia Laura. 2005. *Globalizing consumption: Coffee trade and consumption in imperial Germany.* Paper presented at the first World History Conference, in Leipzig, Germany.

Roche, Julian. 1998. *The international banana trade*. Cambridge, UK: Woodhead Publishing.

Rodrik, Dani. 1997. *Has globalization gone too far?* Washington, DC: Institute of International Economics.

Roseberry, William, Lowell Gudmundson, and Mario Samper K. 1995. *Coffee, society and power in Latin America*. Baltimore: Johns Hopkins University Press.

Ross, Robert, and Kent Trachte. 1990. *Global capitalism: The new Leviathan*. Albany: State University of New York Press.

Rostow, Walt W. 1960. *The stages of economic growth: A non-Communist manifesto*. Cambridge, UK: Cambridge University Press.

Roy, William G. 1997. *Socializing capital: The rise of the large industrial corporation in America*. Princeton, NJ: Princeton University Press.

Sachs, Jeffrey. 1998. International economics: Unlocking the mysteries of globalization. *Foreign Policy* 110: 97–111.

Saddi, Victoria. 2002. *The role of coffee in the creation of institutions in Brazil: 1830–1930*. Ph.D. dissertation, University of Southern California.

Samper K., Mario. 2003. The historical construction of quality and competitiveness: A preliminary discussion of coffee commodity chains. In *The global coffee economy in Africa, Asia and Latin America, 1500–1989*, ed. William Clarence-Smith and Steven Topik, 120–153. New York: Cambridge University Press.

Samper K., Mario, and Radin Fernando. 2003. Historical statistics of coffee production and trade from 1700 to 1960. In *The global coffee economy in Africa, Asia and Latin America, 1500–1989*, ed. William Clarence-Smith and Steven Topik, 411–462. New York: Cambridge University Press.

Sanderson, Steven. 1986. The emergence of the "world steer": Internationalization and foreign domination in Latin American cattle production. In *Food, the state, and international political economy*, ed. F. Lamond Tullis and W. Ladd Hollist, 123–148. Lincoln: University of Nebraska Press.

Sayer, R. Andrew. 2003. De(commodification), consumer culture, and moral economy. *Environment and Planning D: Society and Space* 21(3):341–357.

Schelling, Thomas C. 1978. *Micromotives and macrobehavior*. New York: W.W. Norton.

Schivelbusch, Wolfgang. 1992. *Tastes of paradise: A social history of spices, stimulants and intoxicants*. Trans. David Jacobson. New York: Pantheon Books.

Schmitz, Hubert, ed. 2004. *Local enterprises in the global economy—Issues of governance and upgrading*. Cheltenham, UK: Edward Elgar.

Schrank, Andrew. 2004. Ready-to-wear development: Foreign investment, technology transfer, and learning-by-watching in the apparel trade. *Social Forces* 83(1):123–156.

Schultz, T. Paul. 1998. Inequality in the distribution of personal income in the world: How it is changing and why. *Journal of Population Economics* 11(3):307–344.

Schurman, Rachel. 2004. "Fighting Frankenfoods": Industry structures and the efficacy of the anti-biotech movement in Western Europe. *Social Problems* 51(2):243–268.

Schurman, Rachel, and William Munro. 2006. Ideas, thinkers, and social networks: The process of grievance construction in the anti-genetic engineering movement. *Theory and Society* 35(1):1–38.

Schweiger, T. 2001. Europe: Hostile lands for GMOs. In *Redesigning life? The worldwide challenge to genetic engineering,* ed. Brian Tokar, 440. London: Zed Books.

Scott, Allen. 1988a. *Metropolis: From the division of labor to urban form.* Berkeley and Los Angeles: University of California Press.

———. 1988b. Flexible production systems and regional development. *International Journal of Urban and Regional Research* 12:171–186.

———. 2006. The changing global geography of low-technology, labor-intensive industry: Clothing, footwear, and furniture. *World Development* 34(9):1517–1536.

Scott, John. 1991. Networks of corporate power: A comparative assessment. *Annual Review of Sociology* 17:181–203.

Shapiro, Bob. 1999. Sci/Tech: Bob Shapiro: In his own words, BBC News, Friday, October 8; available at http://news.bbc.co.uk/1/hi/sci/tech/468147.stm.

Shreck, Aimee. 2005. Resistance, redistribution, and power in the fair trade banana initiative. *Agriculture and Human Values* 22(1):17–29.

Skocpol, Theda R. 1979. *States and social revolutions.* Cambridge, UK: Cambridge University Press.

Smith, David A. 1996. *Third World cities in global perspective: The political economy of urbanization.* Boulder, CO: Westview.

———. 2005. Starting at the beginning: Extractive economies as the unexamined origins of global commodity chains. In *Nature, raw materials, and political economy,* ed. Paul Ciccantell, David A. Smith, and Gay Seidman. New York: Elsevier.

Smith, David A., and Roger J. Nemeth. 1988. Research note: An empirical analysis of commodity exchange in the international economy: 1965–1980. *International Studies Quarterly* 32:227–240.

Smith, David A., and Douglas White. 1992. Structure and dynamics of the global economy: Network analysis of international trade 1965–1980. *Social Forces* 70(4):857–893.

Smith, Sally, Diana Auret, Stephanie Barrientos, Catherine Dolan, Karin Kleinbooi, Chosani Njobvu, Maggie Opondo, and Anne Tallontire. 2003. *Ethical trade in African horticulture: Gender, rights and participation.* Preliminary report for multistakeholder workshop. Institute of Development Studies, 26 June, in Sussex, U.K.

Snyder, David, and Edward Kick. 1979. Structural position in the world system and economic growth, 1955–1970: A multiple network analysis of transnational interaction. *American Journal of Sociology* 84(5):1097–1126.

Specter, Michael. 2000. The Pharmageddon riddle. *The New Yorker,* April 10, 58–71.

Spice Mill. January 1912, 28.

Spulber, Daniel F. 1996. Market microstructure and intermediation. *Journal of Economic Perspectives* 10(3):135–152.

Stark, David. 1996. Recombinant property in East European capitalism. *American Journal of Sociology* 101(4):993–1027.

Stark, David, and Láslô Bruszt. 1998. *Postsocialist pathways: Transforming politics and property in East Central Europe*. New York: Cambridge University Press.

Steiber, Steven. 1979. The world system and world trade: An empirical exploration of conceptual conflicts. *Sociological Quarterly* 20(1):23–36.

Stein, Stanley J. 1985. *Vassouras, a Brazilian coffee county, 1850–1900: The roles of planter and slave in a plantation society*. Princeton, NJ: Princeton University Press.

Stinchcombe, Arthur L. 1997. On the virtues of the old institutionalism. *Annual Review of Sociology* 23:1–18.

Storper, Michael. 1995. The resurgence of regional economies, ten years later: The region as a nexus of untraded dependencies. *European Urban and Regional Studies* 2(3): 191–221.

———. 1997. The regional world: Territorial development in a global economy. In *Perspectives on economic change*, ed. Meric S. Gertler and Peter Dicken. New York: Guilford Press.

Strange, Robert, and James Newton. 2006. Stephen Hymer and the externalization of production. *International Business Review* 15(2):180–193.

Strange, Susan. 1996. *The retreat of the state: The diffusion of power in the world economy*. New York: Cambridge University Press.

Sturgeon, Timothy. 2001. How do we define value chains and production networks? *IDS Bulletin* 32(3):9–18.

———. 2002. Modular production networks. A new American model of industrial organization. *Industrial and Corporate Change* 11(3):451–496.

———. 2007. How globalization drives institutional diversity: The Japanese electronics industry's response to value chain modularity. *Journal of East Asian Studies* 7(1):1–34.

Sturgeon, Timothy, Johannes Van Biesebroeck, and Gary Gereffi. 2007. *Prospects for Canada in the NAFTA automotive industry: A global value chain analysis*. Industry Canada, Research Report.

Swedberg, Richard. 1997. New economic sociology: What has been accomplished, what is ahead. *Acta Sociologica* 40(2):161–182.

———. 2003. *Principles of economic sociology*. Princeton, NJ: Princeton University Press.

Sweigart, Joseph. 1987. Financing and marketing Brazilian export agriculture: The coffee factors of Rio de Janeiro, 1850–1888. New York: Garland.

Talbot, John M. 1997a. The struggle for the control of a commodity chain: Instant coffee from Latin America. *Latin American Research Review* 32(2): 117–135.

———. 1997b. Where does your coffee dollar go? The distribution of income and surplus along the coffee commodity chain. *Studies in Comparative International Development* 32(1):56–91.

———. 2002. Tropical commodity chains, forward integration strategies and international inequality: Coffee, cocoa and tea. *Review of International Political Economy* 9(4):701–734.

———. 2004. *Grounds for agreement: The political economy of the coffee commodity chain*. Lanham, MD: Rowman and Littlefield.

Taylor, Peter Leigh. 2005. In the market but not of it: Fair trade coffee and forest stewardship council certification as market-based social change. *World Development* 33(1):129–147.

Teece, David. 1986. Profiting from technological innovation: Implications for integration, collaboration, licensing and public policy. *Research Policy* 15(t):285–305.

Teece, David, Gary Pisano, and Amy Shuen. 1997. Dynamic capabilities and strategic management. *Strategic Management Journal* 18(7):509–533.

Thompson, Grahame F. 2003. *Between hierarchies and markets: The logic and limits of network forms of organization.* New York: Oxford University Press.

Thurber, Francis Beatty. 1886. *Coffee: From plantation to cup. A brief history of coffee production and consumption.* New York: American Grocer Publishing Association.

Tiberghien, Yves, and Sean Starrs. 2004. *The EU as global trouble-maker in chief: A political analysis of EU regulations and EU global leadership in the field of genetically modified organisms.* Paper presented at the Conference of Europeanists, Council of European Studies (CES), March 13, in Chicago.

Tilly, Charles. 1978. *From mobilization to revolution.* Reading, MA: Addison-Wesley.

———. 1984. *Big structures, large processes, huge comparisons.* New York: Russell Sage Foundation.

Tokar, Brian. 2001. *Redesigning life? The worldwide challenge to genetic engineering.* London: Zed Books.

Topik, Steven. 1996. *Trade and gunboats: the United States and Brazil in the age of empire.* Stanford, CA: Stanford University Press.

———. 2002. The hollow state. In *Studies in the formation of the nation-state in Latin America,* ed. James Dunkerley. London: Institute of Latin American Studies.

———. Forthcoming. Coffee consumption in Latin America. In *The Culture of Consumption in Latin America,* ed. Colin Lewis and Rory Miller. London: Institute of Latin American Studies.

Topik, Steven, and Mario Samper K. 2006. The Latin American coffee commodity chain: Brazil and Costa Rica. In *From silver to cocaine: Latin American commodity chains and the building of the world commodity,* ed. Steven Topik, Carlos Marichal, and Zephyr Frank, 118–146. Durham, NC: Duke University Press.

Traidcraft. 2006. *Buying matters: Sourcing fairly from developing countries.* London: Traidcraft; available at www.responsible-purchasing.org.

Tuchscherer, Michel. 2003. Coffee in the Red Sea areas from the sixteenth century to the nineteenth century. In *The global coffee economy in Africa, Asia and Latin America, 1500–1989,* ed. William Clarence-Smith and Steven Topik, 50–66. New York: Cambridge University Press.

Ukers, William. 1935. *All about coffee.* New York: Tea and Coffee Publishing Company.

United Kingdom House of Commons Environment Food and Rural Affairs Committee. 2002–2003. Gangmasters, Fourteenth Report of Session; available at www.publications.parliament.uk/pa/cm200203/cmselect/cmenvfru/691/69102.htm.

United Nations. 1963. *Commodity indexes for the standard international trade classification,* Revision 1. Statistical Papers M: 38(II). New York: United Nations.

United States Federal Trade Commission. 1954. *Investigation of coffee prices.* Washington DC: Government Printing Office.

Uzzi, Brian. 1997. Social structure and competition in interfirm networks: The paradox of embeddedness. *Administrative Science Quarterly* 42:35–67.

Uzzi, Brian, and Jarrett Spiro. 2005. Collaboration and creativity: The small world problem. *American Journal of Sociology* 111(2):447–504.

Van Yoder, Steven. 2001. Beware the coming corporate backlash. *Industry Week,* April 2:38–42.

Varian, Hal R. 2007. An iPod has global value. Ask the (many) countries that make it. *New York Times,* June 28.

Vega Jimenez, Patrícia. 2004. *Con sabor a tertulia. Historia del consume del café en Costa Rica, 1840–1940.* San José: Editorial de la Universidad de Costa Rica.

Vernon, Raymond. 1966. International investment and international trade in the product cycle. *Quarterly Journal of Economics* 80(2):190–207.

———. 1971. *Sovereignty at bay: The multinational spread of U.S. enterprises.* New York: Basic Books.

———. 1979. The product cycle hypothesis in a new international environment. *Oxford Bulletin of Economics and Statistics* 41(4):255–267.

Wade, Robert. 1990. *Governing the market: Economic theory and the role of government in East Asian industrialization.* Princeton, NJ: Princeton University Press.

Wakeman, Abram. 1911. Reminiscences of lower Wall St. *Spice Mill,* March.

Waldinger, Roger. 1986. *Through the eye of the needle.* New York: New York University Press.

Waldinger, Roger, Howard Aldrich, and Robin Ward, eds. 1990. *Ethnic entrepreneurs: Immigrant and ethnic business in Western industrial societies.* Beverly Hills, CA: Sage.

Wallerstein, Immanuel. 1974. The rise and future demise of the world capitalist system: Concepts for comparative analysis. *Comparative Studies in Society and History* 16(4):387–415.

———. 1979. *The capitalist world economy.* Cambridge, UK: Cambridge University Press.

———. 1988. Development: Lodestar or illusion? *Economic and Political Weekly* 23(39):2017–2023.

———. 1994. Development: Lodestar or illusion? In *Capitalism and development,* ed. Leslie Sklair. London: Routledge.

———. 2000a. Introduction to special issue on commodity chains in the world economy, 1590 to 1790. *Review* 23(1):1–13.

———. 2000b. Globalization or the age of transition? A long-term view of the trajectory of the world-system, *International Sociology* 15(2):249–265.

———. 2005. After developmentalism and globalization, what? *Social Forces,* 83(3):1263–1278.

Wasserman, Stanley, and Katherine Faust. 1994. *Social network analysis: Methods and applications.* Cambridge, UK: Cambridge University Press.

Waugh, Paul. 1999. British stores Tesco and Unilever ban genetically manipulated products. *The Independent,* April 28.

———. 2000. MPs demand destruction of GM rape crop. *The Independent* (London), May 19.

Webber, Michael, and David Rigby. 1996. *The golden age illusion: Rethinking postwar capitalism.* New York: Guilford.

Weiss, Brad. 2003. *Sacred trees, bitter harvests: Globalizing coffee in Northwest Tanzania.* Portsmouth, NH: Heinemann.

Weller, Susan, and Kimball Romney. 1990. *Metric scaling: Correspondence analysis.* Sage University Papers Series: Quantitative Applications in the Social Sciences. London: Sage.

Whatmore, Sarah, and Lorraine Thorne. 1997. Nourishing networks: Alternative geographies of food. In *Globalising food: Agrarian questions and global restructuring,* ed. David Goodman and Michael Watts, 287–304. London: Routledge.

White, Douglas R. 1984. REGE: A regular graph equivalence algorithm for computing role distances prior to block modelling. Unpublished manuscript, University of California, Irvine.

White, Douglas R., and Karl P. Reitz. 1983. Graph and semi-group homomorphisms on networks of relations. *Social Networks* 5(2):193–235.

Whitley, Richard D. 1992. *Business Systems in East Asia.* London: Sage.

———. 1996. Business systems and global commodity chains: Competing or complementary forms of economic organisation? *Competition and Change* 1(4):411–425.

———. 1999. *Divergent capitalisms: The social structuring and change of business systems.* New York: Oxford University Press.

Wickizer, V. D. 1961. *Coffee, tea, and cocoa: An economic and political analysis.* Stanford, CA: Stanford University Press.

Williamson, Oliver. 1975. *Markets and Hierarchies.* New York: Free Press.

———. 1981. The modern corporation: Origins, evolution, attributes. *Journal of Economic Literature* 19(4):1537–1568.

———. 1985. *The economic institutions of capitalism: Firms, markets, relational contracting.* London: Macmillan.

———. 1991. Economic institutions: Spontaneous and intentional governance. *Journal of Law, Economics, and Organization* 7:159–187.

Womack, James P., and Daniel Jones. 1996. *Lean thinking: Banish waste and create wealth in your corporation.* New York: Simon & Schuster.

Woo, J. E. 1991. *Race to the swift: State and finance in Korean industrialization.* New York: Columbia University Press.

Woolf, Marie. 2001. U.S. may provoke row over GM food labeling. *The Independent,* August 14.

World Bank. 1993. *The East Asian miracle: Economic growth and public policy.* New York: Oxford University Press.

———. 2006. *World development indicators.* Washington DC: World Bank.

Yeung, Henry Wai-chung. Forthcoming. Situating regional development in the competitive dynamics of global production networks: An East Asian perspective. *Regional Studies* 42.

Yeung, Henry Wai-chung, Weidong Liu, and Peter Dicken. 2006. Transnational corporations and network effects of a local manufacturing cluster in mobile telecommunications equipment in China. *World Development* 34(3):520–540.

Zanfei, Antonello. 2000. Transnational firms and the changing organization of innovative activities. *Cambridge Journal of Economics* 24(5):515–542.

Zimmerman, Siegfried. 1969. *Theodor Wille.* Hamburg: n.p.

Index